Facts On File Encyclopedia of

Black Women

IN AMERICA

The Early Years, 1619–1899

Encyclopedia of
Black Women in America

Facts On File Encyclopedia of

IN AMERICA

The Early Years, 1619–1899

Darlene Clark Hine, Editor

Kathleen Thompson, Associate Editor

☑® Facts On File, Inc.

Facts On File Encyclopedia of Black Women in America: The Early Years, 1619–1899

Copyright © 1997 by Darlene Clark Hine

Facts On File, Inc.
11 Penn Plaza
New York NY 10001

Library of Congress Cataloging-in-Publication Data

Facts on File encyclopedia of Black women in America / Darlene Clark
Hine, editor ; Kathleen Thompson, associate editor.
p. cm.
Includes bibliographical references and index.
Contents: v. 1. The early years, 1619–1899 — v. 2. Literature —
v. 3. Dance, sports, and visual arts — v. 4. Business and professions —
v. 5. Music — v. 6. Education — v. 7. Religion and community —
v. 8. Law and government — v. 9. Theater arts and
entertainment — v. 10. Social activism — v. 11. Science, health,
and medicine.
ISBN 0-8160-3424-9 (set : alk. paper)
ISBN 0-8160-3425-7 (The Early Years)
1. Afro-American women—Biography—Encyclopedias. I. Hine,
Darlene Clark. II. Thompson, Kathleen.
E185.96.F2   1996
920.72′408996073—dc20   96-33268

Text design by Cathy Rincon

Cover design by Smart Graphics

Printed in the United States of America

RRD FOF 10 9 8 7 6 5 4 3 2 1

This book is printed on acid-free paper.

Contents

How to Use This Volume

SCOPE OF THE VOLUME

This volume includes entries on individuals and organizations whose most significant achievements occurred before the twentieth century; however, some whose accomplishments spanned the nineteenth and twentieth centuries are also included. The entries cover all areas of life. In rare cases, an individual was deemed to be so important in her field that an entry for her is included in a subject-area volume, as well.

HOW TO USE THIS VOLUME

The introduction to this volume presents an overview of the history of black women in America before the twentieth century. A chronology following the main entries in this volume lists important events in this history.

Individuals and organizations are covered in alphabetically arranged entries. If you are looking for an individual or organization that does not have an entry in this volume, please check the alphabetically arranged list of entries for all eleven volumes of this encyclopedia that appears at the end of this volume.

Names of individuals and organizations for which there are entries in this or other volumes of the encyclopedia are printed in boldface. Check the contents list at the end of this book to find the volume where a particular entry can be located.

Facts On File Encyclopedia of

Black Women

IN AMERICA

The Early Years, 1619–1899

Introduction

In the bright sunlight of a Chicago summer, the white buildings of the **World's Columbian Exposition of 1893** were blinding in their glory. Glorious, too, were the thousands of exhibits charting the progress of humanity and celebrating—one year late—the anniversary of Columbus' landing in the New World.

It was, in an era that loved its world fairs, the biggest and best that had ever been. But, looking back, it was more than that. It marked the end of one part of our history and the beginning of another.

Right in the middle of all those buildings, for example, was one devoted entirely to women. And it contained an exhibit collected and arranged by black women. Also, on this afternoon, in a nearby lecture hall, there stood a tall, well-dressed woman, speaking to a large crowd of men and women, both black and white. A lawyer's wife and a prominent member of Chicago society, Fannie Barrier Williams was talking about the progress of her sisters—black women. And outside on the streets of the fair, a fiery orator, Ida B. Wells, declared for all to hear that that progress was too slow as she passed out pamphlets entitled *The Reason Why the Colored American Is Not in the Columbian Exposition*. In the journey from slavery to freedom, a corner had been turned.

SLAVERY

The history of America is a story of innocence lost, of the brightest promise the world has ever known tarnished by greed and inhumanity. The two everlasting stains on America's brightness are the virtual destruction of Native-American peoples and the enslavement of Africans.

The first black women who came to the British colonies probably arrived in Virginia in 1619. The summer before, the English ship *Treasurer* had left Virginia on its way to get goats, salt, and other provisions for the colony. That was the official story, anyway. Shortly after it left Virginia, however, the *Treasurer* met up with a Dutch man-of-war. The two ships sailed on together and happened upon, perhaps by carefully arranged accident, a Spanish frigate with a cargo of African slaves en route to the West Indies. The crews of the *Treasurer* and the Dutch ship took the cargo of slaves for themselves.

The ships were separated and delayed by bad weather, and their provisions began to give out. Most of the slaves died from starvation before the ships reached land. When the Dutch man-of-war arrived at Jamestown in August 1619, it carried only twenty of the one hundred slaves it had taken aboard. Of these twenty slaves, some undoubtedly were women. The *Treasurer*, which had taken the other part of the African cargo, landed only one black person in Virginia, a woman her captors called Angela.

It is not certain what became of this lone African woman, Angela, or the few others who arrived at the British settlement in 1619. Slavery was not a formal, legalized institution in the colony at the time, although Europeans had been taking Africans as slaves to Europe and to the New World for more than a century. Virginians first regarded these African women as indentured servants. (The colony of Georgia outlawed the importation of black slaves until 1750.)

In 1661, however, Virginia officially recognized slavery. The following year, the fate of the next several generations was sealed in law. In response to questions regarding the status of children born to black women and white men, the colonists decided that "all children borne in this country shall be held bond or free only according to the condition of the mother." Other colonies followed suit, reversing traditional British law and patriarchal custom that gave a child his or her father's status.

This law had a profound effect. Because of the shortage of European women in the early colonies, significant numbers of white men fathered children by African women. If the father's status had determined whether a child was free or slave, a free mulatto class of some size might have emerged. The law of 1662 prevented that.

In the next several decades, all of the colonies recognized slavery as a legal institution and declared that the children of slave mothers would be slaves. So African women were brought into a land where they and their children would be enslaved for generations.

To the white colonists, these women were interchangeable. They were simply workers. In fact, however, they were a varied group that came from African villages, cities, and states with differing social rules, and in which they played diverse roles.

Some of them were from patriarchal societies, and others were not. Some practiced polygamy, while others embraced monogamous marriages. Many brought with them their Islamic beliefs and rules of social behavior. Others clung to the rituals and moral ideology of indigenous African religions.

These women came from societies with rich and ancient heritages in which women were traders, farmers, weavers, warriors, leaders, and mothers. Now, they were strangers in a foreign land. They were forced into a completely different life by strange-looking people who spoke a new language and behaved in ways that were incomprehensible to them. They were stripped of freedom, respect, and comfort of any kind.

But their anguish and alienation did not begin on the coasts of the New World. Long before they ever reached North America, African girls and women suffered incredibly at the hands of the European and African traders who captured or bought them. Torn out of the lives they knew, these women, many of whom were already married and had children of their own, were forced to leave their families, their culture, and their ethnic identities behind. Once daughters and mothers and valued members of their society, they now became commodities that African merchants bartered for iron bars, gunpowder, rum, cloth, and crystal beads.

Conditions on the ships that brought these captives to America were unimaginably horrible. Huge numbers of them died before they reached these shores.

Women were only a small portion of these first black slaves, because the slaveowners were looking for manual laborers and believed young men would be superior workers. However, the trade in women increased during the pre-Revolutionary eigh-teenth century.

Georgia was the last southern colony to embrace the institution of slavery. It was legally forbidden at the colony's founding, but, amid persistent settler criticism, that law was repealed in 1750. Advertisements in the colony's *Gazette* soon read like so many others of the era: "To be Sold on Thursday next, at publick vendue, Ten Likely Gold Coast New Negroes, Just imported from the West Indies, consisting of eight stout men and two women."

Black women were brought, not just to the South, but to the middle and northern colonies as well. In all of these places they faced frightening disorientation. On board ship, they may have formed ties to others who shared their language and customs. But when they left the docks with their new masters, they were alone and, to some degree, they remained alone, or, at least, existed in a kind of social isolation. The ways they might have reached out to others were under the control of the masters.

Community and family were critically important to an African woman's sense of identity and purpose. But seventeenth-century masters quickly established the right to define and structure the most intimate connections and activities of their slaves and servants. They even chose to control various aspects of their sexual behavior and family life through their power in the colonial legislature.

The colonial households that these African women helped to form, therefore, often were not defined by blood relationships, race, or culture but rather by economic considerations. Family for many of the first African and black Creole people in North America was nothing but a memory of those whom they had been forced to leave behind.

And yet, another kind of family arose among the slaves and servants in the colony. Living as a slave meant hard work, poor rations, sometimes brutal beatings, lost families, and illness. It also meant negotiated marriage but marriage nonetheless, children who learned how to care for their elderly or ailing kin, communities of friends, and, between the hard times, some laughter, pride, romantic love, song, dance, and God.

WORK

Despite the importance of family and marriage to slave women, their principal role in American society was that of laborer. Work is what they were brought to these shores to do.

In the New England and middle colonies, most worked on small farms, raising vegetables and tending livestock. Others were house servants who cooked, cleaned, butchered livestock, nursed and reared children, served at table, and acted as caregivers to their masters' families.

Throughout the British part of North America, black women were allowed to perform little skilled labor except that of midwives, nurses or herbalists, seamstresses, weavers, or cooks. Few slaveowners believed women were suited for other kinds of work. Accordingly, jobs in iron works, distilleries, and tanneries, in the lumber, whaling, and fishing industries, and as blacksmiths, coopers, and carpenters, were left almost exclusively to men. So, too, was the mobility associated with these types of work.

The just man shall be in eternal remembrance

The First Poetical
Writer of Race,
1776.

Transported by slave ship to the American colonies in 1761, Phillis Wheatley eventually became a master of eighteenth-century poetic forms, producing work that gained recognition in England and Europe as well as in America. Her book Poems on Various Subjects, Religious and Moral *was the first published by a black person in America.* (SCHOMBURG CENTER)

However, the work of raising crops was in itself skilled labor. And the women who worked the fields were not just strong backs. These women from Africa often brought with them to the New World agricultural skills and methods that were similar to those used in the American South.

Slave women rose early in the morning to the sound of an overseer's horn and worked until nightfall for six days a week. Except for the initial clearing of the land, they usually were responsible for every aspect of the crops' cultivation, from planting to preparing them for market. With rare exceptions, supervisory positions in the fields, like other skilled occupations, were held by men.

Slave women and girls were particularly important to rice production. Prices of slaves in Savannah document that planters were willing to pay equally for prime male and female rice hands. In a slave inventory dated 1852, for example, twenty-seven-year-old Callie May, a woman described as a "Prime Woman, Rice," was priced at $1,000; equally priced was Deacon, a twenty-six-year-old "Prime Rice Hand."

Women produced many of the domestic objects their families used as slaves. They made cloth, baskets, containers, and buttons. They also introduced the cultivation and preparation of various West-African foods. And women helped create the songs slaves sang to set the rhythms of their work, to comfort themselves, to celebrate their small joys. They also helped keep alive African religious beliefs, medicinal and birthing practices, dress and hairstyles, dancing, and courtship and marital rituals.

Women were also more likely than male slaves to acquire some form of education in English and the European tradition of knowledge, because of their work in the slave owners' homes. An extraordinary example of this is **Phillis Wheatley**, who was purchased as a child directly off a slave ship. She was to be trained as a personal servant to the wife of merchant John Wheatley. However, she picked up knowledge so quickly and thoroughly from the Wheatley family that she became known throughout Massachusetts. Soon, she was writing poetry that was published, first in newspapers, then, in 1773, as a book entitled *Poems on*

Various Subjects, Religious and Moral. It was the first book of poetry published by an African American and only the second by an American woman.

Wheatley was one of the almost 30,000 black women who were freed in the Northeast and Midwest as the colonial era passed and slavery disappeared in those areas. To the south, however, the number of female slaves grew steadily, as did the amount of slave territory. The acquisition of Florida, the Louisiana Purchase, and the annexation of Texas, along with the forced relocation of Native Americans in the Deep South, provided a tremendous boost to the expansion of the institution of slavery. The profitable cultivation and ginning of short staple cotton, as well as the development of Sea Island cotton, provided raw fiber for a growing textile industry in Britain and the Northeastern United States. It also almost guaranteed an increase in the number of persons enslaved.

The increase in the number of slaves during the pre–Civil War era occurred at a time when the concentration of the Southern black population also was shifting drastically, from the Upper South to the cotton states of the Deep South. This dramatic shift in slave concentrations caused profound changes in the lives of slave women, thousands of whom lost husbands, sons, daughters, and other kin and friends to traders who took them south. The rapid "peopling" of the South in general and the cotton belt specifically meant that slaveholders were placing tremendous pressure on slave women to begin to have children earlier and to have them regularly. Procreation literally became part of their job.

In the Deep South, cotton was king. As slaves, women participated in every aspect of cotton production. When masters owned at least sixteen slaves, they usually divided them into hoe gangs and plow gangs. Generally, women did not participate in plow gangs to the same degree as men. But slave women, with boys and elderly men, dominated the hoe gangs. Of course there were many exceptions. One traveler to Mississippi noted, for example, "Seeing a wench ploughing, I asked him [the overseer] if they usually held the plough. He replied that they often did; and that this girl did not like to hoe, and, she being a faithful hand, they let her take her choice." And, on farms with small holdings, there were tasks assigned to men or women exclusively. Women were compelled to participate in every aspect of cotton production.

Everyone participated in the harvest, although on farms of intermediate or large size the number of female pickers was usually greater. Overseers and drivers forced workers to pick as quickly, carefully, and thoroughly as possible, and beat them if they didn't measure up.

Slave women and girls were energetic and diligent pickers, sometimes even surpassing men. The average daily yield of a prime picker in the latter part of the antebellum era was about 150 pounds per day. Betsy, a slave on a Yazoo River plantation, picked 712 pounds in four days. Ellin, another woman on the same plantation, picked 818 pounds.

Women who were too old to continue to do fieldwork were employed in cotton gins and as spinners and weavers. Among those slaveholdings with sufficient numbers of women to allow full-time diversification, younger women also held these positions.

Older slave women were also plantation seamstresses and knitters. This too was difficult labor. Although "cloth houses" provided physical shelter for female workers, mistresses insisted on closely supervised work regimentation. They established routines that often exceeded the physical capabilities of elderly women, who may have suffered from general fatigue and other illnesses, as well as rheumatism and arthritis.

An important minority of native-born women performed domestic service in the homes of their owners or were rented out to others. Some worked part of the time in the house and the rest in the field. On large plantations there were full-time household servants, who often lived in special quarters in or just behind their owners' homes.

Some women preferred the position of domestic to fieldworker. There were several reasons for this. First, they did not have to perform the same kind of hard, physically demanding labor that tobacco, rice, sugar, or cotton cultivation required. Second, most of the work was done inside their owners' homes, away from the heat, cold, and rain that fieldworkers sometimes faced. In addition, domestic slaves usually had better food, clothing, and, occasionally, housing. Some felt that being around whites would speed the process of cultural assimilation. Others hoped that they would be able to establish close ties with powerful whites who might reward them—or even give them their freedom.

But domestic slavery was still slavery. Domestic slave women had little time to tend to the needs of their own families. They worked very long hours, especially when they lived in their masters' houses and were accessible to their owners twenty-four hours a day. They were subject to overwhelming emotional strain because they worked so

closely with and under the constant scrutiny of those in authority.

In order to have an efficient staff, most white women believed it was necessary for their domestic slaves to learn white cultural domestic skills and behavior. Thus, many small slave girls selected to be domestic servants entered into a long and intense period of apprenticeship.

The tragedy of this emotionally wrenching process was that it sometimes caused house slaves to be alienated from the rest of the slave community. As they grew to young womanhood, they were robbed of the comfort and support other slaves could offer.

And plantation mistresses were not gentle. Most were perfectly willing to punish slaves they considered slow, lazy, inefficient, or ungrateful, either verbally or physically. Although they often grew attached to their domestic servants and allowed them certain favors, slaveholding mistresses were quick to assert their authority if they felt it challenged in any way.

Field-workers also began their training at an early age. Owners wanted obedient, disciplined, efficient laborers who knew the work routine and the punishment for not adhering to it. Most little girls started performing some tasks at about six years of age. Slave girls selected to be agricultural workers not only picked up stones, pulled weeds, and carried water but also learned to care for livestock and fowl and performed other tasks such as collecting fallen fruit and nuts and picking berries for their owners' tables. Slave children on tobacco farms were responsible for pulling hornworms from tobacco leaves. Girls on cotton farms and plantations helped their mothers pick cotton and worked in trash gangs composed of children, older slaves, pregnant women, and others who were physically less able.

Once slave girls began to work, they came under the direct supervision of white owners and overseers. And they began to suffer psychological and physical abuse similar to that endured by their mothers. It was not unusual for supervisors of slave children to physically punish them. Owners also threatened to sell young slaves who didn't do as they were told. The idea of being sold away from parents and family was, of course, terrifying for young children.

Young girls now also came into contact with and fell prey to the sexual aggression of white males. Some slave masters purchased adolescent females for the purpose of establishing sexual relationships with them.

Childhood, in slavery, ended early and cruelly. Motherhood was filled with pain. And yet, all the records and narratives reveal that slave parents loved and cared for their children, and that families found joy in each other.

MARRIAGE

Marriage and family are at the center of most people's lives. This is true in almost all cultures, and it was certainly true in both America and the African nations from which slaves came. And there, at the very heart of life, slaves were completely vulnerable.

Unfounded in law, though oftentimes consummated in love, slave marriages were fragile relationships in which couples struggled to survive given the immense and divisive pressures of slave life. Even the strongest marriages could be torn apart by the sexual aggression of a white owner, by the sale of one of the

partners, or by the sheer horror of life. And many slave marriages were not made in heaven. They were made in the big house, for the convenience of its owner.

Owners made the final decision as to whether or not a slave could marry, when he or she could do so, and to whom. If the couple had the same master, there was usually no problem in gaining permission, although sometimes the owner would question each party as to his or her feelings before consenting to the marriage. If the couple had different owners, however, they had to receive permission from both masters

Discipline among slaves was maintained by force. This woodcut from a book entitled Picture of Slavery. . . *by George Bourne (published in 1834) is entitled "Ladies Whipping Girls."* (LIBRARY OF CONGRESS)

SLAVE AUCTION AT RICHMOND, VIRGINIA.

This wood engraving of a slave auction at Richmond, Virginia, was published in The Illustrated London News, *September 27, 1856.* (LIBRARY OF CONGRESS)

and usually continued to live on separate farms after the marriage.

Slaves regarded marriage as an important commitment and tried to impress their children with the seriousness of the institution and its responsibilities. Most slaves hoped that marriages would be permanent and therefore expected young people to consider well their choice of spouse before they married. Although most slaves had to ask their owners for permission to marry, it was the custom in some slave communities for the couples to seek the blessing of an authority figure within their family or community. Caroline Johnson Harris, for example, recalled that when she wanted to marry she had to ask "Aunt Sue" for permission. Harris said of the elderly slave's response: "She tell us to think 'bout it hard fo' two day, 'cause marryin' was sacred in de eyes of Jesus." After reflecting for two days, Caroline and her intended, Moses, returned to Aunt Sue's, "an' say we done thought 'bout it an' still want to git married." Aunt Sue then "called all de slaves arter tasks to pray fo' de union dat God was gonna make. Pray we stay together an' have lots of chillun an' none of 'em git sol way from de parents."

Although some slave marriages were forced, and couples suffered from the negative implications of such arrangements, many black women who were former slaves dearly loved their husbands and cherished memories of their courting days, weddings, and marriages.

Slave marriages, like those of any group, varied in terms of quality, length, and goals. Slave women wanted long, loving, affectionate, faithful marriages. Most did not expect that their spouses would be able to protect them from some of the most violent and abusive aspects of slave life, but hoped that they would understand their wives' lack of choices.

Slave husbands expected the same kind of love, support, and respect from their wives. Regardless of the commitment that slave couples made to each other, however, the intervention of slave owners could be devastating. The impact of white male sexual aggression toward married slaves created a great deal of tension in the relationships between slave husbands and wives. Rape was meant to be a violent and dehumanizing experience for black women, and an emasculating one for the men who could not afford to interfere with such activities. Many did, and they suffered the consequences, such as severe beatings, murder, or permanent separation from their families.

The most devastating problem that slave couples faced was the threat of owner-imposed permanent separations. Large numbers of slave couples were pulled apart as a result of the sale of one or both persons. Slave women and especially slave men between the ages of thirteen and twenty-five comprised a large percentage of slaves sold, most without their spouse or children.

It was difficult, if not impossible, for slave women to retain close ties to husbands who had been sold. Some never heard from their husbands again, while others tried to maintain communication by writing or having others write for them. Many such wives remained unattached for years, hoping that by some miracle they would be reunited with their spouses. Others moved on with their lives more quickly, finding some other man to love and cherish, and hoping that they could establish new, loving families in which to rear their children.

IT TAKES A VILLAGE . . .

Almost everyone has heard the African saying that it takes a whole village to raise a child. That was certainly true in the days of slavery.

Think about the dangers of a situation in which slave owners have virtually life-and-death control over their slaves. Consider the fact that either parent—or both—could be sold away at any time. It is not difficult to understand that childrearing was a shared responsibility in the slave quarters. Grandparents, stepparents, older siblings, aunts, uncles, and sometimes cousins and other community members contributed to the upbringing of slave children if circumstances made it necessary to do so.

Slave owners significantly shaped the domestic relations of slaves and the upbringing of their children. Their insistence on the importance of the mother in the slave family, particularly in regard to childrearing, is one example. Most owners believed that slave women had a natural bond with their children; therefore, it was more their responsibility than the fathers' to care for their offspring. Some slave owners frowned upon separating mothers from children under twelve years old. Others did not. But rarely did *any* owners afford fathers the same measure of consideration.

So, most slave children under twelve years of age lived with their mothers and many did not have consistent contact with their fathers. Men who lived on neighboring farms could usually visit their families only on Sundays and holidays. Others might see their children rarely, if at all. Slave men who were rented out usually did not see their families except during the Christmas holidays. For all of these reasons, slave mothers reared the children.

When slave mothers needed help, they usually called on older daughters, nearby grandmothers and single aunts to help feed young children, care for and repair their clothing, wash them, teach them, and attend to their medical needs. This sharing of childrearing and other domestic tasks strengthened the bonds between generations of women and prepared the younger generation to assume the duties of those who had come before them.

Slave parents and white owners certainly held the most important positions of authority in the lives of slave children. Yet the balance of power was both delicate and complex and could shift quite suddenly. While their parents were the most important authority figures in the lives of young slave children, as they grew older they increasingly realized that their parents' authority and power were limited. It was undoubtedly a confusing and difficult situation for children, although most eventually managed to comprehend it.

Slave parents particularly resented the intrusion of white authority in the lives of their daughters. First, it was a reminder of the power whites held over their most personal concerns. Second, slave mothers knew that the childrearing techniques and goals of whites often were harmful to their children's development into healthy, moral, and

This pencil drawing done by the artist Edwin Forbes in 1864 depicts the "Interior of a Negro cabin." (LIBRARY OF CONGRESS)

psychologically sound adults. Not surprisingly, some slave mothers argued openly with their owners regarding control of their children. One slave woman in Virginia, for example, recalled an argument that she had with her mistress: "I said to my Missis if folks owns folks, then folks owns their own children. 'No, they don't' [her mistress responded] ... 'white folks own niggers. "Well," replied the slave mother, not to be outdone, "the Government owns *you* and everything."

Slave owners balked at attempts by slave kin or any other potential authority figure to retain control of the lives of black children. They were especially outraged at the notion that their authority on the plantation might be challenged by one they viewed as threefold inferior—black, female, and slave. A successful challenge to their authority by a slave mother would certainly encourage others.

Those who did bear and raise daughters as slaves prepared them to resist dehumanization and to survive their experience. Slave kin could not afford to challenge white authority figures and the abuse they inflicted on their daughters. Those who did so usually failed and risked even greater abuse for themselves and the girls. Parents could, however, try to teach their children to defend themselves.

Slave mothers and other relatives attempted to teach their daughters that the best protection against the brutalities of the slave system was for the individual to develop an approach to whites that was in keeping with her personality and the expectations of her owners. This technique for interacting with masters allowed the slave to walk the line between her position as property and that of human being.

Slaves began to teach their girls survival methods during early childhood. They used children's stories, religious lessons, and example. According to Della Harris, slave mothers taught their children to be seen but not heard and to respect the authority of older slaves. Parents expected children to complete assigned tasks without opposition. Slave mothers tried to teach their daughters the difference between right and wrong and other lessons of morality essential to acceptance in the slave community as well as in the world of whites.

Most believed rigid behavioral and moral standards would not only make the children good citizens of the slave community but also would help them survive as slaves. A child's failure to obey her parents' orders or those of older relatives and to follow established rules of behavior might be met with the same type of punishment that whites would impose, a sound beating. But mothers combined an emphasis on discipline and obedience with words of encouragement and acts of kindness that reassured these girls of their worth and humanity.

Secret religious services emphasized to all members of the slave community the equality of the races before God and slaves' inevitable freedom from bondage. Slave women taught their daughters to turn to God in times of trouble and to pray for divine protection. Mothers hoped to teach their daughters how to survive as individuals in a slave society, the importance of family and community, and their responsibility to help other slaves.

These were revolutionary lessons in a society where behavior was based on the assumed inequality of African Americans. Young women learned not to lie or steal from other slaves, to keep the secrets of the quarters from whites, to protect and hide runaways, to help sick and disabled slaves with their work, and to help other slaves whenever possible. Slave parents taught their girls to protect other slaves and to show them the courtesy and respect that they deserved. Ex-slave Jane Pyatt eloquently explained the relations between slaves, in contrast to those between slaves and whites, when she stated: "The respect that the slaves had for their owners might have been from fear, but the real character of a slave was brought out by the respect that they had for each other. Most of the time there was no force back of the respect the slaves had for each other, and yet, they were for the most part truthful, loving and respectful to one another."

Perhaps the most difficult task for slave mothers was how to teach their daughters to avoid the sexual advances of white men and how to live with their frequent inability to do so. Most mothers did not want their daughters to become sexually active until they were married, but the details of sex were seldom discussed. Instead, mothers warned their girls against getting too close or familiar with any man, black and white.

Despite the oppressive and inevitably painful experiences of parents rearing children as slaves, bondwomen and men loved their children and invested much of their time and energy to assure their well-being. Often slave mothers named their daughters for themselves as well as other relations, especially grandmothers, aunts, and sisters. Slave children were the future of slave families. Parents often spoke of their daughters as people they could depend on for love, comfort, and service when they became older. Their sons would probably be sold away.

RESISTANCE AND REBELLION

A question that must be asked at this point is, "Did they resist?" Did these women and girls try to fight back against their situation and its abuses? The answer is yes. In spite of the tremendous power slave owners had over them, these women resisted. They rebelled. And they ran away.

They resisted when they were exploited and abused beyond their endurance. They had a work ethic that was part of the overall moral code of the slave culture. It demanded that, in exchange for labor and obedience, owners would provide material support, acceptable physical and emotional treatment, and some freedom in their most personal relations. Slaves who felt that this unwritten agreement had been violated rebelled against their owners.

A slave revolt in 1708, which included black women, resulted in the deaths of seven whites on Long Island, New York. In 1712, another rebellion of slave men and women led to the deaths of nine white men.

Rebellion of a different kind came from a women named **Jenny Slew**. She went to court in 1765 to bring suit against her "master" for kidnapping and unlawful enslavement. Because her mother was white and therefore not a slave, she argued, she was born free, according to the law that said a child's condition followed that of the mother. Her "master" claimed that she had no legal right to take him to court. Slew won. She was awarded her freedom, four pounds, and court costs.

Another woman, **Elizabeth Freeman**, also known as Mum Bett, went to court in 1780 in search of freedom. She insisted that, since the Massachusetts state constitution declared all men free and equal, slavery was illegal. Illiterate herself, she found a lawyer who would present her case and they filed a writ. She, too, was granted her freedom. It was a landmark case in American law and the decision should have meant freedom for all the remaining slaves in the state. It didn't.

These court cases occurred in the North, where slavery was under attack from abolitionists. In the South, resistance took more desperate forms. Despite the fear of physical torture, perhaps sale, separation from their children, or rape, African women and their descendants continued to resist enslavement. Some ran away. Of the 562 runaway slaves that owners advertised for in the Huntsville, Alabama newspapers between 1820 and 1860, for example, 15 percent were women.

Fewer women ran away than men, of course, because for women running away usually meant leaving children behind. (Men were too often already separated from their families.) But some fugitive slave women took their children with them. Many of the women also ran *to* family members, trying to get to loved ones from whom they had been separated.

Owners pursued fugitive slave women fiercely. They literally hunted these women, or paid others to do so, and demonstrated little mercy when they found them. The point was not just to recover one's property. It was to prevent others from trying to escape. Slaveholders believed brutal and public retaliation was the best deterrent.

Nonetheless, slave women ran away, refused to maintain certain work quotas, talked back to authority figures, stole food, met secretly with other slaves, plotted against masters, and brought whites physical harm. The earliest records of female slave activity document patterns of resistance and rebellion that continued throughout the antebellum era.

In 1777, for example, Jenny, a slave woman to John Lewis, was condemned and executed for conspiracy against her owner. The following year, Rachel, a slave of Lockey Collier, was executed for murder. Between 1819 and 1831, seventeen female slaves in Virginia were accused of sundry crimes such as stealing and arson and were transported out of the state. Six were found guilty of capital crimes such as murder, conspiracy, and arson and were executed.

While these numbers seem small, one must remember that most acts of resistance were not handled by local officials but by individual slaveholders. Hundreds, perhaps thousands, of slave women were sold because of such acts. Many more were beaten.

Slave women also resisted their enslavement and that of future generations by refusing to have children. Sometimes slave owners promised female slaves material rewards such as larger food allowances, better clothing, or more spacious cabins if they would have children.

Some undoubtedly accepted these incentives. Yet, unless seriously threatened with sale or severe corporal punishment, many slave women did not allow whites to control this most private activity. Slave women used crude contraceptive methods in order to maintain control over their procreation. Although owners suspected them of trying to prevent pregnancy or induce miscarriage, they rarely were able to find them out.

There are also isolated incidences of slave women who went even further to make certain that their children did not grow up as slaves. Perhaps the most famous case of a slave mother killing her child is that of

One of the most widely recognized instances of infanticide among slave women is the case of Margaret Garner, "the modern Medea." Garner's story inspired Toni Morrison's novel Beloved. (LIBRARY OF CONGRESS)

Margaret Garner of Kentucky, who attempted to escape with her husband, four children, and several others across the Ohio River in 1856. When discovered by slave hunters before she and her family could complete their escape, she slit the throat of one of her young children and tried to kill the others before she was subdued.

FREE BLACK WOMEN IN THE SOUTH

Long before the Civil War and the Emancipation Proclamation, hundreds of thousands of African Americans already lived outside the bounds of slavery. In fact,

by 1860, more than 260,000 free people of color lived in the South. The majority of them (53 percent) were women. Freedom, of course, was limited. And its definition changed over time.

The experiences of free black women directly reflected the South's system of slavery. So, during the formative years of the colonial period, when slave codes were not yet established, many Africans who had been brought to the South lived and worked not as free white people did but not exactly as slaves, either. As the seventeenth century drew to a close, and white Southerners increasingly committed themselves to black slave labor, fewer and fewer displaced Africans were able to attain, or maintain, nonslave status. Thus, most women who found themselves enslaved during the final years of the seventeenth century remained enslaved into the eighteenth century.

During the American Revolution, there was a great deal of passionate talk about natural rights. In New England and the mid-Atlantic region, where the land wasn't suitable for large plantations, this talk had some effect. Many slaveholders in these places freed their slaves.

In the South, although a few slaveholders took the revolutionary ideals to heart and emancipated some slaves, the overwhelming number of people of African ancestry remained in bondage. Southern slaveholders staunchly defended their constitutionally confirmed right to own people. The first federal census of 1790 confirms the Southern commitment to slavery. Of the nearly 700,000 Africans and their descendants who lived in the South, only slightly more than 32,000 were not enslaved.

At the end of the eighteenth century, and early into the nineteenth century, the free nonwhite population of the South increased as a result of several factors. In the Upper South—Maryland, Delaware, Kentucky, Virginia, Tennessee, and even North Carolina—slaveholders found that it was cheaper to hire workers—black or white—than to buy and support slaves. In addition, fugitive slaves often disappeared into the anonymous and transient ferment of port cities such as Baltimore or the sparsely populated countryside, thus swelling the region's free nonwhite population. These economic considerations, combined with the growing demand for abolition, meant that many slaves were freed.

Slaveholders in the Lower South—Alabama, Georgia, Louisiana, Mississippi, and South Carolina—were less tolerant of the fledgling abolitionist movement. Slavery remained a viable, productive labor system for them, so they maintained rigid control of the slave population. Most of the increase in the number of free African Americans in the Lower South resulted from natural population growth, as well as the influx of tens of thousands of free nonwhite refugees from Santo Domingo in the wake of the slave revolution of 1801. Thousands more suddenly found themselves on United States soil as a result of the Louisiana Purchase of 1803 and the Adams-Oñis Treaty of 1820 by which Spain ceded Florida to the United States.

White Southerners who felt threatened by the increasing number of free African Americans and the growing abolitionist movement in the North began to close, even more securely, the already narrow gateways to freedom, especially in the Lower South. Between 1810 and 1860, Southern states strengthened their laws to prevent any further increases in the number of free African Americans. Through expulsion, emigration, or reenslavement schemes they even attempted to eliminate the free population entirely.

Of course, nonslave status never guaranteed real freedom or equality. Free African Americans knew that in Southern society race was presumed to signify a certain condition and that their collective existence challenged whites' inherent assumptions. Freedom held few promises. Finding themselves neither enslaved nor wholly free, free African Americans recognized that they were out of place in a society based on slavery. They were a group apart from both black slaves and free whites.

BECOMING FREE

In a country where the institution of slavery was so oppressive and slave owners so powerful, how did a black person become free? What circumstances allowed the free black population to grow, even as much as it did? In a sense, the possibilities of freedom were defined by the idea of property.

A slave was, in the context of the time, a piece of property. Someone owned the property. The property could be bought and sold. *And the property could own him or herself.*

That was the crucial point. No advocate of slavery could get around it. The most basic sense of justice recognized that, if a slave could get the money and an owner was willing to sell, the slave could become self-owning. Free. And if an owner wanted to give the slave to him or herself, the owner had a perfect right to do so. And again the slave became self-owning. Free.

And could the child of a free person be a slave? That was a question that had been answered in the courts in 1661. No one could know for sure who the father of a child was, so the legal status of a child always depended on that of the mother. The daughter or son of a slave woman was inescapably defined as a slave. And the child of a free woman—be she black, white, or Native American—was always free, regardless of the father's status.

Therefore, the slave owner who freed a male slave freed only one individual. But if a slave owner freed a woman, all her future offspring and the offspring of her daughters would be free. Clearly, freeing a woman could have a long-term effect on the black population, slave and free, that far outweighed the consequences of freeing a man.

Nonetheless, women were more likely to be freed than men. For one thing, the white population viewed women as less threatening to the social order. For another, slave women seemed less frightening than men, whose physical strength was feared, as was their presumed ability—and tendency—to foment rebellion.

Most former slaves either came from or went to live in cities. The character of urban slavery advanced the opportunity for freedom. Slaves in the cities often worked and

Born in 1800, Clara Brown was a slave for the first fifty-seven years of her life. She was freed after her master's death by his heirs. She moved to the West, settling in Colorado, starting a laundry business, and, ultimately, investing in real estate. She left an estate worth more than ten thousand dollars. (DENVER PUBLIC LIBRARY, WESTERN HISTORY DEPARTMENT)

lived apart from their owners. A sum was agreed upon as the "rent" of the slave, but if the slave could earn more than that, he or she was allowed to keep it. Therefore, slave women who managed to establish lives beyond the direct day-to-day influence of their owners had a better chance to save money toward purchasing their freedom, where that was allowed. But it wasn't much of a chance. Few slave women were able to accumulate enough money for that purpose, even in an urban setting.

Slaves were much more likely to secure their freedom through familial relationships. Some mothers and grandmothers worked their entire lives to purchase the freedom of their children and grandchildren. One such woman was **Coincoin**, a Louisiana slave who was servant and mistress to a French merchant. She had ten children by the merchant, Claude Metoyer. She had already had five before he bought her. Metoyer freed Coincoin and one of her children in 1778, and the couple remained together for another eight years. Before they parted, Coincoin had another child, who was, of course, free.

When Metoyer left Coincoin to get married, he gave her a small piece of land and a small annuity. At the age of forty-three, she began to work her farm. She worked hard and was extremely shrewd, and her farm grew. At the same time, she began to track down her children and grandchildren. She traveled hundreds of miles and spent every penny her farm produced, but she finally purchased and freed all but one of her children, including those still owned by their white father, Metoyer, and virtually all of her grandchildren.

Fathers and husbands sometimes purchased the rights to their daughters or wives in order to free them. On rare occasions, men who were still enslaved worked to free the women they loved at the expense of their own freedom. But most men who purchased and freed women were already free themselves. Free men of color who were legally married to slave women (in the few jurisdictions that allowed slaves to marry), or who cohabited with them, and even white men who were committed to their de facto wives and their racially mixed offspring, sometimes negotiated their freedom.

Women also were somewhat more likely than men to be freed by masters or mistresses for sentimental reasons. Slave women who served as domestics, cooks, nurses, and nannies formed relationships with their owners that demonstrated at best love and caring and at worst fear and hatred. Such relationships, however complicated, sometimes resulted in freedom for those women who lived most closely with their owners and who therefore had greater opportunity to negotiate the terms of their emancipation. Some white slave owners also freed elderly servants who were no longer economically productive.

Becoming free was only the first step for black women. It was a difficult one, and the women who took it were rare. But the next step was, in some ways, even more difficult.

LIVING FREE

Freedom from slavery was not freedom from oppression. It was a limited, socially dangerous, and economically demanding condition. Free black women needed all the help they could get.

Free black women found it considerably easier to live in a city than in the country.

This group photograph of slaves in front of their cabin was taken around 1861. (SCHOMBURG CENTER)

They formed communities that provided protection and social opportunities. They created community support systems such as churches and benevolent societies, which were generally not available to free black women in rural areas of the South. Indeed, the advantage of urban living is reflected in the total number of free African Americans who lived in cities. In 1860, while approximately 85 percent of the white and 95 percent of the slave population lived in the countryside, more than 72 percent of free African Americans lived in cities. The majority of these were women.

Interestingly, it was the Lower South that accommodated the most thriving population of free African Americans in the slave states. These were the racially mixed descendants of African, French, and Spanish settlers of colonial Louisiana and Florida who identified themselves as free black Creoles.

Louisiana's black Creoles became United States residents following the 1803 Louisiana Purchase. Then, in 1812 and 1821, the black Creoles in Spanish west Florida joined their Louisiana counterparts. By 1860, the approximately 20,000 black Creoles who lived in Louisiana, southern Alabama, Mississippi, and northwest Florida were distinct from both slaves and whites.

Many of the free African Americans elsewhere in the South were viewed by their white neighbors as slaves without masters. Free Creoles considered themselves, and were acknowledged by both whites and slaves, as an intermediate caste. Consequently, black Creoles held a special status in their communities. For the most part, they were socially and legally recognized as free citizens. The law protected their legal status, and members of the white community, to whom they often were related, ensured their social standing.

Throughout most of the pre–Civil War period, free black Creoles retained the right to buy and sell property, including slaves. They were able to marry, bring suit in court, and acquire an education—until fear of slave uprisings and paranoia drove white leaders to limit their freedom. Increasingly after 1850, white politicians in Louisiana, Alabama, and Florida passed laws forbidding free African Americans to transact business without white guardians. As a result, many free black Creoles left the region for France, Cuba, even Mexico, where they hoped to find a racial climate that was similar to the one they had known along the Gulf Coast. Those who chose to remain faced increasing hardships. Most, however, educated their children and worshipped without interference.

Black Creole women celebrated and protected their distinct crosscultural heritage and, as mothers, they transmitted that heritage to their children. Because of their unique social identity, free black Creoles were closely tied to both their Creole white and their black slave kin and neighbors. As part of an intermediate caste, however, free black Creoles usually segregated themselves into communities where they spoke only French or Spanish and continued to practice the Roman Catholicism that the early settlers had brought with them to the New World.

The **Catholic Church** itself reinforced the special identity of black Creoles. Viewing itself as the moral protector of women, the church continued to support black Creole women even as racism deepened. From the early days of settlement, the Catholic Church had educated free black women. So, while many white Southerners remained uneducated, many black Creole women received some formal education.

Beyond the Gulf Coast region, however, most free black women in the rural plantation South lived in areas where they were always a small minority. But in spite of their apparent isolation and small numbers, these women knew themselves to be the daughters, sisters, wives, and mothers who anchored family and community. In addition, as was the case with many free Creoles, free African Americans in the plantation belt maintained familial ties with white Southerners.

In spite of links with both the free white and the enslaved black communities, the preferred alliances clearly were those that bound the small number of free black families to one another. Free African Americans who lived in the Lower South often clustered together in enclaves where they formed tight-knit communities.

The Cane River region of Louisiana and Chastang Bluff and Mon Luis Island in Alabama are examples of rural communities in which free African Americans were in the majority and thus able to enjoy their separate status. However, even in regions such as Georgia's rural plantation belt, where free African Americans constituted only a small percentage of the population, they were not scattered like isolated grains of sand across a landscape of plantations worked by slaves and owned by hostile whites. Rather, they usually lived near one another in small towns or on adjoining farms. They formed loose neighborhood clusters in which they maintained small but protective and nurturing communities of people who shared life's everyday rituals.

In addition to family and community, free black women identified themselves through their work. A few were comfortably situated, but most had to work to provide, or at least supplement, their family's income.

Black women were caught in the middle when it came to sex roles. They had not been spared hard manual labor in the fields as slaves, but they were usually limited to "women's work" when it came to finding employment. They were household servants, spinners, weavers, and dressmakers. Still, there were those who worked as independent farmers, often raising both crops and animals and toiling at rigorous physical labor just like men.

Women who hoped to strengthen their position in the free community worked diligently to buy homes. Home ownership, of course, not only gave free black women a place to house their families, but extended their economic and political security. Some free black women carried on their work within their households, turning their homes into boardinghouses or devoting rooms to seamstressing, laundering, or baking goods to sell.

A few free black women even owned slaves, many of whom were female and some of whom were relatives. A free woman of color might own her mother, sister, or even her children, whom statute or local authorities forbade her to free. Other free black women, however, like white slaveholders, owned slaves for economic reasons, and because they generally needed slaves who shared or supplemented their own skills, they usually owned other women.

Many free black women were permitted to own property and transact business with few restrictions until the early to mid-nineteenth century, when state laws began to heap insult on injury by limiting their political, social, and economic independence. These new laws, designed to restrict the independence of free African Americans, pertained to both women and men. In many jurisdictions, free African Americans were required to register annually at county courthouses. They also had to acquire and maintain legal guardians and usually could transact business only through those guardians. Many occupations were closed to them, and they often bore an unequal tax burden. Most jurisdictions considered them residents but denied them the rights of citizenship. Few Southern states allowed free African Americans to become educated, and, for the most part, criminal codes placed free African Americans on the same footing as slaves.

Of course, all women, including free black women, lacked many of the rights extended to white men. In most jurisdictions, married free black women, like married white women, were denied the right to own property and control their children. Their rights, as defined by common or civil law, were subsumed by their husbands. However, if they were widowed or remained unmarried, they retained rights to both property and their children.

So, many free black women remained unmarried. This was not considered proper behavior for good Christian women, but it gave them a fair degree of control over their lives as well as their children and property. Also, because free African Americans could enter into contracts only through the agency of a white person, and because marriage is a contract, there is some question as to whether marriages between free African Americans would have been recognized in most jurisdictions.

In some respects, the day-to-day experience of free black women changed little after general emancipation. Most of these women celebrated when they saw friends and family members freed. A few regretted the loss of their own slaves. Nothing prepared them for the great social changes that would take place as a result of the Civil War.

Freedom—the status that had separated free black women from female slaves—was no longer unique. Some free black women struggled against all odds to maintain what had been a relatively prestigious social position. Threatened by increasing racism in the white community, and by the possibility of submersion into the larger group of former slaves, many members of this group tried to maintain their distinct identity, but they were not generally successful.

After the war, the dominant society defined everyone who was nonwhite, free persons of color as well as freedpeople, as black, and African Americans quickly began to coalesce into a new, all-inclusive community. That community was not without its own social and economic diversity and stratification, however. In many cases, those who had been free prior to general emancipation—often because of nothing more than good fortune—gravitated toward the top of the newly emerging nonwhite community.

Before emancipation, many of them had enjoyed the advantages of owning property, getting an education, participating in busi-

ness, and having close relationships with white people. In a great many cases, these people parlayed such advantages into positions in the upper echelon of their new community—however oppressed that community might be. Thus, during Reconstruction, formerly free African Americans became the nucleus of an emerging African-American middle class.

FREE BLACK WOMEN IN THE NORTH

Freedom came to Northern slaves primarily through legislation, not purchase. Starting with Vermont in 1777, all Northern states abolished slavery either outright or through strategies of gradual emancipation. Within two generations only 1,100 slaves remained in a Northern population of more than 170,000 black Americans. On the eve of the Civil War, the number of Northern slaves had dropped to eighteen.

In the North, therefore, free African Americans were not surrounded by a slave society in which their friends and loved ones might still be in bonds. They were not exceptions. But their freedom was still highly limited.

The work lives of most African-American women in the North did not change much with freedom. They were still domestic workers in white households. In nineteenth-century Philadelphia, New York, and Boston, two-thirds of black women were household servants. Yet the general title "servant" often obscured the variety of jobs that these women did.

The largest group performed traditional household work, cleaning, laundering, and cooking. Many provided child care for white families and a few performed more specialized services such as dressmaking and gourmet cooking. The nature of their work often depended on the social and economic status of their employers and carried with it significant social and economic meaning. To work in the home of a prominent family was to have potential access to influence. Such a position might make a woman important to her friends and neighbors.

The establishment of black institutions also provided opportunities for women. Early African-American schools founded in many cities were staffed by white reformers. Elie Neau, a white New Yorker, founded the first slave school in British North America in New York at Trinity Church in 1704. Other schools were established by Puritans in New England and by Quakers in Philadelphia and other towns in Pennsylvania and New Jersey.

In 1793, a former slave named **Catherine Ferguson** opened an integrated Sunday school in her home. She took in forty-eight black and white children from the streets of her neighborhood and the almshouse nearby. She taught them Scripture and how to take care of themselves. She helped many find homes and even took some of them into her own home. She supported this whole venture through her work as a caterer to wealthy white families. Later, she received some support from a neighborhood church.

From the beginning, black women played important roles as classroom assistants in some of the early schools and as teachers in many of the later ones. Eleanor Harris was the first black teacher in Philadelphia, and Sarah Dorsey and **Margaretta Forten** were among those who followed in her footsteps. In the early 1830s, **Sarah Mapps Douglass** returned from New York City, where she

had been a teacher, to open a school for black girls in her native Philadelphia. Hers was, at the time, the only high school for black girls in the nation. Douglass took the bold step of teaching science to her female students and later, after taking courses in medicine at the Female Medical College of Pennsylvania and at Pennsylvania Medical University, she traveled widely, lecturing to black women.

Throughout the North in the early decades of the nineteenth century, black women provided and even supervised the education of black girls and, less frequently, black boys as well. These were far more desirable jobs than those in white households, but they were few and required education far beyond the reach of most free black women of the period.

There were black women in other occupations as well, though they were in the minority. Some of them were outright mavericks. **Jarena Lee**, for example, believed that she had a vocation to preach the gospel. As early as 1809, she asked to be allowed to preach at the Bethel African Methodist Church of Philadelphia. Her request was denied, but years later, after the death of her minister husband, she became a traveling minister. Many more black women would become active, though unordained, ministers during the nineteenth century.

Elizabeth Clovis Lange founded an order of Roman Catholic nuns called the **Oblate Sisters of Providence** in Baltimore, Maryland, in 1829. **Elizabeth Keckley** had a career as a dressmaker that took her all the way to the White House, as clothing designer for Mary Todd Lincoln. She also wrote the "first behind-the-scenes-at-the-White House" memoirs. **Elleanor Eldridge** built up a painting and wallpapering business before she went into real estate. **Elizabeth Taylor Greenfield** went on the concert stage and, in 1854, performed for Queen Victoria at Buckingham Palace. All of these women had one thing in common. They were either unmarried or widowed.

A DOUBLE BURDEN

In nineteenth-century America, women were instructed by their families, churches, schools, and popular culture to assume dependent, subordinate, supportive postures in society. Theirs was the domain of the home, the responsibility of the moral maintenance of the family, and the role of helpmate to their husbands.

These were absurd ideals for poor women—black or white—as they are now. If they stayed home to care for their families, their families would starve. They had to work. Then they had to come home to cook, clean, and tend the children. But this issue of a woman's role was further complicated for African-American women by their history.

Because slavery did not respect gender, female slaves were protected neither by traditional Western assumptions about female frailty, nor by presumptions about their emotional delicacy. When heavy fieldwork was required and black males were not available in sufficient numbers to perform such labor, female slaves were field hands. Moreover, the obedience, humility, and dependency demanded of male slaves deprived black men of the traditional privileges accorded men in American society. They were expected to exhibit "male qualities" of physical strength and "female qualities" of subordination, not only to their masters but to all white people.

If slavery sought to defeminize black women and emasculate black men, most believed that freedom should reestablish traditional gender roles. As free black communities formed in the early nineteenth century, this message appeared in the sermons of black ministers, in the expectations of family life, and even in the pages of black newspapers. The socializing agencies of black society instructed black women and men in the gender expectations of America.

The economic realities of black life frustrated all African Americans but posed special problems for black women. Forced to work long hours at inadequately compensated employment, they also were expected to fulfill the duties of wife and mother. Society implicitly recognized the full-time nature of housework and child care in its expectation that such work might be done by domestic staff, yet women were expected to perform such tasks in addition to their full-time compensated employment.

Such expectations burdened not only black women but all working-class women. However, racial discrimination limited job and income possibilities for black males so that black women were more likely to remain employed after marriage. And their situation was even more complex. Whereas white women might be expected to do double duty solely because of their gender, black women were also charged with such duty as part of their special responsibility to their race. If black men were to regain their status as true men by predominating in the family, black women must be true women by subordinating themselves to their husbands' wills.

Such beliefs put women in particularly difficult situations, as in the case of Chloe Spears who, with her husband, Cesar, ran a boardinghouse in nineteenth-century Boston. In addition, Chloe did domestic work for a prominent Boston family. During the day, while she was at work, Cesar saw to the cooking and other duties at the boardinghouse. When Chloe returned in the evening, he retired and turned the operation over to her while he rested. At this point, what had been seen as work during the day became housework at night, fit not for the man of the house, but for the housewife.

Thus, after working all day at her job, Chloe cooked dinner for her family and the boarders and cleaned the house. Then, in order to make extra money she took in washing—more women's work—which she did at night, setting up lines in her room for drying the clothes. She slept a few hours while the clothes dried, then ironed them, and prepared breakfast for the household before going off to work for the day.

It was important that Cesar not be expected to participate in the housework, for that was not man's work, and both Cesar and Chloe had an obligation to uphold every black man's manhood as a part of their duty to the freedom and manhood of the race, a duty reinforced by the teachings of almost every authority in black society. This was one of the ways that race complicated black life.

Yet, in some ways black women benefited from their critical economic roles in black society. Despite the custom and law in American society that husbands control the family finances, Chloe did not routinely place her wages under Cesar's management. Instead, she controlled her own money and, when she decided to acquire an unfurnished house, Cesar was surprised that she had the $700 needed to do it.

In fact, the only reason Cesar became involved in the transaction was the law that prevented a married woman from buying a house in her own name. Chloe's independence in financial matters was limited not by the customs or admonitions of black society but by laws that limited all women in American society.

A WIDER SCOPE

Black women, generally, had certain advantages within their communities not extended to other women in American society. White women, in theory at least, were restricted to the private sphere of home and children. Black women were allowed, even expected, to take part in the public arena of community politics. Like their white counterparts, they organized their own women's organizations. But they also joined with black men to work for such common political and social goals as the abolition of slavery and improvement of life conditions for free black Americans. Whether in the cause of education, temperance, community service, civil rights, antislavery, or the Underground Railroad, black women were central players.

Mary Ann Shadd Cary of Philadelphia and later of Canada, **Sojourner Truth** of New York, **Maria Stewart** of Boston, and **Ellen Craft** who escaped from slavery in Georgia were among the many black women who, with the full support of black men, traveled the nation speaking out against slavery and for racial justice. These and other black women, such as **Sarah Remond** of Boston, also journeyed to Europe in the cause of freedom to be received by the royalty of the Old World. Theirs was not the retiring role of the traditional nineteenth-century feminine ideal. In the female antislavery societies, the less formal vigilance groups that sheltered and defended fugitive slaves, and the literary societies that placed the issues of freedom and justice before the public for discussion and debate, black women were among the leaders.

Yet these women paid a price for their expanded role. Although they traveled the globe as cosmopolitan representatives of their race, they were expected to perform the household duties as well. For black women, any service they provided to the community was service in addition to that they provided for their families—it was a second job.

To the extent that they took on full-time responsibilities in the public sphere, it was with the assistance of other black women. Mary Ann Shadd Cary's sister assisted with the care of Cary's children while she was on the road speaking against slavery. Ellen Craft had no children for whom she was responsible while she worked for the cause. Zilpha Elaw, an itinerant minister, relied on relatives to care for her daughter in her absence. Whereas black men like Frederick Douglass, William Wells Brown, and Charles Lennox Remond could rely on their wives to shoulder the day-to-day family responsibilities while they tended to their careers in the protest movement, female reformers relied on female relatives and friends.

The domestic expectations of married women sometimes encouraged black women to postpone marriage, allowing them time to establish public careers first. Sarah Mapps Douglass remained single until well into middle age. Some black women refused to marry because they found few black men capable of supporting them. One consequence of the limited occupational opportunities for black men was the disproportionate number of single black women and black families headed by women, ranging as high as one-third of free black families in the antebellum North.

Yet this situation, like most others for African Americans at the time, was more complex than it at first appears. One important reason for the absence of black men from black families was their high death rate, brought about by the dangerous jobs they were often forced to take and the high mortality rate among poor people generally in American society. The absence of a father from a black family was most often a consequence of death or the adjustment to a racially restricted job market.

The lives of free black women in the antebellum North were thus molded by economic and social forces that were often beyond their control. Race complicated gender, forcing black women and men to make adjustments in their relationships and their expectations of one another. Under these circumstances, black women experienced some benefits but most often bore a special burden.

NORTHWEST TERRITORY

The lives and historical experiences of black women in the midwestern states of Illinois, Michigan, Wisconsin, Ohio, and Indiana that were carved out of the Northwest Territory are known only through widely scattered and fragmented sources. Although the much-heralded Northwest Ordinance of 1787 prohibited slavery and mandated that this region be free, slavery in various guises—ranging from outright lifetime indenture to long-term apprenticeship—existed into the 1850s.

As late as the 1840s, there were still approximately 350 slaves in the region, most located in the river counties of southern Illinois. One of the connecting threads in the history of black women in the Northwest is their relentless quest for freedom and for the equal enjoyment of educational, social, and economic opportunities.

From the outset, black women in the Northwest region established a pattern of fighting for the freedom of their children. For example, beginning in the 1830s, a number of petitions were filed in Illinois courts on behalf of black women challenging the indenture and apprentice claims of their white masters on their children. In the case of *Boon* v. *Juliet* (1836), Bennington Boon claimed that although his indenture agreement with Juliet had expired, he retained the rights to the service of her three children under the provisions of an 1807 statute. Juliet, with the aid of white antislavery supporters, won the suit, the state court ruling that the children of African Americans registered under the territorial laws of Indiana and Illinois were unquestionably free. However, not until 1845 did the Illinois Supreme Court declare the holding of all black apprentices illegal.

A small number of black women in the nineteenth century were born and raised in the Northwest Territory, and others were transported into the region as members of freed slave families from North Carolina, Virginia, Kentucky, and Tennessee. Still other black women came to reside in the Northwest after escaping slavery via the Underground Railroad. Margaret Garner was made famous through the fictionalized tale,

by novelist **Toni Morrison** in *Beloved*, of her escape and subsequent killing of her daughter. She crossed the frozen Ohio River in the winter of 1856 and arrived in Cincinnati, where she was ultimately captured by local police and returned to slavery in Louisville. Finally, a few free black women living in Southern or border states voluntarily migrated to the Northwest.

As in other parts of the country, most black women worked as domestics, cooks, washerwomen, and agricultural laborers. Like white women, they could not vote or hold political office. Other rights were even more circumscribed. Ohio denied African Americans the benefits of welfare relief, and schools were segregated by law. Indiana and Illinois denied public education to black children altogether.

In spite of these limitations, some black women were able to make strides toward greater freedom and independence. They had many advantages over their sisters in slavery. Life in the small midwestern towns afforded more opportunities to become involved in church and community activities. A few black women and their families found islands of racial tolerance in frontier settlements in Wisconsin. Like Lucy, the wife of Free Frank of Illinois, these women cultivated gardens, raised poultry, sold dairy produce, and engaged in a number of other income-producing tasks.

Black schoolteachers were often the only professional women in the Northwest region prior to the Civil War. Those black women interested in acquiring higher education found Oberlin, Ohio, a particularly promising haven. **Oberlin College** was the first coeducational and interracial institution of higher learning.

Sarah Jane Woodson (Early), born on November 15, 1825, in Chillicothe, Ohio, was one of the first black women to attend Oberlin College. She was the youngest of the eleven children of Thomas and Jemimma Woodson, two emigrants from Greenbriar County, Virginia. After moving into Ohio in 1820, the Woodsons had joined several other families to found an all-black farming community at Berlin Crossroads, Jackson County, Ohio. In 1852, Sarah enrolled at Oberlin. During vacations, she earned money by teaching in the segregated schools in Circleville and Portsmouth, Ohio. After her graduation in 1856, Woodson served on the faculty of Wilberforce University in Ohio, becoming one of the first black women to teach at the college level.

Black women played a crucial role in the development of religious and social welfare institutions within small black Northwest communities. Virtually all of the black churches, regardless of denomination, depended on the fund-raising activities and support of black women. Sarah Woodson, an astute observer of black women's participation in community efforts, recorded that while black women seldom occupied visible positions of leadership, they often bore a heavy burden. "In raising funds with which to build churches," she said, "no difficulties deterred them from their efforts and no dangers affrighted them from their purpose. Through heat and cold and storms and fatigue and hardships they gathered a little here and there, while they made what they could with their own hands, which many times was only the widow's mite; but when these small sums were put together they were sufficient to raise a monument in the name of God to dedicate to his worship."

As the number of black women increased in Northwest communities, so too did the number of clubs devoted to self-improvement and social or racial advancement. In 1843, a group of black women in Detroit formed what eventually became known as the Detroit Colored Ladies Benevolent Society. Similar organizations were established in Chicago, Cleveland, and other midwestern communities. These clubs worked to lessen the suffering of the poor, aged, orphaned, and sick. They also helped combat the image of the morally unsound black woman that white society had created.

Women on the frontier, and especially black women, seldom had the luxury of living within the role of the ideal woman. With the men, they worked in the fields and helped to create and sustain the major community institutions. They also bore a great deal of the responsibility for maintaining family ties, socializing the young, providing elementary education and basic health care, and working in the home. The survival of African Americans in the Northwest depended on the full participation of every member of the community.

THE ABOLITIONIST MOVEMENT

The North was largely free. The Northwest and West were moving toward freedom. But in the South, slavery was growing and becoming more widespread. And so was the demand to end it.

Slavery was not the only issue at hand, however. Closely related was the position—social, economic, and political—of free African Americans who were victims of increasing legal and customary discrimination. Most Southern states, for example, required free African Americans to carry evidence of their status, or "certificates of freedom," wherever they went. Those who could not immediately produce this kind of documentation were held in jail until they could. Some eventually were sold back into slavery.

The Northwest and West provided few additional expressions of freedom for the black minority. Many of the so-called black laws enacted in these regions were drawn directly from Southern legislation and tradition. Free African Americans fared better in the Northeast than other parts of the nation, but their reception was far from welcoming.

Where discrimination was not founded in law, its basis was often custom. None of the Northern states, for example, had laws barring African Americans from the courtroom, but social convention often prevented them from sitting on juries anywhere except Massachusetts. Likewise, Northern free African Americans generally were not segregated in places of public accommodation or in publicly owned institutions, except schools, but they routinely were denied admission to hotels, restaurants, theaters, public lyceums, hospitals, and even cemeteries patronized by whites.

It was not just that free African Americans faced growing opposition, which limited their opportunities, resources, and fundamental rights. There also was a movement building to force black people out of the country permanently.

The American Colonization Society was formed in 1816 for that express purpose. The black community widely opposed colonization, and their campaign against this effort, coupled with the inability of the society to fund their removal, kept the organization from achieving its goals. In the end, only about 1,400 persons moved to the West African colony of Liberia, despite the support of leading United States statesmen and the federal government.

And the number of free black people in the population did not diminish. There was actually a steady increase from 108,435 persons in 1800 to 233,634 in 1820, to 386,293 in 1840, to almost half a million in 1860. Most lived in the Northeast, in urban areas. And it was in such places that abolitionist activities were centered.

Black women had powerful reasons for participating in the fight for black rights. Most of them worked all their lives, beginning as older children and continuing through old age, yet rarely achieved financial security. Their poverty had an incredible social impact on the free African-American community because these women headed a significant minority of households. Given the tragic effect of racial oppression on their daily lives, it is no wonder that many free women of color became involved in efforts to extend the rights of black Americans.

In the most fundamental sense, African-American women's participation in abolitionist efforts began with African girls and women who resisted their enslavement at every juncture. This tradition is perhaps most easily seen in the courageous work of **Harriet Tubman**, a slave from Maryland who was not content to win her own freedom but risked her life at least nineteen times in order to help approximately 300 other slaves find their way to safety and freedom. Tubman's determination to end slavery did not cease with these brilliantly planned and executed escapes funded principally by her own sporadic work as a domestic. She also served as a nurse, a scout, and a spy for the Union Army during the Civil War. Like

Tubman, some of the most important female participants in organized abolitionist activities during the antebellum era were fugitive slave women.

African-American women involved in abolitionist efforts derived much of their inspiration and legitimacy from the self-help and self-improvement traditions of the black community. Many such organizations were formed throughout the Northeast as well as in Southern cities such as Baltimore, Alexandria, Richmond, Charleston, and New Orleans. Most, however, arose in Northeastern urban centers. They included such groups as the African Female Benevolent Society of Newport, Rhode Island, formed in 1809; the Colored Female Religious and

Moral Society of Salem, Massachusetts, in 1818; the Coloured Female Roman Catholic Beneficial Society of Washington, D.C., in 1828; the Colored Female Charitable Society of Boston in 1832; the Minerva Literary Association of Philadelphia in 1834; the Ladies Literary Society and the Female Literary Society, both of New York City, in 1834 and 1836; the Ladies Literary and Dorcas Society of Rochester in 1836; and the Young Ladies Literary Society of Buffalo in 1837.

Most of these reformers were middle-class or relatively well-to-do women who had some formal education and were involved in organizations devoted to improving the community. Many had grown up in homes and among friends who,

Harriet Tubman, a slave woman from Maryland, was not content to secure her own freedom; she risked her life at least nineteen times in order to help some 300 other slaves reach freedom. Here she stands (far left) with some of the passengers on the Underground Railroad. (SCHOMBURG CENTER)

as influential reformers and revolutionaries in their own right, set high standards for the young.

The number of elite black people in many communities was so small that some of their reform organizations resembled extended families. Therefore, race, class, gender, and sometimes even family lines influenced the work they performed.

Of course, there were many exceptions to this middle-class standard. The Daughters of Africa in Philadelphia, for example, consisted of working women who pooled small amounts of their income in order to provide a collective fund to serve their members in times of emergency. Yet it was difficult for individuals, particularly pioneers such as Maria Stewart, to have a significant impact on the African-American community or the abolitionist movement without the benefit and support of a network of sponsoring black reformers.

Literary societies were popular among free women of color throughout the antebellum years. Given the lack of educational opportunities or intellectual and artistic outlets for black women, it is not difficult to imagine why many joined these organizations. Yet the African-American women who supported these literary and debating societies had political interests as well. Many invested as much time in efforts toward abolition and equality as in literary pursuits and intellectual stimulation.

As the decades passed and abolition became the dominant reform issue, some organizations shifted emphasis to address this priority. Therefore, although the title of a group might suggest simply a literary society, often the primary interests of its members were abolition and the struggle for black rights.

Many raised money to support these movements by selling some of their original texts, writing letters for persons who were illiterate, running bake sales, and holding fairs. The Ladies Literary Society of New York, for example, held numerous fundraising events in September 1837 in order to assist the *Colored American*, an African-American antislavery journal. They also donated funds to the New York Vigilance Committee.

Even at the most fundamental level, African-American women who were active in literary groups believed that their goals supported abolition and black rights, maintaining that the intellectual acuity and high moral standards demonstrated by their work undermined racist notions of innate black inferiority and debasement. "As daughters of a despised race," the Female Literary Association of Philadelphia asserted in 1831, "it becomes a duty . . . to cultivate the talents entrusted to our keeping that by so doing, we may break down the strong barrier of prejudice."

Their intellectual endeavors also helped inspire a core of dedicated teachers who worked among free black people and, later, Southern freedpeople. Many abolitionist women, including Maria Stewart, Mary Ann Shadd Cary, **Margaretta and Charlotte Forten, Frances Ellen Watkins Harper,** and Sarah Douglass, believed that their teaching careers were laudable expressions of their abolitionist sentiments. As Frances Harper declared in 1852:

> There are no people that need all the benefits resulting from a well-directed education more than we do. The condition of our people, the wants of our children, and the welfare of our race demand the aid of every

helping hand. It is a work of time, a labor of patience, to become an effective school teacher; and it should be a work of love in which they who engage should not abate heart or hope until it is done.

The literature of these women carried powerful statements affirming the African-American cause. Mary Prince's *The History of Mary Prince, A West Indian Slave* (1831), a horrifying document of Caribbean slavery, was the first slave narrative written by a black woman in the Americas. The following year, Maria Stewart became the first free African-American woman to publish a book of hymns and meditations. In 1835, Stewart also published a collection of her works, including political speeches, essays, and religious meditations.

Ten years later, **Ann Plato** became the first African American to publish a book of essays, and **Harriet Wilson** was the first black person in the United States to publish a novel. Her 1859 book, *Our Nig: or, Sketches from the Life of a Free Black*, recounts some of the excruciating problems faced by free families of color, and the abuse of African-American servant children and female domestics, whose only chance of financial survival was to work under conditions similar to those of chattel slavery. Two years later, **Harriet Jacobs'** *Incidents in the Life of a Slave Girl* personalized the plight of the Southern female slave through her account of psychological torture, sexual abuse, physical intimidation, and loss of family in her own life. Jacobs' testimony, which expresses her determination to resist abuse and claim her humanity and femininity as much as it describes her life as a slave, was an invaluable defense of abolition and the black female character.

Some women also published in various antislavery journals and literary magazines. The writings of Charlotte Forten, for example, appeared in the *Liberator*, the *Christian Recorder*, the *Anglo-African Magazine*, the *National Anti-Slavery Standard*, the *Atlantic Monthly*, and the *New England Magazine*. An avid scholar and educator, Forten also impressed her "society" of friends with her linguistic abilities, translating for publication the French novel *Madame Thérèse: or, The Volunteers of '92* by Emile Erckmann and Alexandre Chatrian.

One of the most prolific writers of her generation was Frances E. W. Harper, a free woman of color from Baltimore who had worked as a domestic, seamstress, and teacher before turning to writing and lecturing for the Maine Anti-Slavery Society on a full-time basis. Harper's poems were published in three volumes: *Poems on Miscellaneous Subjects* (1854), *Poems* (1871), and *Sketches of Southern Life* (1872). Eager to provide financial support as well as inspiration and information to the abolitionist movement, Harper used much of the income derived from her first book of poems to support William Still and his efforts on behalf of the Underground Railroad.

Mary Ann Shadd Cary was not only an influential abolitionist writer and activist but also the first African-American female editor. Determined not to have her political views or social critiques censored, Shadd Cary founded her own newspaper, the *Provincial Freeman*, in 1853. For six years Shadd Cary juggled positions on the fledgling antislavery and emigrationist journal, serving as its editor, writer, promoter, and fund-raiser. She was a pioneer in an all-male profession, however, and few were willing to provide her with long-term support.

Shadd Cary's personal cause was not helped by her conflict with Henry Bibb, a fugitive slave with considerable power in abolitionist circles whom she accused of illegal and unethical activities. Exposing Bibb's activities resulted in the loss of funding from the American Missionary Association for a school she had founded in Windsor, Canada. Shadd Cary continued to agitate, however, and part of her message was a scorching criticism of black male sexism. "Better far to have a class of sensible, industrious wood-sawyers, than of conceited poverty-starved lawyers, superficial professors, or conceited quacks," she asserted regarding the African-American male leadership in the United States and Canada in *Provincial Freeman*, May 5, 1855.

Shadd Cary was born in Wilmington, Delaware, but grew up in Pennsylvania. Like many of her female peers, she was reared in an African-American abolitionist household and as a child came to understand the kinds of sacrifices that one had to make in order to promote black freedom and equality. Yet her solutions differed substantially from those of many others. For one thing, Mary Ann Shadd Cary supported emigration to Canada, and she spent much of her time and energy during the 1850s promoting the exodus that eventually included approximately 15,000 people.

In 1852, she wrote a lengthy pamphlet entitled, *A Plea for Emigration or, Notes of Canada West, in its Moral, Social and Political Aspect*. Like other emigrationists, she believed that free black people could live better outside the United States. She also knew that Canada was one of the few places

on the continent where fugitive slaves could live without constant fear of being captured.

During the 1830s, 1840s, and 1850s, free women of color were at the forefront in establishing and maintaining female antislavery societies. For example, they are credited with founding the first women's abolitionist society, the Salem (Massachusetts) Female Antislavery Society, in 1832. Although many of these organizations did not include white members, some were racially integrated. **The Philadelphia Female Anti-Slavery Society**, for example, was founded in 1833 by both white and black women, including four from the prominent black Forten family.

Other integrated organizations were established in Rochester, New York, and Lynn and Boston, Massachusetts. Members sponsored many revenue-producing projects, public lyceums, exhibitions, and lectures, and they circulated abolitionist literature and various petitions directed at local, state, and national government agencies. Gaining a sense of their unique contributions to—and their general self-assurance within—these politically charged reformist circles, black women acted as representatives at regional and national antislavery conventions and helped initiate the earliest organized activities in the fight for women's rights.

Integrated abolitionist societies, however, did not eliminate demonstrations of racial bias. Many white abolitionists did not believe in racial equality or social integration. Often they refused to embrace black antislavery advocates socially, allow them to take leadership positions in various organizations, or support them as journalists and lecturers. Many spoke to or about black abolitionists in a condescending or patronizing manner, willing to tolerate some African-American participation in the movement but demanding that white activists retain ultimate control.

Black women abolitionists did not ignore these conflicts. "Our skins may differ, but from thee we claim / A sister's privilege and a sister's name," **Sarah Forten** wrote in a poem commissioned for the 1837 Convention of American Women. That same year, in a letter to **Charlotte Grimké**, she said, regarding prejudice, "Even our professed friends have not yet rid themselves of it. To some of them it clings like a dark mantle obscuring their many virtues and choking up the avenues of higher and nobler sentiments. I recollect the words of one of the best and least prejudiced men in the Abolition ranks. 'Ah,' said he, 'I can recall the time when in walking with a colored brother, the darker the night, the better Abolitionist was I.' . . . how much of this leaven still lingers in the hearts of our white brethren and sisters is oftentimes made manifest to us."

A few people were able to move beyond the bounds of racism and sexism not only to participate in local abolitionist organizations, but also to lecture as representatives of some of the largest and most powerful national antislavery societies. Younger generations of African-American women were able to take advantage of the opportunities painfully opened by their predecessors.

Sarah Parker Remond, for example, born in Salem, Massachusetts into a family of activists, was a member of several antislavery groups, and became a lecturer for the American Anti-Slavery Society in 1856. She lectured throughout the Northeast, England, Scotland, and Ireland from 1859 through the Civil War era, at first supporting the abolitionist cause and then hoping to influence the British not to support the Confederacy.

Many black women abolitionists defied a nineteenth-century convention that saw women as fragile and weak. Consider, for example, the life and work of Sojourner Truth. Born a slave in New York at the end of the eighteenth century, Truth (named Isabella Bomefree while a slave) was the victim of a series of cruel masters and devastating personal experiences, including separation from her parents as a child and having her own children sold away from her.

At about the same time as her emancipation, Sojourner Truth embraced Christianity and came to believe that it was her religious duty to further the cause of black men and women, slave and free. She was a tireless lecturer, often appearing unexpectedly but fascinating a charged crowd whenever she spoke. Refusing to be turned away by antagonists, Truth helped redefine womanhood in order to embrace the African-American woman's experience. "Nobody ever helps me into carriages, or over mud puddles, or gives me any best place!" she declared at a women's rights convention in Akron, Ohio, in 1851. "And ain't I a woman?"

Free women of color continued their various activities in support of abolition and black rights through the antebellum era and beyond. Not content to end their efforts with the initiation of the Civil War, they continued their agitation, hoping to convince the United States government and the American people to demand general emancipation as a condition for peace.

Other women joined forces to collect food, clothing, schoolbooks, and medical supplies for the thousands of slaves who escaped to Union lines during the war. Their efforts inspired younger women, many just finishing their formal education, to travel to the South during and after the Civil War to educate black Southerners. Teachers such as Charlotte Forten, **Sara Stanley**, Lucie Stanton Day, and Blanche Harris helped educate the first generation of literate former slaves. As always, their work, pursued under trying social and economic conditions, reflected their determination to fulfill their twofold duty as women and African Americans.

THE WAR TO END SLAVERY

The emancipation of slaves was unquestionably the single most significant event in the history of African-American women in the United States. This dramatic shift in legal status for the majority of women of African descent—a shift precipitated by war and followed by sectional and political crises that continued throughout much of the century—marked a new era. Although most former slaves were given "nothing but freedom," and although most African-American women found that the word *freedom* had different meanings for men and women, America would never again be the same.

Guns were fired at Fort Sumter, South Carolina, in April 1861, and within months the North and South were mobilized for battle. Southern states declared their independence and formed a Confederacy, while the North waged a fight to preserve the Union. African Americans in the United States were affected dramatically by the war's outbreak, with nearly four million slaves residing almost entirely within the Confederate states.

The typical experience of most of those held in bondage was the plantation, where slaves lived in groups of twenty or more on one estate. The war threatened to disrupt this system. First, masters and able-bodied men enlisted, leaving many plantations without male supervision. Second, many plantation mistresses who were left alone felt isolated and vulnerable. Third, the chaos of war created both opportunities and disadvantages for slaves left behind on estates.

The war turned many power relations upside down on the home front. Kate McClure, a plantation mistress left behind in Union County, South Carolina, banned Maybery, the overseer hired by her husband, from entering her household. She deputized a slave, Jeff, and admitted him into her home, since she trusted her slaves more than the white man left in charge. Her resistance to the overseer's authority and her discovery of his coercive sexual relationship with a slave named Susan forced Maybery to flee the plantation. Alliances between mistresses and slaves were rarely documented during wartime, but glimmers of these bonds remain nonetheless.

A large body of anecdotal evidence was supplied by plantation owners to demonstrate the loyalty, and by implication, contentment, of slaves within the Confederacy. Much of this evidence is based on recollection, consisting of often exaggerated and perhaps fictionalized accounts meant to repudiate the cause of Yankee invaders. Slave women were reported to have cooperated in efforts to protect supplies from Yankee requisitioning. Yet there is an equal body of evidence within the records of planters as well as documents preserved by the Union army to show that flight and "Confederate treason" (also known as "Union

In 1862, the First Confiscation Act prohibited the return of runaway slaves to their masters, and the Second Confiscation Act granted slaves their freedom when they fled the South for federal protection, unless they were owned by masters in border states who remained loyal to the Union. This photograph shows a school for the runaways, or contrabands. (NATIONAL ARCHIVES)

heroism") equally typified the wartime experience of slaves.

Slaves fleeing behind federal lines provided the Union with a public relations coup as well as a dilemma. Why were these people escaping slavery if it was the pleasant paternalistic system their owners painted? But beyond the abstract, what was the army to do with these hundreds, and soon thousands, who sought refuge from the Confederacy? General Benjamin Butler classified the runaway slaves as "contrabands"—the enemy's property—appropriating them for Union use. When slaves appeared in droves at Fortress Monroe, having deserted their posts building Confederate fortifications, Butler put the runaways to work finishing a bakehouse for his troops. Congress formally ratified this policy with the

First Confiscation Act of 1862, prohibiting the return of runaways to their masters, which had been a practice of some Union officers. Further, with the Second Confiscation Act of 1862, all slaves were granted their freedom when they fled the South for federal protection, except those owned by masters in the border states which remained loyal to the Union. This gave many slave families the opportunity to escape to freedom and to remain together.

Former slave Eliza Sparks remembered a lost Union soldier seeking guidance while she was nursing her child. She directed him to his destination, and he pulled out some money from his pocket, admired her child, and asked his name. He said, "Well, you sure have a purty baby. Buy him something with this; an' thankee fo' de direction.

Goodbye Mrs. Sparks." Sparks recalled the incident clearly because it was the first time she had been addressed as "Mrs." She remarked, "Now, what do you think of dat? Dey all call me 'Mrs. Sparks'!"

These charitable acts—granting former slaves the dignity they deserved—were uncommon. Most slaves were aware that Union soldiers were not fighting against slavery but for patriotism, or merely for pay. Despite this, most slaves, freedpeople, and free African Americans saw the Union cause as their own. Further, after the Emancipation Proclamation on January 1, 1863, the fight to preserve the Union was transformed into a battle against slavery. Black men enthusiastically enlisted for this cause.

African-American soldiers suffered enormous hardship and deprivation in their battle for recognition of their manhood. Many were rejected by those who saw the war as "a white man's war." But black participants volunteered, most notably in Massachusetts. By the war's end more than 180,000 African Americans had served in the Union army.

Perhaps the most famous African American who volunteered to serve the Union was Harriet Tubman, who had earned wide recognition and respect as a conductor on the Underground Railroad.

Acting on information gathered during Tubman's secret missions, Colonel James Montgomery, commander of the Second Carolina Volunteers, was able to lead

During the war, runaway slaves were classified by the Union forces as "contraband"—enemy property—and were put to work by the Union forces. In this contraband camp women served the officers of the Fifth Army Corps Headquarters at Harrison's Landing, James River, Virginia.
(NATIONAL ARCHIVES)

several successful raids on ammunition de-pots, supply warehouses, and other vital Confederate strongholds along the Comba-hee River. Although the Confederacy put a steep price on Tubman's head, honor was her only reward, as she received less than $200 from the army during her three years of service.

The wives and families of black soldiers, too, suffered during the war. Black women were suddenly thrown into economic chaos by a male relative's war service, as Jane Welcome complained to President Lincoln in her letter of November 21, 1864: "Mr. Abaraham lincon I wont to knw sir if you please wether I can have my son relest from the arme he is all the subport I have now his father is Dead and his brother that wase all the help that I had he has bean wonded twise he has not had nothing to send me yet." The reply was curt: "The interests of the service will not permit that your request be granted." Husbands and fathers at the front were sometimes deeply pained by news from home, especially when learning of the tribu-lations of loved ones left behind in slavery. One Missouri wife confided: "They are treating me worse and worse every day. Our child cries for you. Send me some money as soon as you can for me and my child are almost naked." The destruction of family harmony and the fears of wives and mothers wreaked havoc within the black community, slave and free.

But wartime provided some black women—especially slaves—with new op-portunities. Unlike white women, who were taking on men's roles and responsibilities for the first time in the fully mobilized Confed-eracy, slave women had always been forced to shoulder equal burdens on the planta-tions. The absence of white male rule and the increasing fears of white women on many plantations put slaves in better bar-gaining positions. Many African Americans on plantations took advantage of this situ-ation to improve their lot.

Others took the ultimate advantage. In the words of the time, they voted with their feet. They simply left their slave homes and freed themselves. The Sea Islands of South Carolina and other areas deserted by Confed-erate planters were pioneering communities of former slaves where education, family farms, and civil rights became a reality for African Americans within the occupied South.

Most slaves stayed behind—recalcitrant, re-bellious, and, in the end, an effective fifth column. Historians suggest that the failure of nerve and the failure of control in the plantation South undermined Confederate independence. And they document women's roles in disrupt-ing plantation work patterns and, in some cases, initiating work stoppages or strikes in the fields. These and other activities by black women behind the lines disheartened planta-tion mistresses, at the least. At the most, they prevented the plantation owners from main-taining discipline and productivity at a time when continued productivity was crucial to Confederate success.

Whatever the causes of defeat, the advent of emancipation marked the beginning of the end of slavery. Surrender on April 9, 1865, was only the formal recognition of the loss of Confederate control.

AFTER THE WAR

The war's end was celebrated by most slaves in an intense, dramatic fashion. Most former slaves interviewed by the Works Progress Administration during the 1930s recalled the momentous occasion of Union victory.

This store for freedpeople was located in Beaufort, South Carolina, in 1864.
(NATIONAL ARCHIVES)

The mother of author Paul Laurence Dunbar, Mathilda Dunbar, said, "I was in the kitchen getting breakfast. The word came—'All darkies are free.' I never finished breakfast! I ran 'round and 'round the kitchen, hitting my head against the wall, clapping my hands and crying 'Freedom! freedom! freedom! Rejoice, freedom has come!' Oh, how we sang and shouted that day!"

Thousands of similar celebrations echoed throughout the country, in both North and South, as black households expressed their jubilation. Many women, freed from the domestic tyranny of abusive mistresses, celebrated in ways calculated to offend their former owners. Using dress and fashion as

weapons, they paraded in fine clothing, often liberated from their mistresses' wardrobes. One former slave recalled with exasperation his wife's demand that the master's bed be dragged into their cabin, even though the massive piece of furniture occupied the entire floor space so the couple could not walk around inside their home. The freedwoman didn't care. She wanted to sleep in the bed that she had made for almost half a century.

Indeed, freedom had dramatically different meanings for slave men and women. The passage of the Thirteenth Amendment in December 1865 abolished slavery. But the Fourteenth Amendment (introduced in

1866 and ratified in July 1868) extended citizenship rights only to males of the former slave class. This was reinforced by the Fifteenth Amendment, introduced in 1869 and ratified in 1870. By federal statute, black women would be subjected to the same unequal status as white women.

And their way was, of course, even harder. The Freedmen's Bureau was set up to intervene when children were unlawfully apprenticed, when white employers drove black people off the land without compensation for their labor, when a husband deserted a family, or when destitution became desperation. A look at the petitions for relief to the bureau in one Alabama county in 1867 shows that almost 90 percent of the petitioning households were without adult males.

African-American women struggled against the tide of violence and resentment loosed by the war, seeking respectability as a shield in increasingly perilous times. But there was a bleak and abusive double standard. An article in a black newspaper in Augusta questioned, "Why is it that the wives and daughters of freedmen, though they be chaste as ice, and pay the same fare that white people do on railways, are put into filthy freight cars and compelled to submit to all kinds of vulgar and insulting language?" Black leaders vehemently objected to women's ejection from the "ladies car" and protested the use of the term "colored females," demanding the appellation "ladies."

Freedpeople did not seek social status—the niceties of ladyhood were irrelevant—but racial dignity and personal integrity were absolute priorities. Former slaves sought the protection of women and, by extension, all persons of African descent who were handicapped by the racism that continued to poison Southern society. Both black men and women suffered dehumanization as victims of the ridicule, caricature, and eventual violence that white racists promoted. Increasing numbers of white Southern men, frustrated by the postwar economic gloom and blaming former slaves, joined in the crusade to "redeem" and restore white supremacy in the South.

Some of these campaigns involved hooded men on nighttime raids, lynching, and the

These refugee quarters were located in Hilton Head, South Carolina. (NATIONAL ARCHIVES)

The harsh fieldwork done by black women during Reconstruction may have seemed identical to the labor of slave women, but to emancipated African-Americans, the opportunity to contribute to the family economy—their own, rather than a master's—symbolized freedom. (NEW YORK HISTORICAL SOCIETY)

sexual violation of African-American women. In Louisiana, during the fall of 1868, the Freedmen's Bureau compiled a massive record of complaints of violence under the heading, "Murders and Outrages." By October, more than one hundred freedpeople were reported dead, and terrorism against African Americans was on the rise. The conquered Confederates did not so much surrender as take the war home.

THE MOVEMENT FORWARD

Despite the perils, Reconstruction was a period during which institutions that had been invisible during slavery came to the surface. African-American women were in the forefront of movements for education. Southern black women teachers, such as **Mary S. Peake** and **Susie King Taylor**, and black women from the North (celebrated by W. E. B. DuBois as the "tenth crusade") worked together to make the next generation better prepared to enjoy the freedom that had been thrust upon them.

Black Southern women were essential in organizing the cooperatives, burial societies, and savings and loan associations established in the wake of the war. The ground swell of self-help organizations in devastated Southern towns and cities sustained African-American migrants fleeing harsh conditions in the countryside. The bulwark of the black community, the black church, was sustained by women whose charity and good works filled every corner of the South. Finally, women banded together to plant the seeds for the club movement that would flourish by the century's end. Through these bonds of black womanhood, mighty strides were made. Gains were even more impressive when measured against the overwhelming odds against freedpeople during the era of Reconstruction.

Most African Americans remained in the rural South and continued to perform agricultural work after emancipation. But women migrated to Southern cities in disproportionate numbers as they were pushed off farms and plantations where male laborers, or whole family units, were preferred. They took jobs performing the same kind of work many had done as slaves in the big house. Few occupations were open to these women except those of cook, general maid, child-nurse, and laundress. Some more specialized positions were available as chambermaids, kitchen helpers, or pastry cooks. A relatively small number found other work as seamstresses, midwives, nurses, and teachers.

In 1860, 11 percent of the African-American population (which numbered 4,488,000) was free. At that time, 15 percent of free black women were dressmakers and hairdressers, including those women who owned their own businesses. Five percent ran boardinghouses or small shops. The remaining 80 percent were laundresses and domestics, including day workers and those in service. In the urban South, this proportion did not change with the coming of freedom.

Most black women could expect to enter domestic service between the ages of ten and sixteen and remain in it throughout their lives. Their only choice lay in deciding which kind of domestic work to do. Positions as child-nurses tended to attract young, single women. Laundresses were usually older married women with children. They constituted the largest proportion of domestic workers, especially in large cities where the total numbers significantly exceeded those employed in smaller towns and rural areas. Women with families took in washing because it gave them greater independence and flexibility.

Washerwomen picked up dirty bundles from their patrons on Monday and did the wash in their own homes during the week. This allowed them to fit their outside work in with their own housework and child care. It also encouraged them to work together in communal spaces within their neighborhoods. Women often gathered to wash clothes in backyards or at common wells and streams. They got to know each other and, therefore, to help each other. The practical value of this support system was realized at critical moments when there was a need to spread vital news or share resources.

Cooks, child-nurses, and maids tended to work in relative isolation in most white households that employed only one or a few domestic workers. Still, one of the most distinguishing characteristics of domestic service in the South was that workers lived in their own homes. In order to emphasize the difference between slavery and freedom, most African-American women refused to live with their employers. White Southerners had mixed feelings about close contact with black servants, so the arrangement was convenient for employers as well.

More important for the development of the South, was that the domestics living apart from their employers could actively participate in the creation of community institutions. Laundresses led in combining

This perhaps posed photograph is entitled "Coming from the Well." It was taken at Wormsloe, Island of Hope, Georgia. (NEW YORK HISTORICAL SOCIETY)

By the end of the nineteenth century, black women were beginning to organize with a vengeance to protest their status in American society. This photo depicts the "First Congress of Negro Women, Atlanta, Georgia, December 1895." (SCHOMBURG CENTER)

the sustaining of family with the sustaining of neighborhood in their daily activities, but cooks, maids, and child-nurses also contributed toward the common good.

Workers and employers disagreed about many issues, with disputes over wages topping the list. Household laborers toiled long hours, often for twelve hours a day every day of the week, and their pay was terrible. In addition, their meager incomes sometimes provided the sole financial support of their families.

Paltry wages certainly diminished black women's living standards, but the complete denial of cash wages could wreak even greater havoc. Many employers readily engaged in questionable practices that bilked workers of their rightful earnings. At the end of the week

or month, for example, a domestic might discover exorbitant deductions from her wages, for damaging household objects or breaking household rules. She could even end up in debt to her employer.

Conflicts between employers and workers were not easily resolved. When negotiations failed and black women could not obtain the proper redress, they developed a variety of overt and covert methods to demonstrate their grievances and seek justice. Quitting, for example, proved to be a vexing way to deny employers total control. The ease with which black women moved from job to job became a popular complaint among employers bemoaning the perpetual "servant problem."

Mutual aid organizations such as the Daughters of Friendship, the Sisters of Love, and the Daughters of Liberty provided benefits to the sick, infirm, unemployed, widowed, and orphaned. But they also provided opportunities for worker unity and political and social expression. Benevolent societies enhanced the ability of individual wage earners to quit spontaneously and provided a surreptitious mechanism for exacting justice against unfair and unscrupulous employers through informal boycotts.

Strikes were rare but profound expressions of household workers' opposition to oppression. Washerwomen, taking advantage of their relative autonomy, led the vanguard of such mobilizations. They organized strikes in Jackson, Mississippi, in 1866; Galveston, Texas, in 1877; and Atlanta, Georgia, in 1881. Household workers in Norfolk, Virginia, joined a strike with tobacco stemmers and waitresses in 1917.

The demand for self-regulation—the ability to maintain control over their occupations—loomed large throughout these strikes. The strikers gathered wide support among other African Americans by canvassing their neighborhoods and knocking on doors, conducting mass meetings, and building on groups and organizations previously established. They sent petitions to local officials and newspapers to argue their cases and demonstrated remarkable resilience and skill in the face of the considerable forces marshaled against them.

The ability to negotiate was considerably less in rural areas, where hundreds of thousands of poor black women had little or no opportunity to improve their deteriorating economic lot. By 1870, eight out of ten black children remained illiterate. Southern state legislatures were preparing to write

into law Jim Crow practices enforcing segregation, which began in Tennessee in 1881. The withdrawal of federal troops from the South in 1877 signaled a halt to African-American gains, and dreams slipped away with Yankee guardians.

White backlash decreased black hopes of a steady path to permanent progress. Rather, the march to equality would be marked by

Born into the black elite of Memphis, Tennessee, in 1863, Mary Church Terrell was sheltered from racism as much as possible by her parents. As her awareness of discrimination grew, so too did her resolve to prove the abilities of African Americans in general and of African-American women in particular. (LIBRARY OF CONGRESS)

Dr. Hallie Tanner Johnson was the first woman licensed to practice medicine in Alabama. See Science, Health, and Medicine *for a history of black American women health professionals.* (SCHOMBURG CENTER)

obstacles, detours, and deterrents along the way, even after the great signpost of freedom that had accompanied the Civil War. African-American women would nevertheless continue the course, journeying forward on the path taken by those before them, down the road to a better life for those who would follow.

THE LAST DECADES

The seeds were sown in the small black schools of the late 1700s. The plants were nourished by the mutual benefit societies and the literary groups of the 1800s. Then,

in the last decades of the nineteenth century, a garden of determined, educated black women began to bloom.

When **Fannie Barrier Williams** stood on the platform at the **World's Columbian Exposition** and spoke of a new day for black women, she represented thousands like herself around the country. All were committed to using their education, and even their ambition, in the service of the African-American people.

Many of these women came from a middle class that had its roots in free black society before the Civil War. But the black middle class was not defined primarily by money or family background. In a society where economic opportunities were so limited for African Americans, that was hardly possible. Instead, social status was based largely on behavior, on upholding extremely strict standards of respectability and morality. A laundress could easily be considered middle class, so long as she behaved like a duchess.

In *Black Women in America*, Sharon Harley defines three groups within the black middle class—the upper-middle-class social elite, the new professional middle class, and the lower middle class.

In the first group, the women often came from prominent families, had white ancestors, and were very light-skinned. Most came from generations of free blacks. These women were considered highly desirable wives for successful black men. They were also the first black women to be accepted by white women in clubs and political organizations.

Mary Church Terrell was one of the black elite. The daughter of black millionaire Robert Church, she became one of the most active clubwomen and activists in the black community. **Josephine St. Pierre Ruffin** moved with her husband to England to escape American racism but returned to fight for abolition. She remained to found or co-found many black and interracial activist organizations. Fannie Barrier Williams was the daughter of a New York merchant and the wife of a successful lawyer. In addition to speaking at the Columbian Exposition, she founded and raised money for hospitals, settlement houses, and other social causes. She was also the first black woman member of the elite Chicago Women's Club.

The second group was made up of women who earned their status through education and professional achievement. Many were teachers and librarians who dedicated their lives to the belief that education would be the salvation of black people in America. Others worked in, or owned, black businesses. Some were doctors, lawyers, and other professionals.

Rebecca Lee Crumpler, in 1864, had been the first black woman to become a licensed physician in the United States. In 1867 and 1870 respectively, she was joined by **Rebecca J. Cole** and **Susan McKinney Steward**. In 1891, **Halle Tanner Johnson** was the first woman—of any race—to be licensed to practice medicine in Alabama. Between 1869, when it opened its doors to women, and the end of the century, twenty-three black women graduated from Howard University Medical School.

In 1879, **Mary Eliza Mahoney** became the first African American in the United States to receive a diploma in nursing, but there was a number of black women who served as nurses before licensing was required.

In 1872, **Charlotte E. Ray** became the first black woman lawyer in the United States. In 1883, Mary Ann Shadd Cary became the second black woman to earn a law degree in the United States. Not until 1925 was a black woman licensed to practice in a Southern State.

In 1875, **Anna and Emma Hyers** sowed the seeds of the black theater movement when they produced a play based on the black experience, called *Out of Bondage*.

Ida B. Wells-Barnett became a leader in the antilynching movement when her close friend Tom Moss was murdered by a mob. She is pictured here (left) with his wife, Betty, and his children, Maureen and Tom, Jr. (c. 1893). Wells-Barnett protested the treatment of black women at the World's Columbian Exposition in Chicago shortly thereafter. (THE JOSEPH REGENSTEIN LIBRARY, THE UNIVERSITY OF CHICAGO)

They would continue to produce and tour with a musical theater company for many years.

In 1895, **Maggie Lena Walker** started her career with the Independent Order of St. Luke, a mutual benefit society. Under her guidance, the organization opened the St. Luke Penny Savings Bank, and Walker became the first woman bank president in the United States.

There were musicians and composers such as **Marie Selika, Sissieretta Jones, Flora Batson,** and **Nellie B. Mitchell**. There were writers and journalists such as **Ida B. Wells-Barnett, Gertrude Mossell,** and **Frances Ellen Watkins Harper**. There were business-women such as **Mary Ellen Pleasant,** who owned restaurants, laundries, and boarding-houses in San Francisco, and **Madame C. J. Walker,** who founded a cosmetics empire.

The third group that made up the emerging middle class were women who simply worked hard at whatever job they had, were constructive members of their communities, supported their churches, and maintained that mandatory high level of respectability. As Harley says, "Education and means (however limited) obligated members of the black middle class to assume important community roles and to work to better their race. Thus, free time that could have been devoted to purely leisure-time activities often went to conducting mothers' meetings, operating kindergartens, teaching Sunday school, and aiding working women." Belonging to the middle class, she goes on to say, was more a duty than a status symbol.

The women gathered together in clubs and political groups. They fought against lynching and for the vote. They raised money for schools and hospitals. They made the churches and the community strong. In short, they became the foundation on which the civil rights movements of the twentieth century would build.

These black women, from the first slaves who arrived in 1619 to the lawyers and doctors and nurses of the late nineteenth century, faced appalling obstacles. Many died in pain and sorrow. Others lived to enjoy respect and prosperity. All of them left behind a legacy of pride, and remarkable, moving stories.

[This introduction was adapted from the following articles in the *Black Women in America: An Historic Encyclopedia*: "Abolition Movement," by Brenda E. Stevenson; "Civil War and Reconstruction," by Catherine Clinton; "Domestic Workers in the South," by Tera Hunter; "Free Black Women in the Antebellum North," by James O. Horton; "Free Black Women in the Antebellum South," by Adele Logan Alexander and Virginia Gould; "The Middle Class," by Sharon Harley; "Northwest Territory," by Darlene Clark Hine; "Slavery," by Brenda E. Stevenson; "World's Columbian Exposition," by Wanda Hendricks.]

A

African Methodist Episcopal Preaching Women in the Nineteenth Century

Throughout the nineteenth century, hundreds of African-American women traveled the country preaching the gospel of Christianity. Fewer than three were ever officially ordained into the ministry though most were successful in the type of ministry they practiced. Within the African Methodist Episcopal (AME) Church, the collective efforts of preaching women served as a cutting edge that pierced the fabric of the all-male church hierarchy. When the denomination was organized in 1816, there was no organizational position for women. By 1900, however, church structure had been expanded to include three positions for women's service. In addition, the radical question of ordaining women to the ministry had been considered by church officials on eight occasions. The existence and success of preaching women were major reasons for church actions to officially include women and their service.

Nineteenth-century AME preaching women would never have considered themselves a radical element in their church, but they were extremely committed to their supreme call to preach the gospel and were devoutly religious in their Christian faith. To surrender a call from their God because a worldly organization did not approve would have meant a serious breach of their religious beliefs. However, throughout the century, preaching women carrying out their call consistently caused church officials to reconsider women's absence in denominational structure.

Jarena Lee was the first woman preacher of the AME Church, and she began her gospel work before African Methodism was organized; in fact, no one has been found who precedes her in preaching activities.

Between 1816 and 1849, the year Lee published her autobiographical *Journal*, a number of women were active as preachers within the AME Church network. Sophie Murray, for example, was an early member of the Philadelphia Bethel African Methodist Church, as was Elizabeth Cole. Each woman was referred to as an evangelist of the congregation and was reported to have "held many glorious prayer meetings [where] many souls were brought to the saving knowledge." In New Jersey, Rachel Evans distinguished herself as a better preacher than her acclaimed husband and was referred to as "a preacheress of no ordinary ability. She could rouse a congregation at any time." In Washington, D.C., Harriet Felson Taylor also earned a reputation for her preaching abilities. As one of the first members of that city's 1840 Union Bethel congregation, Taylor was identified as "first female exhorter and local preacher." Similarly, **Zilpha Elaw** was a preaching woman within African Methodism from 1816 to 1849. Not only did she visit the annual conference of the Bethel AME Church of

Baltimore in 1828, but, like Lee, she published an autobiography.

None of these women, or the many others not named, was ordained. In the context of Christianity of the time, there was no authority that sanctioned women as preachers. Independent denominations like the AME Church had separated themselves from white bodies over issues of a racially inclusive worship, but no group had ever questioned the church's patriarchy or the authority of an exclusively male clergy. The preaching women themselves were not as interested in altering the organizational arrangements of their church as they were in garnering recognition for their right to preach. However, their activities and their reputations as successful preachers threatened the exclusive authority of men in the ministry.

Although the AME Church had not formally responded to women preachers, by the 1844 meeting of the General Conference the issue had gained so much public attention that it required official consideration. Reverend Nathan Ward and others, as authorized members of the decision-making body, presented a petition requesting that the church "make provisions for females to preach and exhort." This petition was defeated, but at the next meeting of the conference, in 1848, another request was made that women be licensed to preach in connection with "ministerial privileges, akin to those of men."

The significance of the challenge posed by these petitions is reflected in the fact that the reigning church thinker of 1848, Reverend Daniel Payne, soon to be bishop, "filed a protest against the licensing of females to travel in the connection." In writing an official history of the church in 1891, after serving thirty-nine years as bishop, Payne trivialized women's preaching activities and the petitions for their licensing:

> The origin of the question is found in the fact that certain women members of the AME Church, who believed themselves divinely commissioned to preach by formal licenses, subsequently organized themselves into an association with avowed intention of laying out a field of usefulness for themselves, and making out appointments for such a field after the manner of our Annual Conferences. They held together for a brief period, and then fell to pieces like a rope of sand.

None of this stopped women from preaching, and at the next meeting of the General Conference a distinct action, as called for in the episcopal address of Bishop William Paul Quinn, was secured. By a large majority vote, the all-male body defeated the bishop's 1852 request that the church consider licensing women to preach. The question of authorizing women preachers quieted for a while, but the women's activities did not. More significantly, the issue reflected the larger problem of a lack of positions for women within the denominational structure.

Between 1816 and 1852, the AME Church expanded its membership tremendously, and women were the majority of participants in that expansion. Individually and collectively, women were the essence of African Methodism: they helped construct church buildings; they supported denominational programs; they converted and socialized new members; they led worship; they sustained fledgling congregations; they fed and clothed ministers; they visited the sick in the name of the church; they buried the dead; and they financed church work.

However, every officially designated position within the church structure was reserved for men.

In 1868, male leadership could no longer avoid taking some type of action to correct this serious omission. Men had dismissed the question of women's ordination at the 1864 General Conference by not discussing it. However, they could no longer justify women's absence from church positions, given their overwhelming majority in the growth and development of African Methodism. At the 1868 conference, delegates created the position of stewardess and allowed pastors to nominate a board of stewardesses. As conditional and male-dependent as this was, it was still the first and official position for women in the denomination.

Preaching women were not seeking just any service, however; they had been called to proclaim the Christian gospel. The position of stewardess might suffice for the services of many AME women, but there remained a group who would continue to preach. Between 1868 and 1900, the number of women functioning as preachers increased tremendously, and their work did not go unnoticed. Amanda Berry Smith was among the more internationally known preaching women of the period, and Margaret Wilson of the New Jersey Annual Conference was known for her work at the Haleyville Mission in 1883. Emily Calkins Stevens and Harriet A. Baker had support from bishops of the church, including Bishop John Mifflin Brown. Lena Doolin Mason was exceptionally active in her preaching.

By the 1884 meeting of the General Conference, the preponderance of women preachers, and their renowned successes, were once again challenging the male-dominated church hierarchy. Part of the problem was the increasing number of pastors willing to give license to female evangelists in order that their congregations be the beneficiaries of the women's successful proselytizing work. These local licenses were not under the control of the denominational church, and the 1884 conference was urged to take action.

To concede the reality of preaching women and their successes, the conference gave denominational approval to licensing women, but with severe restrictions. The concession of the female evangelist position was the second organizational change made by the church to accommodate its women members. However, the change did not sanction women's call to the gospel ministry, and it did not authorize them to ordination. Preaching women refused to be satisfied and continued their activities. The issue was brought to a head again with the 1885 ordination of Sarah A. H. of North Carolina. The 1888 meeting of the General Conference once again had to consider the topic of ordaining women.

The all-male leadership of the conference began making a definitive decision by first reprimanding Bishop Henry McNeal Turner for ordaining a woman. They then proceeded to issue a strongly worded resolution absolutely prohibiting the ordination of women. The resolution passed, and bishops were officially "forbidden to ordain a woman to the order of a deacon or an elder."

In spite of limitations from the denomination, women persevered with their work. Mary C. Palmer, Melinda M. Cotton, Emma V. Johnson, and Mary L. Harris made extensive reports of their 1896-98 preaching activities to the Philadelphia Annual Conference, for example. Margaret Wilson also continued and reported on her preaching success to the 1897 New Jersey Annual

Conference. African Methodist women labored to preach despite church restrictions.

As the nineteenth century came to a close, the male hierarchy of the church made another attempt to channel women's activities from those that challenged men's exclusive authority to ministry. At the 1900 meeting of the General Conference, delegates agreed to create another position for women. This final organizational, gender-specific position was that of deaconess. There were formal rituals for becoming a deaconess, but the position was never part of the ordained ministry like that of deacon for men.

It would be another forty-eight years before the African Methodist Episcopal Church authorized women into the ordained ministry, but without the persistence of preaching women, the inclusion of women's activities by way of other structural positions might have been delayed.

JUALYNNE E. DODSON

Albert, Octavia   (1853–c.1890)

Octavia Victoria Rogers Albert was a teacher and author, known for her religious commitment and for writing a collection of slave narratives. She was born a slave on December 24, 1853, in Oglethorpe, Georgia. After emancipation, she attended Atlanta University, where she trained to become a teacher. Her first teaching position was at a school in Montezuma, Georgia, where she met A. E. P. Albert in 1873. On October 21, 1874, they married and moved to Houma, Louisiana. They had one child.

In 1875, she joined the African Methodist Episcopal (AME) Church in Oglethorpe, under the leadership of Bishop Henry McNeal Turner. When her husband was ordained a minister in the Methodist Episcopal Church

in 1877, she converted to Methodism and was baptized in 1878.

Albert's home in Houma became a gathering place for former slaves. She taught them to read and write, read them the Scriptures, and encouraged them to discuss their lives during slavery. A skilled interviewer and writer, Albert recorded their experiences. Having been freed from slavery before she was old enough to understand the institution, Albert felt compelled to create an accurate record of slavery in the United States. The resulting book, *The House of Bondage*, was published posthumously in 1890 by her husband and daughter. It consists of seven slave narratives, recorded fifteen years after the end of slavery. The narratives are vivid accounts of the inhumane treatment of slaves. She also records the progress of some freedpeople during the Reconstruction period.

Albert wrote to correct and re-create history, not just to satisfy her artistic talent. Her evangelism was evident in her writings. She believed that God would make the entire nation accountable for the sins of slavery and charged that slavery under Catholic slaveholders was more oppressive than under Protestants.

She compared slavery in the United States to the Egyptian bondage of the people of Israel. Noting the differences between black and white racial attitudes, she preached a gospel of spiritual development. Albert shows that Christianity survived in the black community despite slave owner's refusal to allow slaves to practice religion.

VIVIAN NJERI FISHER

Allen, Sarah   (1764–1849)

Although she is usually ignored, or thought of only as the wife of Richard Allen, first bishop of the African Methodist Episcopal (AME) Church, Sarah Allen was also instrumental in establishing the first official role of women within the church and providing the assistance necessary for AME ministers to carry out their mission. Most biographers accept that Sarah Allen was born in 1764 on the Isle of Wight, but no verification has been found. At the age of eight, she was brought as a slave to Philadelphia, and though it is not yet known how she acquired freedom, she married Richard Allen in 1800. She died July 16, 1849, in Philadelphia at the home of her daughter Ann.

Most of Allen's life was devoted to raising her four sons and two daughters while securing the household resources and home atmosphere that fostered her husband's ministry. She was undoubtedly, however, the guiding force behind the formation of Daughters of Conference organizations of the predominantly African-American AME Church.

As the small group of itinerant ministers of African Methodism returned to Philadelphia for the young church's first annual conference, their appearance and clothing were at best bedraggled. Allen organized women of the church to remedy the condition of the men's attire.

Allen continued to lead conference women in feeding, repairing garments for, and improving the appearance of AME pastors. These activities spread beyond Philadelphia as a tradition was formed. In 1827, the organizations were officially designated Daughters of Conference, wherein AME women assumed responsibility to provide material improvements for ministers assigned to their annual conferences.

Long after Allen's death, the Daughters of Conference organizations provided an es-

When she saw the bedraggled state of her husband and his colleagues at the African Methodist Episcopal Church's first annual conference, Sarah Allen formed a group of women to clothe and feed the dedicated black ministers. Daughters of Conference, Allen's group, became a crucial part of the support system for impoverished black churches and their clergy. (SCHOMBURG CENTER)

sential supplement to AME minister's meager salaries and insured the survival of church clergy.

JUALYNNE E. DODSON

Anderson, Naomi (b. 1843)

Developing survival strategies for herself and the people of her race characterized Naomi Anderson's adult life. Born free in Indiana during the antebellum period, Anderson exemplified nineteenth-century feminism, self-help, and westward migration, and was a pioneer in the black woman's club movement.

Naomi Bowman was born March 1, 1843, in Michigan City, Indiana. Her parents, Elijah and Guilly Ann Bowman, were free black Americans, natives of Ohio. Her mother's goal was to educate Naomi so that she could graduate from **Oberlin College**, but Guilly Ann's death in 1860 prevented Naomi from going to college.

From that time on, Naomi Bowman shared the plight of African-American women during and after the Civil War. Her

As one of the strongest black voices in the women's suffrage movement, Naomi Anderson gained the respect and affection of Susan B. Anthony and Elizabeth Cady Stanton for her fight against racism. (SCHOMBURG CENTER)

marriage to William Talbert in 1863 marked a hopeful time, but the events that followed—the deaths of Naomi's brother, sister, and her first born of four children, plus her husband's failing health—brought hardships. Throughout this period, Naomi Talbert struggled to keep the family together. Her husband died in 1877, after the family had moved three times, settling in Chicago.

Despite the tragedies, Talbert began a career of feminism and public service, including temperance and suffrage work. She delivered a controversial pro-women suffrage speech at the women's rights convention held at Chicago in 1869 and engaged in the temperance work of the International Organization of Grand Templars (IOGT). Throughout the late 1870s, Naomi Talbert made several lecture tours in Illinois, Indiana, and Ohio, promoting women's rights and, while living in Portsmouth, Ohio, she helped to organize a home for orphaned African-American children.

After William Talbert's death, Naomi became the main provider for her three surviving children and her aging father. She learned the hairdressing trade and later passed the Ohio Board of Examiners examination for public school teachers. By 1879, she and her family had moved to Columbus, Ohio, where she practiced cosmetology and wrote articles on temperance and women's rights. Talbert was one of a growing number of African-American women who felt the sting of both racism and sexism and decided to speak out.

Talbert met Lewis Anderson in Columbus. They married in 1881 and moved to a farm outside of the city. "Kansas fever" attracted them, however, and like many

African Americans, they headed west, settling in Wichita, Kansas, in 1884. Anderson became a successful financier, freeing Naomi to campaign for women's rights.

In Kansas, Naomi Anderson promoted the efforts of the woman suffrage movement and the Women's Christian Temperance Union (WCTU). In 1892, she campaigned with white suffragists for the state woman suffrage referendum, only the second in the nation. Nonetheless, she realized the prejudices of white women in both the suffrage and the temperance movements. As a result, she sought to convince her white neighbors that African Americans were not foreigners, but Americans entitled to full rights of citizenship. An example of the prejudice she fought occurred when the white clubwomen in Wichita organized a children's home that barred black children. In response, Anderson organized the women of her race to raise funds for a children's home for African Americans. By 1890, the women had rented a small facility and obtained a monthly stipend from the county to help support it.

By 1895, Naomi Anderson had left Kansas for California. Whether she was joined by her husband and her adult children is not known. However, in San Francisco, Anderson, then in her fifties, became active in the woman suffrage movement, representing African-American women at the state level in their efforts to lobby the legislature. In so doing, she earned praise for her work from noted woman suffragists Susan B. Anthony and Elizabeth Cady Stanton.

Apparently Anderson continued a life of service to women and to black people, leaving legacies throughout her westward trek from Ohio, to Kansas, to California. After 1895, her name did not appear again in the proceedings of the National American Woman Suffrage Association. Presumably she remained in California until her death, the date of which has yet to be established.

ROSALYN TERBORG-PENN

B

Batson, Flora (1864–1906)

Born on April 16, 1864, in Washington, D.C., Flora Batson was one of the most famous black concert singers of the late nineteenth century, known as "The Double-Voiced Queen of Song" because of her

Flora Batson was known as the "Double-Voiced Queen of Song" when she sang before enthusiastic audiences throughout the United States and Europe, and as far afield as the Samoan Islands. (SCHOMBURG CENTER)

phenomenal baritone to soprano range. Her youth was spent in Providence, Rhode Island, where she made her first public appearances. Although she had already won some recognition in the United States and Europe through singing with churches and in programs promoting the temperance movement, she reached the height of her fame with the Bergen Star Company after becoming its star singer in 1885. The same year, she married Colonel John Bergen, the white manager of the company, and their collaboration continued until 1896.

Another phase of Flora Batson's concert career began in 1896 with a new manager, Gerard Millar, a black basso. The two performed concerts together and sang as a featured duo with the South before the War Company. Batson's last years were spent in Philadelphia, where she was still called upon to perform in concert and in dramatic presentations. Flora Batson was adored by American audiences, who gave her impressive gifts of jewelry that she regularly wore at concerts.

Concert appearances outside the United States included visits to Europe, Great Britain, the Samoan Islands, New Zealand, Australia, India, Fiji, China, and Japan, highlighted by performances for Pope Leo XIII and royalty, such as Queen Victoria of England and Queen Liliuokalani of Hawaii. Flora Batson died in Philadelphia on December 1, 1906.

DORIS EVANS McGINTY

Beasley, Mathilda (c.1833–1903)

Mathilda Beasley made an unsuccessful attempt to establish a convent of black sisters in Savannah, Georgia. A free woman of color, she was born about 1833 in New Orleans of mixed Creole and Native American parentage. Sometime in the 1850s, she married Abraham Beasley, a businessman, restaurant owner, and sometime slave dealer. During Reconstruction he acquired extensive property, including racehorses. Although it was against the law, Mathilda taught slaves. After the death of her husband (c. 1878), she gave her property to the Catholic Church, stipulating that an orphanage for black children be established. At some point after 1880, under circumstances that remain unclear, she went to England to become a Franciscan nun.

After 1885, Beasley returned to Georgia and began a community of black sisters, first in Wilkes County then in Savannah. It is uncertain whether Beasley was a professed Franciscan sister when she returned from England. It is certain that by 1889 she and two other black women had begun the religious life following the Franciscan Rule. By 1896 the Catholic Directory indicated that there were five sisters and nineteen young orphan girls, all black, in Savannah. Mother Beasley sought in vain to affiliate her community officially to the Franciscan Order. From her letters to Mother Katherine Drexel in Philadelphia, the founder of the Sisters of the Blessed Sacrament for Indians and Colored People, we know of her financial needs and her pleas for help in the spiritual formation of her sisters. In the end, she received little help of any kind. In 1898, the community was suppressed, the orphanage was taken over by the Missionary Franciscan

Born a free woman of color, Mathilda Beasley began a community of black sisters in Georgia in the late 1880s. She sought in vain to affiliate her community officially to the Franciscan Order. (GEORGIA HISTORICAL SOCIETY)

Sisters of the Immaculate Conception, and Mother Beasley retired to a small cottage near Sacred Heart Church, at the time a church for black Catholics. Here she lived a life of poverty, prayer, and charitable works. On Sunday morning, December 20, 1903, she was found dead in her cottage in an attitude of prayer. Mother Beasley's work was seemingly a failure; her success was her life of holiness and service, a memory that lives on in the Savannah black community to this day.

CYPRIAN DAVIS, O.S.B.

Becroft, Anne Marie   (1805–1833)

"In spite of ill health this pious girl rendered herself useful" and "had a very sweet disposition joining with it the firmness necessary to make her respected by children." That diary note, written by Father Nicholas Joubert in 1833, describes one of America's most illustrious women—Anne Marie Becroft. Her accomplishments in education in the early nineteenth-century helped shape black Catholic history in the United States.

Anne Becroft, the oldest of seven children, was born in 1805 to freeborn William and Sara Becroft. At age four, she began her formal education at the white-operated Potter School in Washington, D.C. However, hostilities associated with race and slavery forced her to leave that school in 1812. The following year, she resumed her studies at the New Georgetown School, which was operated by a white widow named Mary Billing. Becroft studied with Billing until 1820 when the Denmark Vesey Revolt affected Billing's ability to operate the school. It closed because white involvement in the education of black people was discouraged. That same year, Becroft opened her own school on Georgetown's Dumbarton Street and for eight years operated this small day school for girls, continuing the work of Mary Billing. Then, in 1827, Becroft was invited by the parish priest of Holy Trinity Catholic Church to open a school under the auspices of the church.

Holy Trinity Church was a white church, but as far back as 1787 black Catholics had been parishioners. Given Becroft's extraordinary abilities as a teacher, it is not surprising that Father J. Van Lommel asked her to begin a day and boarding school for black girls. With the assistance of the white Visitation nuns, the academy opened on Fayette Street. The tuition, one dollar a month, was paid by thirty-five students who came from well-to-do and poor families in Washington, Virginia, and Maryland. The school remained in Becroft's hands until 1831 when she turned it over to former student, Ellen Simonds, and left to become the ninth nun of the Oblate Sisters of Providence in Baltimore.

On September 8, 1832, Becroft took her habit and a new name, Sister Aloysius; the following year she took her vows. As a teaching Oblate, she instructed her students in arithmetic, English, and embroidery, but her life as a nun was brief. She had been sickly off and on since age fifteen, but in 1833 her health began to deteriorate rapidly. She died on December 16, 1833, and was buried in the Old Cathedral Cemetery in Baltimore.

Anne Becroft was a courageous woman. She brought education and religion to black females at a time when freedom was a fragile commodity. She lived in a society in which slavery and racism were firmly entrenched, even so she was able to stimulate in her students a desire for educational attainment. No stone monument has been erected on behalf of this righteous woman, but her presence continues to be felt in black history.

GLORIA MARROW

Bowen, Cornelia   (1858–1934)

"One could feel the impact of her dedication and commitment. It was here that my outlook on, and commitment to, life began to take shape. It was here that I began to dream dreams of the life I wanted to live." This brief comment demonstrates the lifelong impression that was made on Solomon Seay (1991), a Montgomery civil rights leader, by Cornelia Bowen, his teacher and principal, whose life was dedicated to the education of black youth.

Cornelia Bowen was born into slavery in 1858, on Colonel William Bowen's plantation home in Macon County, Alabama. She attended Tuskegee Institute, where she was a member of the first graduating class in 1885. Upon graduation, she was named principal of Tuskegee Institute's Children's House. While on a fund-raising tour in the New England area in 1888, Washington telegraphed Bowen with a request that she start a school in the vicinity of Mt. Meigs, Alabama. Toward that end and with the use of funds provided by E. N. Pierce of Plainville, Connecticut, Bowen purchased land and began an industrial school known as the Mt. Meigs Institute. After the state assumed control of the school in the early 1900s, Bowen remained on the board of trustees.

Bowen continued her own education by attending Teachers College at Columbia University and Queen Margaret College in Glasgow, Scotland, among other institutions of higher learning. She also served as an officer of many organizations, including the Alabama State Teachers Association, the Colored Women's Federation of the State of Alabama, and the **National Association of Colored Women**. After a life of stressing the importance of education, Cornelia Bowen died in 1934.

SANDRA BEHEL

Bowser, Mary Elizabeth   (b.c. 1840s)

Jefferson Davis, during the years of the Civil War, made the fatal mistake of underestimating the power—and the intelligence—of a black woman. As a result, military plans discussed in his dining room unerringly, for a time, made their way into Ulysses S. Grant's hands.

The immediate agent of this dazzling piece of espionage was Mary Elizabeth Bowser. She was born on a plantation outside Richmond, Virginia, as a slave; the owners were the Van Lew family. When John Van Lew died in 1851, however, the abolitionist women of his family freed all of his slaves. They are reported even to have bought and then freed the members of their servant's families who lived in other households. Bowser remained at the Van Lew home as a servant, along with another former slave, named Nelson. Nelson, who went North with her after the fall of Richmond many years later, may have been her father. In the meantime, however, the Van Lew family sent Bowser to Philadelphia to receive an education, and she was there at the beginning of the Civil War.

Elizabeth Van Lew, the daughter of the family, was a strong Union sympathizer. For the first few months of the war, she nursed Union soldiers in Libby Prison. Later, her activities became more daring. She became a spy. Feigning weakness of the mind, she allowed herself to be called "Crazy Bet" in order to avert suspicion from herself. Then she began to help prisoners escape from Libby Prison by hiding them in a secret room in her house. While they were there, the prisoners would tell her everything they had been able to learn by listening to their guards while in the Confederate prison. Van Lew wrote down the information in cipher code and sent it through the lines to Grant, General Benjamin J. Butler, and other Union officers.

Van Lew's ardor did not stop there. She decided that she should have an intelligence agent in Jefferson Davi's own home. She sent for Bowser, who soon became a servant in the Confederate White House. Like Van Lew, Bowser pretended to have a mental deficiency. She was therefore disregarded while her sharp wits garnered information from the Davise's conversations with their guests. She also read dispatches as she dusted, and carried all this information home with her in her head. Back at the Van Lew home each night, she recited from memory everything she had learned, and Van Lew put it into code.

The coded messages were carried to the Union officers in a variety of ways. A black servant of Van Lew's—an old man—went from Richmond to the Van Lew farm for provisions every day. He carried a pass that allowed him to make the journey. The story goes that one egg in each batch of provisions was a dummy and that messages were carried in that egg. Another servant, a black seamstress who worked for a family named Carrington, carried the materials of her trade between the homes of Union sympathizers. Cipher messages were worked into her dress patterns.

Elizabeth Bowser recorded much of this espionage activity in a diary. The diary is now owned by a black family in Richmond that has never allowed it to be published or even read by outsiders.

KATHLEEN THOMPSON

Briggs, Martha B. (1838–1889)

University faculty member and public school administrator Martha B. Briggs is noteworthy for her service in the preparation of schoolteachers in the nation's capital.

As a member of the Normal and Preparatory Department of **Howard University**, 1873-79, principal of Miner Normal School, 1879-83, and principal of the Normal Department of Howard University, from 1883 until her death in March 1889, Briggs participated in efforts at the District of Columbia public schools and at Howard University to prepare men and women to teach. These new teachers taught not only in the District but also in schools in the South—serving in the latter almost as young missionaries.

Martha B. Briggs was born of John and Fannie Bassett Briggs in New Bedford, Massachusetts. She was educated in that New England town and first taught there in her father's home. Briggs left New Bedford for Easton, Maryland, then in 1869 moved to Washington, D.C. She remained in the District for the next twenty years.

With four year's experience as teacher and principal in Washington, D.C. public schools, Briggs left the public school system in 1873 to begin her career at Howard University.

The Howard University *Catalogue*, 1873–74, records the Normal Department Faculty and identifies Martha B. Briggs as "Instructor in Normal Department." Briggs is identified in later years as an "Instructor in Mathematics."

The performance of Martha B. Briggs at Howard University as an instructor in the Normal Department for the six-year period 1873-79 drew the attention of the public school leadership. When the board of trustees for the District of Columbia assumed authority over Miner Normal School in 1879 and sought a principal for that institution, the board offered the position to Briggs and she accepted.

Assuming leadership of the institution that had been inaugurated by Myrtilla Miner in December 1851, Martha B. Briggs was praised at the conclusion of her first year. In June 1880, Briggs received the board's commendation:" We express the belief and hope that the Miner Normal School, whose first year has proved so successful under the earnest and faithful charge of its principal, Miss Martha B. Briggs, will eventually not only supply the colored schools of the District with educated and earnest teachers, but that it will in a measure contribute to supply the demand of the South for colored teachers for the colored race."

Miner Normal—often officially recorded as Washington Normal School No. 2—was a relatively new school building. It had been built in 1876 by the trustees of the Miner Fund Board, a legal institution flowing from the creation in 1863 by the U.S. Congress of the "Institute for the Education of Colored Youth." In addition, the Miner Fund Board's financial support for the Normal Department of Howard University in 1871 resulted in Myrtilla Miner Hall (a dormitory for girls at Howard).

Because of illness in 1883, Briggs elected to end her service as Miner Normal School principal and returned to Howard University's Normal Department. The *Catalogue* records her as "Principal of the Normal Department."

Briggs died on March 28, 1889, at the age of fifty. The District of Columbia Certificate of Death records the cause as a tumor. Over the years after her death, the District of Columbia Board of Education named two elementary schools in her honor. Both have subsequently been demolished. However, Brigg's contributions to the preparation of teachers have been more permanently en-shrined in the history of Miner Normal School. By Act of Congress in 1930, it became Miner Teachers College. Housed in a Georgian structure still standing at 2565 Georgia Avenue N.W., this building served Miner Normal School (1913-29), Miner Teachers College (1929-55), and the District of Columbia Teachers College (1955-77), and today it houses some of the teacher-preparation programs of the University of the District of Columbia.

Martha B. Briggs was returned to New Bedford, Massachusetts for her burial. A memorial to her life and service was held by the Bethel Literary and Historical Association. Furthermore, Howard University memorialized her with a tablet placed in the wall of Andrew Rankin Chapel on the campus. In its March 1934 Founder's Day program, Miner Teachers College celebrated her service as the third principal of Miner Normal School.

PAUL P. COOKE

Bruce, Josephine (1853–1923)

"The new found pleasure in doing something really worthwhile is quite sufficient as a motive power to keep things going," Josephine Beall Willson Bruce declared in 1904 in an enthusiastic report on the activities of the **National Association of Colored Women,** an organization in which she figured prominently for more than a decade. Born in Philadelphia on October 29, 1853, and reared in Cleveland, Ohio, Josephine Willson was the daughter of Dr. Joseph Willson, a dentist and writer, and Elizabeth Harnett Willson, a talented musician. After graduating from Cleveland's Central High School in 1871 and completing a teacher-training course, she joined the faculty of one of the city's racially integrated elementary schools, reputedly as the first black teacher to receive such an appointment.

In 1878, Willson married Blanche K. Bruce, a U.S. Senator from Mississippi. Following a six-month wedding trip to Europe, the couple settled in Washington, D.C., where their only child, Roscoe Conkling Bruce, was born in 1879. In addition to assisting her husband in the advancement of his political career and being largely responsible for the rearing of their son, she occupied a conspicuous place in the social life of Washington's black elite and was identified with numerous enterprises designed to promote the welfare of black Americans. Though reared an Episcopalian, she later transferred her membership to the Congregational Church and joined her husband and others in organizing the University Park Congregational Temple in Washington, D.C., in 1896. A strong advocate of industrial education for the black masses, she persistently argued that education, both industrial and liberal, was essential for overcoming obstacles in the path of black progress. Following the death of her husband, she served as lady principal of Booker T. Washington's Tuskegee Institute from 1899 to 1902. Devoting herself primarily to "direct teaching in morals and manners" at Tuskegee, she served as a role model for the women students there, most of whom were from the rural South. After she left Tuskegee, she lived for a time in Josephine, Mississippi (a town and post office named in her honor), and managed her family's cotton plantations. Despite her claims that rural life was superior to life in the crowded cities, she returned to Washington, D.C., in 1906 when her Harvard-educated son became assistant superintendent in charge of the district's black schools.

An early leader in the club movement among black women, she was a founder of the Booklover's Club and the Colored Woman's League, both in Washington, D.C., and the National Association of Colored Women (NACW). She held high offices in the latter organization until 1906, when a controversy over her light complexion precluded her election to the presidency. Though less prominent in the NACW thereafter, she remained active in the Women's

A member of the black elite in Washington, D.C., Josephine Bruce occupied a conspicuous place in the black social life of the city and was identified with numerous enterprises designed to promote the welfare of blacks. (MOORLAND-SPINGARN)

Christian Temperance Union, World Purity Federation, and the National Association for the Advancement of Colored People. Always in demand as a public speaker, she consistently stressed the stewardship role of educated black Americans toward the less fortunate of the race.

Josephine Bruce spent the last few months of her life in Kimball, West Virginia, where her son had become a school principal. She died there on February 15, 1923, at the age of seventy. By her direction, her sizeable estate was to be used to finance the higher education of her three grandchildren.

WILLARD B. GATEWOOD

C

Cary, Mary Ann Shadd (1823–1893)

In the winter of 1856, upon receiving the news that antislavery agents were roaming through Canada, Mary Ann Shadd Cary began to write. She objected to those who, begging on behalf of the fugitive slaves who had fled to Canada, took advantage of antislavery sentiment. Feeling a moral right and duty, she became single-minded in her efforts to expose them. She charged that "begging agents" were "wending their way from Canada to the States in unprecedented numbers." "Bees gather honey in the summer," she wrote, "but beggars harvest in the winter." In typically blunt language, Cary preached integrationism, self-reliance, and independence among black Canadians during the 1850s. A pillar of zeal, she helped found the newspaper known as the *Provincial Freeman* as an instrument for transforming black refugees into model citizens. What she wrote, as the first black North American female editor, publisher, and investigative reporter, marked the beginning of a fierce argument over how to manage ex-slaves.

Born in Wilmington, Delaware, on October 9, 1823, Mary Ann Shadd was the first of thirteen children of prominent free black parents, Harriet and Abraham Shadd. Her father was a leader in the Underground Railroad movement and a subscription agent for William Lloyd Garrison's *Liberator*. In her childhood Shadd developed an abiding sympathy for slaves, an assiduous

Not since Ralph Waldo Emerson had a writer spoken as eloquently for self-reliance as Mary Ann Shadd Cary. Her virulent attacks against antislavery "begging agents" shocked nineteenth-century society, both black and white. (MOORLAND-SPINGARN)

understanding of their issues, and a penchant for lively debate. When she was ten years old, she and her family moved to West Chester, Pennsylvania, where Mary Shadd spent the next six years in a Quaker school. Feeling sufficiently educated to open a school for black children in Wilmington, she returned there in 1840. A few years later, she also secured teaching appointments in New York City and Norristown, Pennsylvania.

Following the passage of the 1850 Fugitive Slave Law, Mary and her brother, Isaac, joined the black exodus from the United States to Windsor, Canada. During this time, Shadd established an integrated school in Canada West supported by the American Missionary Association, met the abolitionists Henry and Mary Bibb, and became embroiled in a dispute with them that helped to launch her biting, vituperative campaign against unscrupulous antislavery agents.

Shadd first published her account of the values of self-reliance in 1849, in a pamphlet entitled *Hints to the Colored People of North America*. Three years later, in 1852, she published *Notes on Canada West*, a forty-four-page pamphlet which promoted black emigration to Canada. Hundreds of miles away, people read Shadd's reports of crop yield, terrain, climate, soil, timber, and the virtues of integrated churches and schools. She rallied their attention with statistical and tangible evidence of Canada's glory. By marshaling primary evidence as she did, Mary Ann Shadd became the first black female to develop and utilize a database for propaganda purposes. She carefully crafted *Notes on Canada West* to stop the ugly stories about the region that Southern slaveholders circulated to thwart black emigration.

In 1853, Shadd declared it was time to counter the programs of the Bibbs, Josiah Henson, John Scoble, and other leaders who advocated the moral, social, physical, intellectual, and political elevation of ex-slaves through the Refugee Home Society, a separatist organization that used agents to secure funds, clothing, and land for fugitive slaves. Shadd considered the techniques of these people, especially begging, to be a threat to her goal of an integrated, self-sufficient society for black fugitives, one free of any tincture of inferiority, floundering, or failure. Shadd's attacks appeared in the *Provincial Freeman*, cofounded by editor Samuel Ringgold Ward, a traveling agent for the Anti-Slavery Society of Canada. In fact, Mary Ann Shadd [Cary] edited the paper.

Once embarked on her mission, Shadd Cary became unshakeable in exposing the malfeasance of the "begging agents," using the *Provincial Freeman* as a vehicle for revealing misconduct and for examining how much money was collected and what was done with it. By nineteenth-century norms, Shadd Cary's caustic, jolting language seemed ill-suited to a woman. She used phrases such as "gall and wormwood," "moral pest," "petty despot," "superannuated ministers," "nest of unclean birds," "moral monsters," and "priest-ridden people," in order to keep her ideas before the public. Shadd Cary also attacked black folk religion in her firm, abrasive style, arguing that it retarded black moral and social development.

Mary Ann Shadd married Thomas F. Cary of Toronto in 1856, three years after the publication of the first issue of the *Provincial Freeman*. They lived in Chatham, Canada, until his death in 1860. They had two children: a daughter, Sarah, and a son, Linton. Spurred on by a worsening economic situation for black Canadians and the financial demise of her paper in 1859, Cary continued to teach in Chatham until 1863, when she returned to the United States. During the Civil War she became a Union army recruiting officer and, through contact with Martin Robinson Delaney, developed an interest in black nationalism. Later, with experience as an organizer of a black regiment, Cary settled in Washington, D.C., where she opened a school for black children and attended the Howard University Law

School. Considered the first black woman lawyer in the United States, Cary received her degree in 1870.

Soon after her graduation, she opened a law office in Washington, D.C., and renewed her political activism by challenging the House of Representatives' Judiciary Committee for the right to vote. She won her case and became one of the few women to vote in federal elections during the Reconstruction period. She also vigorously campaigned for women's rights through the **Colored Women's Progressive Franchise Association**, which she organized in 1880. She exhorted black women to address their specific political and economic condition and to fight for equal rights and opportunities. Cary died in 1893.

Whether Cary's efforts to promote change were successful is difficult to determine. Like most ideologues, she gave advice to humanity, but failed to see that her bulldozer bluntness alienated people. Yet she fought against begging as a way of life and thus contributed, however ideologically, to an African-American movement toward economic independence. Ironically, Cary's adamance ultimately diminished her ability to implement her ideas throughout her life. Nonetheless, as an influential black leader and a remarkable pioneering journalist, she continued to live by her paper's motto, "Self-reliance Is the Fine Road to Independence."

CAROLYN CALLOWAY-THOMAS

Coincoin (1742–1816)

I have conceded to my slave Thérèse the privilege of being sold by me, with her mulatto son Joseph Maurice, age nine years, to her mother, Marie Thérèse, free Negress, for the sum of seven hundred dollars.

—Marie St. Denis, 1790

These words, from a French colonial document created in 1790, personify the life, character, and times of an extraordinary woman. The place was Opelousas, Louisiana. The seller was an acerbic, politically prominent Frenchwoman whose family had, for generations, held this black family in slavery. The buyer was a forty-eight-year-old freedwoman of the upriver post of Natchitoches, who had traversed 120 miles of forests and bayous to buy the freedom of this one child. This she would do again and again, in one direction or another, until virtually all of her offspring were free. The unstinting labor, determination, and family cohesiveness that shaped her life would inspire generations to come. Building on her efforts, the dynasty she spawned would represent outstanding wealth, education, and political clout in the pre–Civil War South.

While most eighteenth-century American blacks were enslaved for life, some managed to acquire freedom. A small number used their skills and acumen to earn a comfortable living and even wealth. Of those who prospered, few were women. Although slave women were more likely to win manumission via sexual favors, they had less potential to prosper in free society. Coincoin was, in most respects, an exception. Born at Natchitoches about August 24, 1742 to imported slave parents, she was given the French name Marie Thérèse at baptism. For the rest of her life, however, she was more commonly known by the African name her parents called her, Coincoin, a name given to second-born daughters by those who spoke the Glidzi dialect of the Ewe people of western Africa. Her family's master was the founder of the post, the chevalier and commandant Louis Juchereau de St. Denis. In the span of her childhood, Coincoin would pass to his widow, their son, and then their daughter. The last transfer was a fortunate one, for Marie de Nieges de St. Denis—wife of a political defector from Mexico named Antonio Bermudez y de Soto—was a spirited and unconventional woman who defied the colony's law by renting her young female slave to a bachelor in need of a housekeeper.

For two decades, Coincoin lived with the French merchant Claude Thomas Pierre Metoyer as his servant and mistress, bearing him ten children. Amid a clerical battle to end their "scandalous alliance" and the threat of a court-ordered sale of Coincoin away from the post, Metoyer purchased and freed her, together with the "infant at her breast." The first six children she had borne him remained in slavery, as did five others to whom she had given birth before her union with Metoyer. For eight additional years she remained with the Frenchman, bearing three more freeborn infants—and burying two of them.

In 1786, Coincoin and Metoyer parted. On the eve of taking a legal wife, Metoyer gave Coincoin a small plot of land and promised an annuity of 120 piasters to support those children already free. At age forty-four, after fifteen childbirths, Coincoin began to build a life for herself and her offspring. She planted tobacco and indigo, raised cattle and turkeys, and trapped bear for their marketable grease and hides. By 1794 she qualified, financially and otherwise, to apply for a land grant from the Spanish government. On the 800 *arpents*

(about 640 acres) of piney woods granted to her a dozen or so miles from her homestead, she set up a *vacherie*—a cattle range—hiring a Spaniard to oversee her herd and raise the corn and other crops necessary to meet the government's grant requirements.

The manner in which Coincoin used her profits speaks eloquently of her values. Eschewing the comforts that money could bring, she set out to manumit those still-enslaved children. Her eldest daughter, in 1786, cost her only 300 piasters—Marie Louise had been crippled in a gunshot accident—yet even that sum represented nearly three years of the annuity that was to support her family. Over the next decade, Coincoin tracked down her enslaved children and grandchildren, from the downriver post of Opelousas to the Mexican outpost of Nacogdoches, Texas; most of their masters consented to their sale—some for cash, some on credit. Only one daughter was unattainable; yet, by sundry means, the grandchildren in this family line were freed over the next two decades.

At the age of sixty, Coincoin renegotiated her annuity agreement with Metoyer. Two of the six slave children she had borne him had been manumitted by him at their marriage. In return for the freedom of the last four, she agreed to forfeit the annual payments that would have provided security in her old age. In the interim Coincoin herself became a slave owner, for the same reasons that motivated other contemporaries—a need for labor. Before her death in 1816, at the age of seventy-four, she had become the mistress of sixteen slaves and a thousand *arpents* of land—no small fortune for a male or female of any color in the late eighteenth and early nineteenth centuries.

Yet it was not material accomplishments that made Coincoin a notable historical figure. A few other slave and free black women did as much and more. It was, instead, the enduring inspiration of her example that enshrined her memory and her legacy in Louisiana lore. Building on the foundation Coincoin laid for them, her offspring—indomitable and ingenious—developed a highly effective economic and social network based on kin loyalty and mutual assistance. Maximizing the legal rights available in their society, they built an agricultural empire on Isle Brevelle in Louisiana's Red River Valley. As the largest slave-owning family of color in the United States, their peak holdings included nearly 20,000 acres of land, 500 slaves, and a dozen plantation manor houses. Their self-contained, Catholic-inspired community centered around their own school and church—allegedly the only nonwhite church in America to operate a white mission. The degree to which their success was based on the labors of their less-fortunate black slaves remains a debatable point. Local lore insists they were kind masters, and extant records do document numerous manumissions by them. In retrospect, the era in which they lived limited the choices they might have made; and whatever their exploitations, they were cut from the same economic cloth that motivates all businesspeople, industrialists, or planters whose society is underpinned more by social class than by color.

Contrary to the belief that few genealogical records exist on early black families, many records to piece together this slave-born family have been found. Coincoin's parents, François and Françoise, had been legally married at Natchitoches on December 26, 1735. There, they produced eleven children, whose stories are told in dozens of church records, lawsuits, property inventories, wills, and deeds. Some would earn their freedom, others would not. Coincoin's own children were as follows: Marie Louise, baptized September 8, 1759; Thérèse, baptized September 24, 1761; Françoise, baptized July 8, 1763, never manumitted; Nicolas Chiquito, born c. 1764-65, died April 12, 1850; Nicolas Augustin, born January 22, 1768, died December 18, 1856, after amassing an estate that exceeded $140,000; Marie Suzanne Metoyer, born January 22, 1768, died July 28, 1838, leaving an estate valued at $61,000; Louis Metoyer, born c. 1770, died March 11, 1832, leaving an estate valued at $132,000; Pierre Metoyer, born c. 1772, died June 25, 1833, leaving $19,969 to his heirs in addition to plantations already given them; Dominique Metoyer, born c. 1774, died c. 1840, leaving $42,405 in addition to donations already made to his seventeen children; Marie Eulalie Metoyer, born January 15, 1776, died 1783–1801; Joseph Antoine Metoyer, born January 26, 1778, died October 9, 1838; Marie Françoise Rosalie Metoyer, born December 9, 1780, died before 1783; Pierre Toussaint Metoyer, born c. 1782, died February 17, 1863; and François Metoyer, born September 26, 1784, died after 1841.

The changes wrought by civil war, emancipation, reconstruction, and industrialization, as well as the intensified racism and segregation of the late nineteenth and early twentieth centuries, destroyed the world that Coincoin and her offspring built. Amid new social and economic conditions, younger generations dispersed to other parts of the nation, developing migratory patterns of import to sociologists and historians. Yet, many descendants remain on family lands, their culture still centered around the values that Coincoin taught. The Church of St. Augustin still stands, named for Coincoin's eldest Metoyer son and dominated by a life-sized oil of him, made in his patriarchal years. Nearby stands Melrose Plantation—the only reasonably intact estate to survive the ravaging of their empire; in 1975, it was declared a National Historic Landmark. The world Coincoin created on Isle Brevelle has, in the twentieth century, become fabled through the work of such Louisiana folk-writers as Lyle Saxon, François Mignon, and Harnett Kane, as well as the more recent studies of sociological, historical, and genealogical scholars.

GARY B. MILLS

Colored Female's Free Produce Society

No, dear lady, none for me?
Though squeamish some may think it,
West India sugar spoils my tea;
I cannot, dare not, drink it.

(Gertrude, *Genius of Universal Emancipation*, 1831

Organized to boycott the products of slave labor, the Colored Female's Free Produce Society sought to overthrow the economic power of slavery, one bolt of cotton and one teaspoon of sugar at a time. A union of black women, the Society joined contemporary free produce unions, such as the Colored Free Produce Society, Philadelphia Free Cotton Society, and the Free Produce Society of Philadelphia, dedicated to promoting the manufacture and marketing of goods produced entirely by free labor.

The minutes of a regular organizational meeting on January 24, 1831, at the Bethel Church in Philadelphia provide the clearest picture of the membership of the Colored Female's Free Produce Society. After a reading of the society's constitution, the members elected President Judith James, Vice President Susannah Cork, Treasurer Hester Burr, and Secretary Laetitia Rowley. The Committee of Correspondence included Hannah Alexander, Elizabeth Baker, Mary Benjamin, Martha Holcombe, Rebecca Hutchins, Lydia Lecompt, Pleasant Lloyd, Maria Potts, Sarah White, and Priscilla Wilkins. Raising the consciousness of members and the wider community, the society fought the direct and indirect economic contributions that consumers made to slavery in the nominally free states. Such discussion allowed the public refutation of the argument that slave produce boycotts would ultimately hurt the position of slaves.

Supported by Frederick Douglass and others in the abolition movement, the Colored Female's Free Produce Society and other groups in the Free Produce movement supplied access to nonslave produce merchants and their goods to its members—sometimes in as much as fifty-pound bags of free sugar at a time—to send a moral and economic message to the community at large. Influential members of the community, male and female, black and white, formed associations as part of a larger effort to overthrow slavery.

The Free Produce movement was, like the majority of abolition organizations, segregated by both race and sex in the early 1830s. It provided, however, a launching platform for the growing prominence of black women political activists such as **Frances E. W. Harper** and Grace Douglass, one of the vice presidents of the Anti-Slavery Convention of American Women held in

1837. Free produce women activists encouraged other women, black and white, to go without slave-produced cotton, rice, sugar, molasses, tobacco, and other goods in order to break the stranglehold of slavery-based economics on the markets of the free states. Encouraging the advertising and patronizing of shops and suppliers of freely produced goods strengthened the effects of the boycott.

Fostered primarily in areas of Quaker concentration, like Philadelphia and Wilmington, Delaware, the greatest impact of the Free Produce Movement was more moral than financial. From an unsweetened cup of tea, to a coarser calico, to a platform for black female activism and an eventual integration of the abolition movement, the Colored Female's Free Produce Society brought the spirit of the cause home.

SUSAN A. TAYLOR

Colored Women's Progressive Franchise Association

The Colored Women's Progressive Franchise Association was organized by **Mary Ann Shadd Cary** in Washington, D.C., on February 9, 1880. The first meeting was held at Mount Pisgah Chapel and was presided over by the church's pastor, Reverend Joseph Nichols. The chief purpose of the organization was to assert the equal rights of women. Toward that goal, the association set forth a twenty-point program, the chief objective of which was gaining the ballot for women. The association sought to assert the equal rights of women not only by gaining the right to vote, but also by working to expand the number of occupations available to women, to establish newspapers under the control of black women, and to support only those newspapers that sup-

ported equal rights for all. The association also tried to improve the situation of the entire community by supporting home missionaries and youth training programs, establishing a job bank and labor bureau for the unemployed, developing leadership among the masses, and establishing a company that would help people start small businesses. Another important objective was the establishment of banks and stores for the community.

Thus, the women of the Colored Women's Progressive Franchise Association worked not only to gain the franchise for women; they also took responsibility for the well-being of their community.

ALLISON JOLLY

Coppin, Fanny Jackson   (1837–1913)

When Fanny Jackson became principal of Philadelphia's **Institute for Colored Youth**, she held the highest educational appointment of any black woman in the nation. While most of Fanny Jackson's attention, before and after her marriage, was given to the institute, Jackson Coppin was also active in the African Methodist Episcopal Church, the **National Association of Colored Women** (**NACW**), and, in later life, as a missionary to Africa.

Fanny Jackson Coppin was born a slave in Washington, D.C., in 1837. Her freedom was bought during her early childhood by a devoted Aunt, Sarah Orr. Jackson moved to New Bedford, Massachusetts, and, by the early 1850s, to Newport, Rhode Island, to live with relatives. While in Newport, Jackson worked as a domestic in the home of George Henry Calvert, great-grandson of Lord Baltimore, settler of Maryland. Calvert's wife, Mary, was a descendant of

Mary, Queen of Scots. With the money earned at the Calvert's, Jackson was able to hire a tutor for one hour a day three days a week. She worked for the Calverts for six years, and during her last year of employment attended the segregated public schools of Newport. In 1859, she attended Rhode Island State Normal School in Bristol.

In 1860, Jackson enrolled in the Ladies Department of **Oberlin College** in Ohio. She was assisted financially by her aunt Sarah, a scholarship from Bishop Daniel Payne of the African Methodist Episcopal (AME) Church, and scholarship aid from Oberlin. Jackson also worked while she was a student at Oberlin. She graduated in 1865 with an A.B., the second African-American woman to do so. While at Oberlin, Jackson was active in all facets of college life. Her outstanding reputation as a teacher resulted in her being chosen as a student teacher of the preparatory department at Oberlin—the first African American to achieve such an honor. Also, during her senior year, she was chosen as class poet.

In addition to Jackson's activities on campus at Oberlin College, she was involved in an array of community events. For example, in 1863 she opened an evening school for freedpeople who were migrating into Oberlin. The classes were highly successful and received favorable press coverage in both local and abolitionist newspapers. As a result of the publicity Jackson received for establishing the evening school, and for her outstanding academic record at Oberlin, she was well known throughout black communities of the nation by the time she graduated in 1865.

After leaving Oberlin in 1865, Jackson was appointed principal of the female department at the prestigious Institute for Colored Youth (ICY) in Philadelphia. The institute was a classical high school founded by the Society of Friends in 1837. It included a preparatory department, girl's and boy's high school departments, and a teacher-training course. In 1869, when the principal, Ebenezer Bassett, was appointed U.S. minister of Haiti, Jackson was appointed to take his place. This was a significant appointment; Jackson was the first black woman to

A brilliant teacher and a daring innovator in black education, Fanny Jackson Coppin advocated vocational training many years before Booker T. Washington while maintaining, as he did not, a firm commitment to the importance of liberal arts in black education. (SCHOMBURG CENTER)

head an institution of higher learning in the nation.

The institute was located in the heart of the Philadelphia African-American community, near the historic Mother Bethel AME Church. The *Christian Recorder*, the newspaper of the AME Church, frequently publicized the institute's and Jackson's activities. In addition to her other work, Jackson wrote children's stories and a woman's column for the paper.

In 1881, at the age of forty-four, Jackson married Levi Jenkins Coppin, an AME minister at least fifteen years her junior. They maintained a commuting relationship for the first three years of their marriage. Levi Coppin pastored a church in Baltimore and commuted to Philadelphia while Fanny Coppin remained as principal of the institute. By 1884 it had become apparent that Fanny Coppin was not going to leave her position at the institute, and Reverend Coppin transferred to a small church in Philadelphia. Fanny Coppin's marriage coincided with a huge campaign she headed to establish an industrial department at the institute. By the 1880s, black Americans were shut out of the growing number of technical and industrial positions in Philadelphia. Fanny Coppin was adamant that black Americans should open their own schools to prepare themselves for these new avenues of employment.

After a decade of fund-raising, the industrial department at the institute opened in January 1889. The new department did not meet the expectations that Coppin had for the school to offer advanced technical courses. However, it did offer training in carpentry, bricklaying, shoemaking, printing, plastering, millinery, dressmaking, and cooking. The department was the first trade school for African Americans in Philadelphia. It was flooded with applications, and a waiting list of hundreds was maintained throughout its existence.

After her marriage, Coppin joined the AME Church. She was elected president of the local Women's Mite Missionary Society and later became national president of the Women's Home and Foreign Missionary Society of the AME Church. In 1888, she represented the organization at the Centenary of Missions Conference in London.

Fanny Jackson Coppin was politically active throughout her life. Although women could not vote during her lifetime, she viewed the franchise as being as important for women as for men. She often spoke at political rallies and most often was the only woman on the program. Coppin was elected one of the vice presidents of the NACW. She also served as a member of the board of managers for the Home for Aged and Infirmed Colored People in Philadelphia for over thirty years (1881–1913).

By the turn of the century, the years of activity had begun to take a toll on Coppin's health. She had spent endless hours working at the institute and had earnestly tried to find employment and housing for her students and other African Americans in Philadelphia. Her speaking engagements were numerous, and her involvement with civil and religious activities was endless. In 1896, she became ill with pleurisy and was confined to her home. She never fully recovered, and in 1901 announced her retirement as principal of the institute, effective June 1902.

Fanny Jackson Coppin was extremely private concerning her personal affairs. She made only one brief mention of her marriage to Levi Coppin in her autobiography,

*Remin*iscences of School Life and Hints on Teaching (1913). However, from all indications, the Coppin's marriage was a close one, and Levi Coppin seemed genuinely proud to be married to such a distinguished and well-regarded woman. He often spoke of her with deep respect, admiration, and appreciation.

Although Coppin was devoted to the institute, during the summers she often traveled with her husband for the AME Church. After Levi Coppin graduated from the Philadelphia Episcopal Divinity School in 1887, he was appointed editor of the *AME Review*, a prestigious position in the AME Church. He maintained this position from 1888 until 1896, when he was appointed pastor of Mother Bethel, where he remained until 1900. He was then elected bishop of the Fourteenth Episcopal District in South Africa.

After her retirement from the institute in 1902, Coppin accompanied her husband to Cape Town, South Africa. Because of her poor health and age, many in the Philadelphia community feared she would not survive the trip. Prior to the couple's departure, testimonials were given in Fanny Coppin's honor. Newspapers reported overflowing audiences at each occasion. Gifts and money were given, and Coppin was deeply touched by this outpouring of affection from the community and her former students.

The Coppins arrived in Cape Town in December 1902, then traveled into the interior of South Africa. As many feared, Fanny Coppin's health worsened. She experienced fainting spells but then recovered and devoted her stay to developing missions among the women of the country. Her impact on these women was profound. At an AME school in Cape Town named Wilberforce Institute, the African missions raised $10,000 to build the Fanny Jackson Coppin Girls Hall as a symbol of their appreciation of her efforts on their behalf.

The Coppins left South Africa in December 1903, a year after their arrival. After visiting several European countries, they returned to the United States in spring 1904. Levi Coppin was then appointed bishop to the Seventh Episcopal District of the AME Church, which encompassed South Carolina and Alabama. Fanny Coppin traveled to South Carolina with her husband. However, the South African trip had badly affected her health. By 1905, she was so physically weak that the remaining eight years of her life were spent primarily confined to her Philadelphia home on Nineteenth and Bainbridge streets.

On January 21, 1913, Fanny Jackson Coppin died at her home in Philadelphia. Thousands, many of whom traveled from cities and towns from around the country, filled Mother Bethel AME Church for her funeral. Following the funeral, memorial services were conducted in Washington, D.C., Baltimore, and Philadelphia.

Known as a champion of the poor, Fanny Jackson Coppin was a captivating speaker who never used notes. Throughout her life she attempted to make education available to all black Americans.

Coppin State College in Baltimore, Maryland, is named in her honor.

LINDA M. PERKINS

Couvent, Marie Bernard (c.1757–1837)

The oldest continuously existing black Catholic school in the United States came into being because, even before public education came to New Orleans, a former slave,

Marie Bernard Couvent, provided in her will for the "establishment of a free school for orphans of color."

The Widow Couvent, as she came to be known, was born in Guinea, West Africa, and was brought to Saint-Domingue (Haiti) where she was enslaved at such an early age that she had no memory of her father and mother. When she died in New Orleans on June 29, 1837, a free black woman speaking a French-derived language, her age was given as eighty. That would mean that the year of her birth was probably 1757. Not much is known about her except that she eventually obtained her freedom, established residency in the Marigny district of New Orleans, and at some time married a free black man, Gabriel Bernard Couvent. Her husband's death preceded hers by eight years, and he left her the property that she later donated for the establishment of a free school for free orphans of color living in Faubourg Marigny. (The present-day boundaries of Marigny are the Mississippi River, St. Claude Avenue, Esplanade Avenue, and Franklin Avenue.)

Madame Couvent dictated her will in 1832 and provided biographical information about herself in the document, which is written in French. A portion of the will states: "I bequeath and order that my land at the corner of Grand Hommes (Dauphine) and Union (Touro) streets be dedicated and used in perpetuity for the establishment of a free school for orphans of color of the Faubourg Marigny. This said school is to be operated under the direction of Reverend Father Manehault . . . or under the supervision of his successors in office."

Henry Fletcher, a free man of color, was named executor. He did not implement the terms of the will within a reasonable time, and the estate was dwindling. Finally, a group of free men of color brought him to court and requested an accounting. These men were leading members of the community of free people of color living in the city. Among them were Emilien Brule, Adolphe Duhart, Nelson Fouche, François Lacroix, and Barthélemy Rey. They succeeded in establishing the school in 1848; however its student population consisted of more than indigent orphans, despite its name. L'Institution Catholique des Orphelins Indigens attracted students from a broad base and included a faculty of notable members of the city. One of its principals was Armand Lanusse, compiler of *Les Cenelles,* the first poetry anthology published by an African American in the United States. Lanusse became principal in 1852.

The Couvent School, as it was locally known, not only attracted an excellent faculty and board, but was also destined to include among its alumni many of the leading citizens among the *gens de couleur libres* (free people of color) and their descendants. Ernest N. Morial, the first African-American mayor of New Orleans, was among the school's alumni. Still in existence and believed to be the oldest continuing black Catholic school in the country, the Institution is now known as Holy Redeemer School. Two blocks away is a public school named in honor of Madame Couvent, but the school she caused to found still bears testimony to her piety and generosity. She dictated her will eight years before public education came to New Orleans, and even then it excluded people of color.

The Widow Couvent is buried in historic St. Louis Cemetery Number 2, Square 3, in New Orleans. Her grave may still be visited, and her will may be read in the Louisiana division of the New Orleans Public Library.

FLORENCE BORDERS

Cox, Minnie M. Geddings (1869–1933)

Minnie M. Geddings Cox was one of America's most significant citizens and was a role model—as an educator, government worker, businesswoman, and homemaker—for blacks throughout the United States.

Minnie Geddings was one of two daughters born to former slaves William and Mary Geddings of Lexington, Mississippi. She was born in 1869. The Geddingses owned a restaurant and used their money to send Minnie to Fisk University. She graduated with a teacher's certificate. She first taught at public schools in Lexington and later taught in Indianola, Mississippi.

Minnie Cox was widely known because of her appointment as postmistress of Indianola. Although she had been appointed by President Benjamin Harrison in 1891, it was her reappointment on May 22, 1897, that was controversial. President William McKinley reappointed Cox at a time when white racists wanted black Americans eliminated from leadership positions. In 1902, white protestors in Indianola claimed that Cox's reappointment permitted "nigger domination." To protect black citizens, Cox, a peaceful and religious Methodist, offered her resignation. It was refused by President Theodore Roosevelt who, in order to show his support for black Americans, suspended postal service in Indianola. However, white supremacists did succeed in displacing Cox temporarily. In January 1903, Cox left Indianola but returned a year later, once the controversy had died down. The controversy surrounding her appointment brought her national attention, placed her in the company of notable leaders such as Booker T. Washington and Theodore Roosevelt, and forced Indianola and racism into the national news.

Minnie Cox had married Wayne Wellington Cox on October 31, 1889. They had a daughter, Ethel Grant Cox. The Coxes became successful businesspeople. They were farmers and owned considerable agricultural holdings in Indianola. They organized the Delta Penny Savings Bank of Indianola, which attracted both black and white customers, as well as the Beneficial Life Insurance Company to serve the black community specifically. Minnie Cox was the secretary and treasurer of the insurance company. Even though white citizens had objected to her as postmistress, she constructed her home in the white residential district and continued to interact with all of the citizens of Indianola.

During the 1920s, Minnie Cox left Indianola. She lived in Memphis, Tennessee, before moving to Rockford, Illinois, with her second husband, George Key Hamilton, whom she married on July 2, 1925. On August 31, 1933, she died in Rockford, Illinois. Throughout her life, Cox was politically active, supporting the Republican party while promoting national awareness of racism. She founded business enterprises, provided jobs for others, and advocated pride, progress, and justice during a period of negrophobia.

VALERIE GRIM

Craft, Ellen (1826–1891)

Ellen Craft was born in 1826 in Clinton, Georgia, to Major James Smith, a cotton planter and slaveholder, and his house slave,

Maria. Craft was given as a gift to Smith's daughter, Eliza, and was moved to Macon in 1837. There she met and later married a fellow slave, William, in 1846. Two years later the young couple fled in what is regarded as the most dramatic escape from slavery ever recorded. Since Craft was a light-skinned quadroon, she dressed as a slave master who was traveling to Philadelphia for medical reasons; William acted as her valet. The couple settled in Boston, and Craft established herself as a seamstress. However, their freedom was threatened after the passage of the Fugitive Slave Act in 1850, when slave catchers tried to return the couple to Georgia. That November, the Crafts fled Boston for the safety of England, where they spent the next nineteen years.

In England the Crafts attended an agricultural school established by Lady Byron in Ockham, Surrey. After completing their course of study, they purchased a home in Hammersmith, London, and Craft continued to work as a seamstress. They were active on the antislavery lecture circuit and were members of the executive committee of the London Emancipation Committee. Craft also worked to raise funds for Southern freedpeople and to establish a school for girls in Sierra Leone. Their five children—Charles, Ellen, William, Jr., Brougham, and Alfred—were born in England.

The Crafts returned to the United States in 1869. Two years later they purchased Woodville plantation in Ways Station, Georgia, where they grew cotton and rice and where Ellen Craft ran a school for local children. Constantly rising debts, opposition from local white farmers, and an inability to raise needed capital worked against them. When Ellen Craft died in 1891, the school had been closed for some time, and the plantation was struggling to make ends meet.

RICHARD J. M. BLACKETT

Davidson, Olivia America (1854–1889)

The daughter of an ex-slave father and a freeborn mother, Olivia Davidson taught in Ohio, Mississippi, and Tennessee before helping to build Tuskegee Institute with her peer and later her husband, Booker T. Washington. In *The Story of My Life and Work*, Washington wrote, "The success of the school, especially during the first half dozen years of its existence, was due more to Miss Davidson than any one else."

Six siblings welcomed Davidson's birth on June 11, 1854, and she in turn welcomed the births of three others. Her father, Elias, had been a slave of Joseph Davidson, whose family participated in the Scot-Irish migration into Virginia by way of Pennsylvania. Her mother, Eliza Webb, is thought to have been one of two daughters of Elizabeth Webb, a "free colored" woman recorded in the Tazewell County, Virginia, census of 1830.

The Elias Davidson family migrated to southern Ohio around 1857, pushed by the intolerance directed against mulattoes in the Upper South. They settled for a time in Ironton Village, where Elias died a few years later. Eliza then took her family farther north into Ohio, settling first in Albany and then in Athens.

Davidson started school in Ironton Village, where a school for black children opened in 1857. The Enterprise Academy, owned and controlled by black educators, opened in Albany in 1864 and was probably

Olivia America Davidson's story is an example of the missing woman in history. Although she is not recognized as such, she was one of the cofounders of Tuskegee Institute. Her husband, Booker T. Washington, attributed the early success of the school "more to Miss Davidson than anyone else." (SCHOMBURG CENTER)

the reason the family moved there. Albany, where several **Oberlin College** graduates had settled, was the scene of strong antislavery sentiment and the site of three routes of the Underground Railroad. As a teenager Davidson knew and interacted with Oberlin

College liberals and black activists connected with the academy. Later she was exposed to the dynamics of an ever-changing urban area when she lived for a time with her sister, Mary, and Mary's husband, Noah Elliott, at Gallipolis, a river town.

Davidson started teaching at the age of sixteen. She taught for two years in Ohio before following a sister to Mississippi to teach freedpeople and their children. She ran a school at Spencer, Mississippi, which was no more than a flag stop on the railroad. In 1886, she addressed the members of the Alabama State Teacher's Association on the topic "How Shall We Make the Women of Our Race Stronger?" She stated that the way to improve conditions for black Americans was to work with the girls, who were the "hope of the race." She did this in part by talking about the lives of noble women.

After two years in Mississippi, Davidson accepted employment in Memphis, Tennessee. Her four-year tenure in the Memphis Public School system overlapped with one of the worst financial periods in the city's history of education. Otherwise, however, Davidson was in an exciting environment. She was caught up in the argument in favor of black teachers teaching at black schools, and she worked for a superintendent who introduced advanced teaching and curriculum changes. Her work in Memphis came to an end as a result of the 1878 yellow fever epidemic; she might have died had she not been in Ohio for a summer break when the epidemic broke out. Davidson wrote to Memphis, offering her services as a nurse, but was advised instead to spend the time studying at the Hampton Normal and Agricultural Institute in Hampton, Virginia.

Davidson enrolled in Hampton's senior class in the fall of 1878 with a scholarship paid for by Mrs. Rutherford B. Hayes. She graduated the following May and delivered one of the commencement essays, entitled "Decision of Character." Booker T. Washington, class of 1875, was the postgraduate speaker at the ceremony. While at Hampton, Davidson was brought to the attention of benefactress Mary Hemenway, who financed two years of study for her at the Framingham (Massachusetts) State Normal School. Once again, she earned a spot on the graduation program, speaking on the topic "Work among the Freedmen." After spending only a few months back at Hampton, Davidson left for Tuskegee, where she served the public roles of teacher, curriculum specialist, principal, fund-raiser, and builder as well as the private roles of confidant, wife, and mother.

Davidson was very ill when she left Framingham and returned to Hampton, the first indication that she was in failing health. Then, after about three years of intense activity at Tuskegee, she became ill again and was forced into inactivity for about a year. During that same year, Washington's first wife, Fannie Smith, died, and he and Davidson wed on August 11, 1886. Davidson, who became stepmother to Washington's daughter, Portia, gave birth to two sons, Booker, Jr., born May 29, 1887, and Ernest Davidson, born February 6, 1889.

A few days after Ernest's birth, the Washington home caught fire. Washington himself was away. Davidson's exposure to the early morning chill after she and the baby had been carried out of the house further weakened her physical condition, and she never recovered. She was taken for medical attention, first to Montgomery and then to Boston, where she died on May 9, 1889, at Massachusetts General Hospital. Washington wrote in a letter to his mentor, General Samuel C. Armstrong, that "Few will ever know what she has done for Tuskegee and for me." Similarly, an unknown writer in *Southern Letters* wrote of Davidson that "in her great earnestness she made the mistake of thinking too little about her own health."

Davidson's story is another example of the missing woman in history, for although she is not recognized as such, she was one of the co-founders of an institution that continues to thrive today. The history of what is now Tuskegee University is not complete without an appreciation of the vast contributions made to its development by Olivia A. Davidson.

CAROLYN DORSEY

Dickson, Amanda America (1849–1893)

Amanda America Dickson, a slave-aristocrat, was born on November 21, 1849, on the plantation of her father, the famous white agricultural reformer David Dickson of Hancock County, Georgia. Her birth resulted from the rape of her slave mother, Julia Frances Lewis-Dickson, when Julia was twelve years old. At the time, David Dickson was forty and the wealthiest planter in the county. Amanda Dickson spent her childhood and adolescence in the house of her white grandmother and owner, Elizabeth Dickson, where she learned to read, write, and play the piano—the accomplishments of a young lady, but not normally the skills taught to a slave. According to the Lewis-Dickson family oral history, David Dickson doted on Amanda America, and Julia Dickson quite openly became his concubine and housekeeper.

In 1866, Amanda Dickson married her white first cousin Charles Eubanks, a recently returned Civil War veteran. The union produced two sons: Julian Henry Dickson (1866–1937), who married Eva Walton, the daughter of George Walton; and Charles Green Dickson (1870–1900?), who married Kate Holsey, the daughter of Bishop Lucius and Harriet Holsey.

By 1870, Amanda Dickson had returned to her father's plantation and reclaimed her name. In 1876, she left her father's plantation

Born the slave of her planter father, Amanda America Dickson became one of the wealthiest women in Augusta, Georgia, when the Georgia Supreme Court upheld her right to inherit under his will in 1885. Her life reflected the power of family and class to erode the boundaries of race in the nineteenth-century South. (JOAN JACKSON)

and her mother's domain to attend the Normal School of Atlanta University, and returned in 1878. In the winter of 1885, David Dickson died leaving the bulk of his estate, which the executors appraised at $307,000 (including 17,000 acres of land in Hancock and Washington counties), to Amanda Dickson and her children. In his will Dickson stated that the administration of his estate was to be left to the sound judgment and unlimited discretion of Amanda America Dickson without interference from any quarter, including any husband that she might have. A host of David Dickson's white relatives immediately contested the will, but the Hancock County Superior Court ruled in favor of Amanda Dickson and her sons in November 1885. The disgruntled relatives then appealed to the Georgia Supreme Court, which in 1887 upheld the lower court decision, stating that whatever rights and privileges belonged to a white concubine, or to a bastard white woman and her children, belonged to a "colored" woman and her children and the "rights of each race were controlled and governed by the same enactments on principles of law."

Prior to the supreme court decision, Amanda Dickson purchased a large house at 452 Telfair Street, in the wealthiest section of the then integrated city of Augusta, Georgia. By the time the courts settled the Dickson Will Case, as it came to be called, she had firmly ensconced herself in this new home decorated with Brussels carpets, oil paintings, and books. While white Georgians were establishing apartheid as the ruling social order in the public sphere, members of the Dickson family went about their private lives. On July 14, 1892, Amanda America Dickson married Nathan Toomer of Perry, Georgia. Toomer had been born the son of a slave woman named Kit and one of the prominent white Toomer brothers who had migrated from North Carolina to Houston County, Georgia, in the 1850s. In his youth Nathan Toomer served as the personal servant of Colonel Henry Toomer and in that position learned the manners of the upper class. The census of 1870 lists Nathan Toomer as worth more than all of the other freedpeople in Houston County combined ($30,000). Toomer and Dickson's marriage lasted until she died on July 11, 1893, of neurasthenia, or nervous exhaustion. Shortly thereafter, Nathan Toomer married Nina Pinchback and became the father of the Harlem Renaissance author Jean Toomer.

Amanda America Dickson's life reflects the power of family and class to erode the boundaries of race in the nineteenth-century South.

KENT A. LESLIE

Douglass, Anna Murray (c. 1813–1882)

One of the first and most important agents of the Underground Railroad, Anna Murray Douglass would have been remembered by history for her contributions to the struggle for freedom if it had not been for one thing—she was married to Frederick Douglass. While her extraordinary husband overshadowed her, however, she was a memorable woman in her own right.

Anna Murray Douglass was born in 1813 in Denton, Caroline County, Maryland. She was the eighth child of Bambarra and Mary Murray and the first to be born free. Her parents gained their freedom just one month before she was born. At seventeen, Anna Murray left the family home and traveled to

Baltimore, where she found work with a French family.

She quickly became involved in the black community, joining the East Baltimore Improvement Society. This organization was a somewhat exclusive group, whose membership was small and limited to free blacks. There was before long, however, one exception to the latter restriction. He was a young, intelligent, articulate slave named Frederick Augustus Washington Bailey. The two young people fell in love.

Bailey was determined not to marry until he was free, so he and Anna Murray began to plan his escape. They used her savings of nine years to finance the plan, and she sewed him a sailor's uniform as a disguise. He borrowed from a friend the papers that would allow him to travel as a free man. In September 1838, he arrived in New York. She followed a few days later, and they were married. They began a new life in New Bedford, Massachusetts, where they adopted the name of Douglass.

While her husband worked in the shipyards, the young Anna Murray Douglass worked as a domestic. She also resumed her involvement in community activities. After her husband became prominent in the abolitionist movement and began to travel a great deal, Douglass reared their five children and helped to support the family by taking work binding shoes.

In 1847, the family moved to Rochester, New York. There, the Douglass home became a stop on the Underground Railroad. Since Frederick was not often home, it fell to Anna to carry out the duties of agent. In the meantime, the Douglass sons worked as conductors, leading fugitive slaves from one stop to another on the path to freedom.

Anna Murray Douglass lived her adult life in the shadow of her husband, Frederick. All four of her granddaughters were active early in the twentieth century in the movement to establish organizations in which they, as women, could achieve an autonomy denied their grandmother. (MOORLAND-SPINGARN)

While working, rearing children, and playing a crucial role in abolitionist activities, Anna Murray Douglass also managed the family finances in a way that freed her husband of practical concerns while he traveled, lecturing and writing for the cause of freedom. For reasons of her own, she chose not to learn to read. She was also uninterested in mixing socially with the white abolitionists who became a large part of her husband's social and professional life. She led her life quietly and almost entirely within the black community.

In 1860, when Douglass was forty-seven, her youngest child died at the age of seven. Shortly thereafter, her own health began to fail. She lived another twenty-two years, however, and died on August 4, 1882, at the age of sixty-nine.

KATHLEEN THOMPSON

Douglass, Sarah Mapps (1806–1882)

Sarah Mapps Douglass served black society as an educator and abolitionist. Born into a prominent free black family in Philadelphia on September 9, 1806, she was reared in comfortable circumstances and was edu-

Sarah Mapps was born into a prominent free black family in Philadelphia in 1806. She was a leading educator and active abolitionist. (LIBRARY OF CONGRESS)

cated by private tutoring. Her family background was one of commercial success and cultural awareness. Her maternal grandfather, Cyrus Bustill, a Quaker, owned a bakeshop and, after his retirement, ran a school. He was also an early member of the Free African Society, the first black benevolent association. Her mother ran a "Quaker millinery store," and her father helped found the First African Presbyterian Church of Philadelphia.

As a young woman, Douglass joined the **Philadelphia Female Anti-Slavery Society,** of which her mother had been a founder. In 1838 the society assumed the financial support of a school for black children that Douglass had opened. Her associates and close friends in the society were the **Forten** sisters, daughters of wealthy black shipbuilder James Forten, and the Quakers Lucretia Mott and Sarah and **Angelina Grimké.** The latter were the daughters of a slave-owning justice of the South Carolina Supreme Court and the only white Southern women to become active antislavery agents. The lifelong friendship between Douglass and the Grimké sisters was remarkable for the time. The letters of Douglass to the Grimké sisters reveal her intelligence, abolitionist commitment, and sensitivity.

Douglass provided the Grimké sisters with support and personal testimony when they challenged discrimination within the Quaker Meeting. Douglass described her indignation when white Quakers were prevented from sitting next to her during meeting. Her mother had been kept from membership; when she attended the funeral of a Quaker she was made to walk behind the carriages with two black servant boys. The information Douglass provided to Sarah Grimké was incorporated into a British pamphlet published in 1840 and widely distributed in the United States and England.

Douglas's friendships, as well as her activities, were quite controversial. When Douglass and her mother attended Angelina's wedding, the Philadelphia press expressed outrage, calling the event an intolerable incident of "amalgamation." Two days later a mob burned down the newly built headquarters of the Pennsylvania Anti-Slavery Society and set fire to the Shelter for Colored Orphans.

Though Philadelphia Quakers did not end discrimination for several decades, Douglass remained a member of the society. In 1853 she became a teacher and later an administrator of the **Institute for Colored Youth,** a Quaker-supported school where she trained many teachers for the public schools until her retirement in 1877. She married Reverend William Douglass in 1855; he died in 1861. After the Civil War, she was vice chair of the Women's Pennsylvania Branch of the American Freedmen's Aid Commission. She died in Philadelphia in 1882.

GERDA LERNER

E

Early, Sarah Jane Woodson (1825–1907)

Sarah Jane Woodson was born to Thomas and Jemimma Woodson in Chillicothe, Ohio, on November 15, 1825. As a pioneer black feminist nationalist, she served the

The first black woman to serve on the faculty of an American university, Sarah Jane Woodson Early was hired by Wilberforce University in 1859. In 1865, the school named her its Preceptress of English and Latin and Lady Principal and Matron. (SCHOMBURG CENTER)

black community through her involvement in the woman's movement, the African Methodist Episcopal Church, and a variety of black educational institutions.

In 1856, Woodson earned an L.B. degree from **Oberlin College**, becoming one of the first black women to obtain a college degree. From 1859 to 1860, while employed by Wilberforce University, she became the first black woman college faculty member. She taught in many of Ohio's black community schools and served as principal of the black public school in Xenia, Ohio, 1860–61. In 1865, she was appointed Wilberforce University's "Preceptress of English and Latin and Lady Principal and Matron."

In 1868, Woodson left Wilberforce to teach at a school for black girls run by the Freedman's Bureau in Hillsborough, North Carolina. On September 24, 1868, she married Reverend Jordan W. Early, a pioneer in the AME Church movement. While continuing to teach in black schools throughout the South, Sarah Early participated in her husband's ministry. She led prayer meetings, taught Sunday school, and ministered to the sick. In 1894, she chronicled her husband's life in *The Life and Labors of Rev. J. W. Early*.

Sarah Jane Woodson Early preached and practiced her belief that the black woman's role in racial uplift and moral reform was crucial. Beginning in 1888, she was appointed Superintendent of the Colored Division of the Women's Christian Temperance Union

(WCTU). She remained active in the WCTU as a public lecturer as long as her health allowed. She died of heart disease on August 15, 1907.

CATHERINE JOHNSON

Elaw, Zilpha (b. c.1790)

As an itinerant evangelist, Zilpha Elaw's life was characterized by an intense journey toward spiritual empowerment, a need to define herself as a black woman in a racist society, and psychological wholeness through preaching the word of God. Born around 1790 just outside Philadelphia, Zilpha was one of three children who survived childbirth. At twelve years of age, following her mother's death in childbirth with her twenty-second child, her father placed her in service to a Quaker family, where she remained until she was eighteen years old.

Coming from a pious home where God's praises were joyously sung, Zilpha found the silent devotion of Quakers unsettling and was drawn, instead, to the emotional appeal of the evangelical Protestants proselytizing in the area. During a period of frustration shortly after her placement in the Quaker home and, undoubtedly, grief over the loss of her father only one and a half years after her mother's death, Zilpha began having visionary experiences. In the initial instance, Jesus came to her as an apparition, with arms opened to receive her, while she was performing one of her chores, milking a cow. As with most black women evangelists of the time, her religious conversion followed this vision around 1804. Visionary experiences, for most black women evangelists, served not only to transform their lives but allowed them to criticize the existing social order, particularly slavery, racism,

and sexism. Following subsequent visionary experiences, which occurred throughout her life, she joined a Methodist Episcopal Society near Philadelphia in 1808.

In 1810, Zilpha married Joseph Elaw and moved to Burlington, New Jersey, where Joseph had found employment. A daughter was born to the couple soon thereafter. Because Joseph had been expelled from the Methodist Episcopal Society and encouraged Zilpha to renounce her religion, her religious zeal strained their marriage. In 1817, during a week-long camp meeting and intense religious revival, Elaw fell into a trance. Recovering from this trance, Elaw believed that she had received sanctification of her soul from God. Encouraged by other women, she gave her first public exhortation at the meeting and, following a second camp meeting, became an exhorter in the Burlington area. The sanctification experience of being totally in harmony with the Divine Will enabled women to withstand societal criticism for their nontraditional ministerial roles.

Elaw's husband died in 1823, and she and her daughter were forced to labor as domestics. Incensed by the racial prejudice that allowed only white children to attend public schools, she opened a school for black children sometime later but closed it after two years, believing the Lord had called her to start her evangelical ministry.

Soon, Elaw was on the itinerant ministry circuit. She became the preaching partner of **Jarena Lee,** the first black woman evangelist on record, for a time in western Pennsylvania. Elaw never preached under the auspices of any religious denomination but relied for guidance on her inner sense of spirituality. In 1828, Elaw displayed her courage by preaching in Washington, D.C., and the slaveholding states of Maryland and Virginia to both black and white converts. Repulsed by both slavery and racial prejudice, Elaw denounced in her messages the abominations of both. She also sought to justify, according to the Scriptures, her right to preach. Her ministry was largely confined to the Northeastern and mid-Atlantic region of the United States until 1840. In that year, believing that God had ordained her for a greater undertaking, Elaw went to central England, where she recorded in her memoirs that she preached over a thousand sermons on the word of God and enjoyed great success. Her memoirs close in 1845, when she writes of her plans to return home from England.

GAYLE T. TATE

Eldridge, Elleanor (1784–c. 1845)

A skilled businesswoman and amateur lawyer, Elleanor Eldridge labored industriously to become respected in the black community. She excelled in her crafts and business ventures, and as an amateur lawyer she assisted her brother, George, in securing an acquittal of charges that he "horsewhipped and otherwise barbarously treated a man on the highway."

Elleanor Eldridge was born on March 27, 1784, in Warwick, Rhode Island. Her father, Robin Eldridge, was an African who was captured with his entire family and brought to America on a slave ship. Her mother, Hannah Prophet, was a Native American. Eldridge was born free in part because of the bill enacted in 1784 that called for gradual emancipation.

Robin Eldridge and two of his brothers had fought in the American Revolution. They were promised their freedom and two hundred acres of land apiece for their service. When the war ended they were pronounced free, but because they had been paid in worthless Old Continental currency, they were unable to take possession of their lands.

Eldridge was the youngest of seven daughters, only five of whom lived to maturity. After her mother died when she was ten years old, Eldridge was invited to live with the family of Joseph Baker, for whom her mother had worked as a laundress. Despite her father's protest, she accepted, receiving wages of twenty-five cents a week, and remained for six years. During her years with the Baker family, she became skilled in spinning, weaving, arithmetic, and all types of housework. She was considered a fully accomplished weaver by the age of fourteen and made carpets and bedspreads, among other things. At the age of sixteen, she went to work for Captain Benjamin Green and his family, first as a spinner and later as a dairy worker, making cheeses recognized as of "premium quality."

After Eldridge's father died when she was nineteen, she traveled 180 miles to Adams, Massachusetts, where her aunt helped her to obtain letters of administration of her father's estate. When she returned to Warwick, she settled the estate and went back to work for Captain Green, where she remained until his death in 1812. She then returned home to live with her oldest sister, Lettise.

Eldridge and her sister went into business, weaving, nursing, and soap making. Eldridge was so successful that she purchased a lot and built a house, which she rented out for forty dollars a year. After three years, she was persuaded by another sister to come to Providence, where she resided for almost twenty years.

She continued various business ventures, and by 1822 her painting and wallpapering business was such a success that she had saved $600. She purchased a lot and built a house costing $1,700, with an addition on the east side for herself and on the west side for a tenant. She borrowed $240 at 10 percent interest in order to purchase two more lots. She agreed to renew the note annually and to purchase a house for $2,000 with a down payment of $500, the balance to be paid within four years. After she contracted typhoid fever in September 1831, it was reported that she died and so the holder of the note for $240 filed an attachment to her property. When she returned to Providence from visiting friends in Massachusetts she discovered that all of her property had been auctioned off to pay the note. Friends persuaded her to enter a lawsuit before the Court of Common Pleas in January 1837 for trespass and ejectment because the sale at auction had not been legally advertised and she had not been notified. Although she lost the lawsuit, her conduct during the legal proceedings won her the admiration and respect of friends and neighbors. Eldridge was entitled, however, to recover her property after payment of $2,700 since there was no record of advertisement.

The Memoirs of Elleanor Eldridge was first published in 1838, one of the few narratives of the life of a free black woman.

VIVIAN NJERI FISHER

F

Ferguson, Catherine (c. 1774–1854)

Catherine Williams was born on a schooner, in about 1774, as her mother was being transported from Virginia to her new slave owner in New York. Her mother was sold again when Katy was eight years old, but before their separation her mother had taught Katy the Scriptures. Katy was allowed to attend church services, but she was not taught to read and write. Reverend John M. Mason of Murray Street Church encouraged her and admitted her as a member.

At sixteen, Katy was purchased by an abolitionist sympathizer who gave her half of her $200 purchase price in exchange for one year's work. A merchant, Divee Bethume, helped her obtain the other half. At eighteen, a free woman, she married a man named Ferguson. She had two children who died in infancy, and her husband died soon after.

In 1793, Ferguson began an integrated Sunday school in her home. From her impoverished neighborhood and the almshouse she gathered forty-eight children (twenty of them white) whose parents were not able to care for them. She taught them Scripture and how to care for themselves, and found them homes; some she took into her home.

Word of Ferguson's school and home placement of children reached Dr. Mason. He visited and invited Ferguson to move her activities to the basement of his new church. He provided her with assistants to teach secular courses along with her teaching the Scriptures. For the next forty years, Ferguson supervised the education and welfare services offered at the integrated Murray Street Sabbath School.

Ferguson's school was New York's first Sunday school. She began it with no knowledge of the Sunday school started by Robert Raikes in England in 1780; it was entirely her own inspiration, and she supported it with her own funds. She worked as a caterer for the parties of wealthy white families, and she was also in demand for cleaning fine laces and other delicate materials. She died of cholera in 1854 in New York. Her last words were "All is well."

Ferguson's contributions to integrated/spiritual education and child welfare services on behalf of the poor were recognized by New York City. In 1920, the city opened the Katy Ferguson Home for unwed mothers, which was described as the only one of its kind for black women in the country.

AUDREYE JOHNSON

Fields, "Stagecoach Mary" (1832?–1914)

In 1959, actor Gary Cooper talked to *Ebony* magazine about a pioneer who had fascinated him when he was only nine years old, growing up in Montana. Strong, fearless, and fierce, this pioneer was a black woman named Mary Fields.

Mary Fields was born a slave in Tennessee in about 1832. Little is known about her early life, but it is said that she lived for a time on the Mississippi River.

By 1884, Fields was in Toledo, Ohio, working as a handywoman for an order of Catholic nuns. Her exact position in the convent is not clear. Some reports say that she met and became friends with the mother superior, Mother Amadeus, and then went to work for the order. Others say that she was a slave, owned by a man named Judge Dunne, who was either Mother Amadeu's brother or father. And still another report says that, before Mother Amadeus took her vows, Fields was her personal servant.

At any rate, the convent sent Mother Amadeus to open a school for Native-American girls in Montana. Fields did not go along, but, when the nun came down with pneumonia, she traveled out to take care of her. She stayed to work for the mission.

One of her jobs was transporting supplies from the town of Cascade, which was some distance away. Traveling alone across the prairie was a tough job, but Mary Fields was a tough woman. She stood six feet tall and weighed more than 200 pounds. She was powerful enough to fight off animals intent on grabbing the convent's salt pork and molasses and strong enough to keep going through midwestern thunderstorms.

In the end, Mary Field's toughness ended her stay at the convent. She had a fierce temper. She fought constantly with the hired men and ended up in a gun duel with one of them. Finally, the bishop ordered the nuns to send her away.

She didn't go far. Mother Amadeus helped her open a restaurant in Cascade. However, Fields had a weakness for giving food to hungry people who couldn't pay, and the restaurant failed.

"Stagecoach Mary" Fields stood six feet tall and weighed more than 200 pounds. She was, as Gary Cooper put it, "one of the freest souls ever to draw a breath or a thirty-eight."

Next, Fields got a job driving a stagecoach for the United States government. This is when the legend really began to grow. It's easy to imagine the reaction of the populace to this huge black woman in her sixties, dressed in men's clothing, smoking a cigar, driving the stage. It must have been the kind of sight that captures the imagination.

When Fields retired from driving in 1903, she did a number of jobs around Cascade, where she was the only black resident. By all evidence, she was respected and loved by the townspeople. When a laundry she ran burned down, the town rebuilt it with donated materials and labor. At the saloons in town, no women were allowed—except Stagecoach Mary. When the owner of the Cascade Hotel leased it to another man, he made it a condition of the lease that Fields continue to receive her meals there free.

The town even closed the schools and had a celebration on Field's birthday. Since no one knew when that was, the town celebrated when Mary Fields felt like it.

As she got older, Fields curbed her legendary temper. She worked for long hours in her garden. She was the number one fan of the Cascade baseball team, presenting bouquets to home-run hitters. And she cared for the altar at Wedsworth Hall for the Catholic Society.

Mary Fields died in 1914. She was, as Gary Cooper put it, "one of the freest souls ever to draw a breath or a thirty-eight."

KATHLEEN THOMPSON

Foote, Julia A. J. (1823–1900)

"Redeemed! redeemed! glory! glory!" Shouting these words, fifteen-year-old Julia Foote sprang from her bed where she had lain semiconscious for twenty hours. Fearing eternal damnation, she had fainted while listening to her minister's powerful sermon on sin and redemption. In her semiconscious state, she had heard voices singing,"This Is the New Song." She awakened joyful, peaceful, and redeemed. This moment of conversion launched her personal commitment to Christian righteousness and evangelism as it emboldened her to confront family, friends, and black ministers who challenged her right to preach a message of Christian salvation.

Born in Schenectady, New York, in 1823, the fourth child of former slaves, Julia was raised in a Christian household as a member of the African Methodist Episcopal (AME) Church in Albany, New York. Her conversion transformed her into an assertive disciple for her religion, and she studied to improve her reading and speaking abilities to enhance her Christian mission. Although her Christian self-affirmation and struggles for self-improvement empowered her with a sense of autonomy and individuality, they placed her in conflict with the prescribed behavior for women in the nineteenth century. In her commitment to proclaim her own salvation and her unyielding determination to preach, Julia defied her parents. After her marriage to George Foote in 1841, she defied him as well. Even under the threat of excommunication, she defied her minister, Reverend Jehiel C. Beman, of the AME Church in Boston.

From the 1840s through the 1870s, Foote traveled throughout New York, New England, and the mid-Atlantic states, and as far as Cincinnati, Detroit, and Canada, preaching the doctrine of sanctification—the belief that the soul can be purified of and liberated from sin, thus providing for a more perfect union with Christ, not only in death, but in life. Her thirty years of itinerant evangelism were sporadically interrupted by the illnesses and deaths of her father, mother, and husband.

Although nothing is known of her activities during the 1880s and 1890s, she became a missionary for the African Methodist Episcopal Zion Church, the first ordained deacon in 1894, and the second woman to be ordained an elder in the church.

Julia Foote's willingness to defy the conventions of Christian female propriety sanctioned her condemnation of all forms of evil and sin, including gender discrimination, racism, and slavery. Julia Foote's story is one of self-determination, individualism, and self-affirmation, ordained not by secular authority but by God.

LILLIE JOHNSON EDWARDS

Forten Sisters

MARGARETTA FORTEN (c. 1815–1875)

Dual careers as an educator and an abolitionist gave Margaretta Forten an uncommon life for a nineteenth-century black woman. During the 1840s she taught in a school operated by Sarah Mapps Douglass before opening her own private grammar school equipped with boarding facilities in 1850. In 1859, her school had an enrollment of ten scholars. Margaretta's antislavery career closely paralleled the thirty-six-year existence of the **Philadelphia Female Anti-Slavery Society**. In December 1833, Margaretta, her mother, and two sisters became charter members of this pioneering women's group. She was one of fourteen women selected to draft the society's constitution.

From 1833 to 1870, Margaretta helped to chart the society's agenda. She served as recording secretary in 1833, then during 1836 she was elected treasurer to assist Esther Moore, the society's president. At the end of that year, Margaretta reported a treasury balance of $114.81. Reelected to a second term as treasurer in 1837, she served with the new president, Sarah Pugh. Margaretta frequently sat on the society's

policy-making board of managers. Periodically, she represented her group at meetings of the Pennsylvania State Anti-Slavery Society. On January 16, 1837, for example, Margaretta and four others traveled to a state meeting in Harrisburg as official delegates of the Philadelphia Female Anti-Slavery Society.

Margaretta combined office holding with extensive committee work. She served on the society's membership committee, the education committee, the annual antislavery fair committee, and the petition campaign committee. During her tenure, the education committee was involved in many activities, including donating books to black schools. As one of several fair coordinators in 1856, Margaretta reported a profit of over $1,700.

Margaretta Forten was also involved in charitable activities. In June 1841, she joined Sarah Pugh and four others to spearhead the society's collection of money for the widow of slain abolitionist Elijah P. Lovejoy. Similarly, in 1856, Margaretta forwarded $25 she had collected to Massachusetts. Those funds were used to build a home for abolitionist William Lloyd Garrison and his family. During November 1863, Margaretta advocated women's rights when she joined society members Louisa Keller and others in securing signatures for a Women's National League petition.

After almost four decades of involvement in the antislavery crusade, Margaretta Forten offered a resolution at the last meeting of the Philadelphia Female Anti-Slavery Society in 1870. Acknowledging the newly ratified post-Civil War constitutional amendments, Margaretta's resolution announced the triumph of liberty and celebrated her society's labors in that noble cause.

While her sisters, Harriet and Sarah Louisa, married and raised children, Margaretta remained single and lived in the Forten family home on Lombard Street in Philadelphia. After the death of her father, James Forten, Sr., in 1842, Margaretta resided with her mother and younger brothers, Thomas Francis Willing Forten and William Deas Forten. Margaretta Forten died on January 28, 1875.

SARAH LOUISA FORTEN PURVIS (1814–1883)

Beginning with its January 29, 1831, issue, the *Liberator* newspaper published Sarah Forten's antislavery views. Writing under the pen names of Ada and Magawisca, Sarah, then only seventeen years old, challenged the institution of slavery with such creative works as "The Slave Girl's Address to Her Mother," "The Abuse of Liberty," and "The Slave." Her poems and essays poignantly described the humanity of the bondspeople while attacking the hypocrisy of slavery in a nation founded on the concept of individual liberty. At the conclusion of one essay, Sarah invoked the image of divine intervention on behalf of slaves when she wrote, "He, that Great Spirit, who created all men free and equal . . . He is just, and his anger will not always slumber. He will wipe the tear from Ethiopia's eye; He will shake the tree of liberty, and its blossoms shall spread over the earth" ("The Abuse of Liberty" 1831).

Two years after her debut as an antislavery author, Sarah joined her mother and two sisters as a charter member of the Philadelphia Female Anti-Slavery Society. Like her siblings, she remained a member throughout the society's thirty-six-year existence. Sarah assumed leadership positions on a number of important committees. In May 1835, she joined with **Angelina Grimké** and eight others to promote the moral and intellectual improvement of Philadelphia's black residents. One emphasis of the committee was to improve educational opportunities for children. From 1835 until February 1838, she also worked on the society's petition campaign to end slavery in the District of Columbia. Sarah's primary responsibility was to secure petition signatures in Columbia County, Pennsylvania. During February and March 1837, U.S. Congressman James Harper and U.S. Senator Samuel McKean acknowledged receipt of the society's numerous petitions.

Because abolitionists often encountered difficulty renting halls to hold their meetings, antislavery groups in and around Philadelphia proposed erecting their own building. During December 1836, Sarah joined Lucretia Mott and eight others to spearhead this effort on behalf of the society. In January 1837, the building committee recommended that the society purchase twenty-five shares at $5 per share, and Pennsylvania Hall was completed a year later. Their triumph was short lived, however, when an angry mob of proslavery sympathizers burned the hall to the ground on the evening of May 17, 1838.

As a member of the society's board of managers, Sarah helped to make policy. During her tenure on the board from 1836 to 1838, the Philadelphia Female Anti-Slavery Society initiated its support for the Philadelphia Vigilant Committee, a group that assisted slaves fleeing Southern states.

Throughout her antislavery career, Sarah maintained a close friendship with Angelina Grimké. Besides serving together on several committees, they wrote to one another. On

April 15, 1837, Sarah wrote to Angelina concerning the upcoming Antislavery Convention of American Women to be held the following month in New York City. Sarah and her sisters were traveling from Philadelphia to attend the gathering. Sarah thanked Angelina for offering to arrange lodging in New York, but told her that the Forten women had accepted an invitation to stay at the home of Reverend Peter Williams, pastor of the African Methodist Episcopal Zion Church.

In 1838, Sarah married Joseph Purvis. Six years earlier Sarah's sister Harriet had become the bride of Robert Purvis, Joseph's older brother. By all accounts, Sarah and Joseph enjoyed a happy marriage. The couple had several children. Her duties as a wife and mother and her residence outside of Philadelphia curtailed Sarah's antislavery activities for several years. However, she did not abandon the emancipation crusade. During the 1860s, Sarah worked with the antislavery fair committees alongside her sisters, Margaretta and Harriet.

Joseph Purvis died in January 1857; he was forty-four years old. Sometime after the death of her husband, Sarah and her children moved to the Forten family home on Lombard Street in Philadelphia. The 1880 census lists Sarah as a widow living with her daughter, Anne, and son, William. Other family members residing in the home during the 1880s were Sarah's mother, Charlotte Forten, and her two younger brothers, William Deas Forten and Thomas Francis Willing Forten.

HARRIET D. FORTEN PURVIS (1810–1875)

During a tour of the United States in November 1852, English abolitionist Sallie Holley visited the Byberry, Pennsylvania home of Harriet and Robert Purvis and recorded her impressions. Holley remarked that "his wife is very lady-like in manners and conversation; something of the ease and blandness of a southern lady. The style of living here is quite uncommonly rich and elegant." The ladylike wife to whom Holley referred was Harriet Purvis, the eldest daughter of abolitionists James Forten, Sr., and Charlotte Forten. When Sallie Holley met Harriet and Robert in 1852, the couple had been married for twenty years and were the parents of five children, Robert, Jr., Charles Burleigh, Henry, Harriet, and Emily.

Harriet Purvis, like her mother and two sisters, Margaretta and Sarah Louisa, was a charter member of the Philadelphia Female Anti-Slavery Society. Harriet's energies went primarily to this group and the Pennsylvania State Anti-Slavery Society. She was active in the Female Society for nearly all of its thirty-six years of existence. Harriet frequently cochaired the antislavery fairs, annual fund-raising events. Besides helping to organize and manage the fairs, Harriet also helped devise the strategy to make these events successful. In February 1841, for example, she and **Sarah Mapps Douglass** were members of a group that evaluated the profitability of the previous fair activity.

Harriet viewed the antislavery fairs as important events. In 1861, at the start of the Civil War, she urged the society to hold a fair even though the fair committee was smaller because of increased war efforts. Harriet's arguments proved persuasive, and the members voted to proceed with the annual event. In time, Harriet had additional assistance from her daughter, Harriet Purvis, Jr., who joined the fair committee from 1866 through 1868.

As a skilled seamstress, Harriet served on the Philadelphia Female Society's sewing committee, and was charged with the responsibility of establishing a sewing school in an economically disadvantaged section of the city. On June 23, 1842, the committee reported that they had located a room for the school, which had been donated rent free, and they had engaged a sewing teacher.

On numerous occasions, Harriet represented the Philadelphia Female Anti-Slavery Society as a delegate to meetings of other groups. In 1838 and 1839, she was one of the society's delegates to the Antislavery Convention of American Women. Also in 1839, she and nine others attended the Free Produce Convention on behalf of their society. The antislavery convention delegates pledged to secure the products of free labor, especially cotton goods, for the Philadelphia area. During May 1841, Harriet and her husband attended the Pennsylvania State Anti-Slavery Society convention where Harriet represented the Female Society during the proceedings.

Besides her role as an antislavery delegate, Harriet's connections in abolitionist circles gave her an array of prominent friends and acquaintances. William Lloyd Garrison, Sallie Holley, Angelina Grimké, and many others frequented the Purvis home. Harriet also knew Boston abolitionist **Sarah Parker Remond**. On December 10, 1857, Harriet introduced Remond to the Female Society, and Remond addressed the group on her emancipation efforts in Ohio. On another occasion, during the post-Civil War era, Harriet accompanied **Frances Ellen Watkins Harper**, a black author, and the Reverend Francis S. Cardozo of South Carolina to a state antislavery meeting.

Harriet also lectured on civil rights topics. On September 13, 1866, she spoke to the Female Society in support of black suffrage. During the speech Harriet denounced the practice of segregating black passengers on Philadelphia's railroad cars. She urged the society's committee on railroads as well as the citizens of Philadelphia to correct this injustice. Harriet reminded her audience of the sentiments of Judge Pitkin, a Republican from Louisiana who believed that it would be difficult to outlaw segregation.

Aside from her public activities, relatively little is known about Harriet's life. Evidence suggests that her forty-three-year marriage to Robert Purvis was an equal partnership. Robert encouraged and even assisted Harriet in pursuing a public life dedicated to the causes of abolition and civil rights. From the time of their marriage in 1832, this couple worked as an effective team. While raising a family, they also attended antislavery meetings, lectured, and raised funds to further the emancipation crusade. As a wife, mother, antislavery activist, lecturer, and hostess, Harriet seems to have successfully combined a public career with the more traditional roles set aside for women of her era.

JANICE SUMLER-EDMOND

Forth, Elizabeth Denison (d. 1866)

Ironies abound in African-American history. Surely one of the most ironic accounts concerns the ex-slave Elizabeth Denison Forth, who bequeathed her fortune to be used to build a church in one of the most exclusive white communities in the country. The daughter of slaves Peter and Hannah Denison, Elizabeth, known as Lisette, was a slave in the Michigan Territory when Congress passed the Northwest Ordinance of 1787 prohibiting slavery in the territory, which would eventually become the states of Michigan, Ohio, Illinois, Indiana, and Wisconsin. When the Denison's owner, William Tucker, died on March 7, 1805, he stipulated in his will that Peter and Hannah were to receive their freedom upon the death of his wife, Catherine. The Denison's eight children, however, were bequeathed to Tucker's sons. Thus the antislavery provisions of the Northwest Ordinance had little effect on the children's status.

A suit for the Denison children's freedom failed when Judge Augustus B. Woodward ruled on September 23, 1807, that the Northwest Ordinance applied only to new slaves, not to existing ones, in accordance with Jay's Treaty of 1794. Lisette and her brother Scipio escaped, with the aid of white friends, into Canada. The exact date of their return to the Michigan Territory is not known, but by the early 1820s Lisette was working as a domestic in the Solomon Sibley household in Detroit.

Having saved her meager earnings and perhaps with the advice of her wealthy employer, Lisette bought four lots, totaling 48.5 acres, on April 21, 1825, in Pontiac, Michigan. On September 25, 1827, she married Scipio Forth, according to records of Saint Paul's Protestant Episcopal Church in Detroit. The records do not reveal the exact date of his death, but apparently within three years, Lisette became a widow.

In 1830, she joined the John Biddle household as a domestic servant. Continuing to invest her earnings, during the 1830s Lisette acquired stock in the steamboat *Michigan* and twenty shares of Farmers and Mechanic's Bank stock. Her investments proved profitable. On May 25, 1837, Lisette bought a lot in Detroit, paying the mortgage off in installments. In 1854, Lisette was living in her own home on the edge of the business section of old Detroit. After journeying to Paris in 1855 to attend to the ailing Mrs. Biddle, she returned to Detroit a year later, where she remained until her death on August 7, 1866.

In her final will Lisette left the bulk of her estate "to be used in the erection of a 'Fine Chapel for the use of the Protestant Episcopal Church' of which I am a communicant." She prefaced this rather unusual bequest with the following:

Ex-slave Elizabeth Denison Forth, known as Lisette, stipulated in her will that her fortune be used to build a church. With the aid of the bequest, the Protestant Episcopal Church established Saint James Chapel, in Gross Ile, Michigan. (BURTON HISTORICAL COLLECTION, DETROIT PUBLIC LIBRARY)

Having long felt the inadequacy of the provisions made for the poor in our houses of worship, and knowing from sad experience that many devout believers, and humble followers of the lowly Jesus, are excluded from those courts, where the rich and the poor should meet together, shut out from those holy services by the mammon of unrighteousness, from that very church which declares the widow's mite to be more acceptable in the sight of the Lord than the careless offerings of those who give of their "abundance" and wishing to do all in my power as far as God has given me the means to offer to the poor man and the stranger "wine and milk without price and without cost."

Lisette's estate amounted to approximately $1,500. In 1867, with the aid of the bequest, Saint James Chapel was built on Grosse Ile, Michigan.

DARLENE CLARK HINE

Fox, Lillian Thomas (1866–1917)

Black journalist, clubwoman, and civic leader Lillian Thomas was born in Chicago in 1866 to the Reverend Byrd Parker, pastor of Quinn African Methodist Episcopal (AME) Church, and Jane Janette Thomas, a schoolteacher. Lillian Thomas was raised in Oshkosh, Wisconsin, until moving to Indianapolis in the early 1880s. She began writing at an early age and by the late 1880s achieved national recognition through her work as a reporter and correspondence editor for the *Freeman*, a nationally prominent black newspaper.

In 1893, Lillian Thomas married James E. Fox, a Jamaican merchant tailor in Pensacola, Florida. That year he relocated his business to Indianapolis, and Lillian retired from the *Freeman*. Although she curtailed her formal work commitment, Fox continued her involvement in community organizations. She also gained national prominence as a public speaker on numerous speaking tours in the Midwest and South for various political and religious organizations as well as at conventions of the Afro-American Council, the Negro Business League, the Anti-Lynching League, the Atlanta Congress of Colored Women at the 1895 National Exposition, and the **National Association of Colored Women**.

After separating from her husband, Fox returned to her writing career. In 1900, the *Indianapolis News* hired her as the first black journalist to write a news column regularly appearing in any Indiana newspaper. For fourteen years she used her contacts with the white community and her position at the *News* to further the social and political agendas of various groups within the black community. A superb organizer, Fox was a founder and member of community organizations, among them Bethel AME Literary Society; the Woman's Improvement Club, which provided health care to black tuberculosis patients; and the Indiana State Federation of Colored Women's Clubs.

EARLINE RAE FERGUSON

Freeman, Elizabeth (c. 1744–1829)

"I heard that paper read yesterday, that says, 'all men are born equal, and that every man has a right to freedom.' I am not a dumb critter; won't the law give me my freedom?" So in 1781 Elizabeth Freeman, an enslaved black woman also known as Mum Bett or Mumbet, with the assistance of counsel, entered a Massachusetts court to demand her freedom.

Despite her enslavement, Elizabeth Freeman, an illiterate black woman, was able to secure a legal counsel and provide him with a legal theory for her case. Freeman, through her counsel, filed a writ of replevin alleging that Colonel Ashley and his son were illegally detaining her and a black male co-petitioner named Brom. The writ declared that the enslavement of Freeman and Brom violated a provision of the newly enacted 1780 state constitution which declared that all men are born free and equal. The state court granted them their freedom.

Historians overlook or marginalize Freeman's contribution to the antislavery cause, citing instead the cases of two black men, Quok Walker and Nathaniel Jennison, which were initiated and decided after Freeman's case. However, Elizabeth Freeman's contribution is significant because, unlike other freedom suits based on individual circumstances or technicalities and designed to secure freedom only for the petitioner, the legal theory set forth in her suit had the potential to free not just the petitioners, but all enslaved blacks in Massachusetts. Clearly this was Elizabeth Freeman's intent since she later told people that she was moved to sue after taking a blow from her physically abusive mistress that was intended for her sister. Thus, Freeman was suing for her freedom as well as her sister's.

Freeman's suit was the first freedom suit to use a state constitution as the basis to challenge chattel slavery. In addition, her suit resulted in the first court decision construing a state constitutional provision as inconsistent with the institution of slavery. Unfortunately, Freeman's suit did not result in the complete emancipation of enslaved blacks in the state.

TAUNYA LOVELL BANKS

G

Gannett, Deborah Sampson (1760–1827)

The back of the tombstone reads, "Deborah Sampson Gannett, Robert Shurtleff, The Female Soldier: 1781–1783." Dressed in men's clothing and using a man's name, Deborah Sampson served for over a year in the Continental Army. Her legacy is one of heroism and adventure as a Revolutionary War soldier.

Deborah Sampson was the daughter of Jonathan and Deborah (Bradford) Sampson. She was born in Plymouth, Massachusetts, on December 17, 1760. One of six children, she could trace her ancestry back to old Pilgrim stock. Her mother's lineage was traced to Governor William Bradford, and Miles Standish and John Alden were among her father's ancestors. Despite their illustrious background, the Sampsons were not wealthy people. As a means to provide a better life for his family, Jonathan Sampson decided to become a sailor. Most likely as a result of a storm or shipwreck at sea, he disappeared and was never seen or heard from again. Deborah Bradford Sampson found herself unable to find work that would allow her to take care of her children.

Due to financial difficulties, young Deborah went to live initially with a cousin. Upon the death of her cousin, when Deborah was about eight years old, she went to live with a pastor's wife, with whom she remained for approximately two years. She was then bound out as a servant in the home of Benjamin Thomas of Middleborough, where she remained until age eighteen. She was able to acquire skills in many of the domestic arts associated with expectations about women, becoming generally adept as a cook and a seamstress. Deborah Sampson, owing in large part to her tall and well-proportioned physique, also plowed the fields, fed the farm animals, and did other chores usually done by men, including carpentry.

Sampson had the advantage of part-time attendance at the Middleborough public school. In time, much of her reading centered on the major issues of her day: the quarrel between Britain and the colonies, the vexing concern about Britain's financial problems, and the hateful regard for the taxes imposed on the colonies by Britain. The venturesome young woman continually busied herself not only with female undertakings but also with her avid interest in colonial and British politics. When Deborah Sampson was twenty-one and the war was still being fought, she began to entertain the idea of active involvement in the colonial army.

From her work in the local school district, Sampson had accrued a sum of $12, which she used for purchasing materials for a man's suit. From this time on, she worked diligently to present herself as a man. On May 20, 1782, disguised in men's clothing and using the alias Robert Shurtleff (or Shirtliff or Shirtlieff), she enlisted as a volunteer in the Continental forces. She was mustered into the service by Captain Eliphalet Thorp, at Worcester, on May 23, 1782, and served in Captain George Webb's company, Colonel Shepard's (later Colonel Jackson's) Fourth Massachusetts Regiment until discharged by General Knox at West Point on October 23, 1783.

During the battle at Tarrytown, Sampson was seriously wounded but was afraid to go to a hospital lest her sex be discovered. However, four months later, she was shot through the shoulder. As a consequence of this injury and exposure to extremely cold weather, she developed brain fever. While hospitalized, Dr. Barnabas Binney of Philadelphia, the attending physician, discovered that she was female, but did not divulge her secret.

After her discharge, Deborah returned to her native New England in November 1783, where she resided with an uncle in Sharon, Massachusetts. She resumed female attire and settled into the community life of Sharon. It was there that she met a farmer by the name of Benjamin Gannett, whom she married on April 7, 1784. They had three children: Earl Bradford, Mary, and Patience; they adopted a fourth, Susannah Shepherd, whose mother had died in childbirth.

Eventually Deborah Sampson's sojourn as Robert Shurtleff in the Continental Army began to attract attention. In the late 1790s Herman Mann published a fascinating account of what many regard as a much romanticized biography of Sampson under the title *The Female Review*.

Beginning with her appearance at the Federal Street Theatre in Boston on March 22, 1802, Deborah Sampson Gannett adapted the lecture written for her by Mann to her own liking and toured several New England towns where she told of her Revolutionary War experience. She was awarded a pension by the state of Massachusetts. On March 11, 1805, she was listed among those receiving pension payments from the United States government.

Deborah Sampson Gannett died on April 29, 1827. She is buried in Rockridge Cemetery in Sharon, Massachusetts. Her decision to serve in the Continental Army represents an intense patriotism, and her life as a soldier dramatically refutes the pervasive belief that women cannot serve admirably in combat.

Deborah Sampson Gannett's life exemplifies the black experience, wherein there are many heroes and heroines. While it is generally accepted that Deborah was a black American, there are those who question the authenticity of this claim.

LARRY MARTIN

Granson, Milla (b. c. 1800)

Although Milla Granson was born a slave around 1800 in Kentucky, she became one of black America's early pioneers of education. Teaching school at midnight, Granson risked her life to educate hundreds of black children and adults in Kentucky and Mississippi.

Granson's interest in education began early. In Kentucky she learned firsthand the value of education. Impressed by the knowledge and power that white people possessed, Granson persuaded her master's children to teach her to read and write because she believed that education was the passage to freedom. Having acquired some rudimentary skills, Granson, with her master's permission, taught other slaves to read and write. With Granson's help many slaves wrote their own passes to freedom. Granson, however, remained a slave and on her master's death was sold to a plantation owner in Mississippi.

In Mississippi, Granson experienced hardships. Because she had been a house slave in Kentucky, she was unfamiliar with fieldwork and could rarely complete her assigned day's work in the Mississippi plantation fields. Consequently, she was beaten. Then, due to ailing health, she was made a house servant.

Granson's reassignment created the opportunity for the black community on this Mississippi plantation to be educated. With more of her time available, she initiated a teaching project in one of the small cabins in the back alley. Granson taught classes from midnight to two o'clock in the morning. When she had educated one group of students to the best of her ability, she graduated them and enrolled another group. Eventually, Granson's efforts led to the implementation of a Mississippi law which made it legal for slaves to teach slaves. To educate more slaves, Granson opened a Sabbath school for those who could not attend the midnight classes.

Although it is not clear when Granson died or whether she married, gave birth, or adopted a religious affiliation, it is apparent that she made a significant contribution to black America. As one of the pioneers of black education, Granson recognized the importance of self-help and through community effort and cooperation, she made a difference in the lives of black people in Kentucky and Mississippi during slavery.

VALERIE GRIM

Greenfield, Elizabeth (c. 1819–1876)

They called her "The Black Swan" and an "African nightingale." She was courted by high society on both sides of the Atlantic. Born into slavery, she sang in a command performance before Queen Victoria of Great Britain.

Elizabeth Taylor Greenfield, the first African-American musician to earn a reputation in both the United States and Britain, was born c. 1819 in Natchez, Mississippi, to a family named Taylor, who were slaves on the estate of Mrs. Holliday Greenfield. When Elizabeth was only a year old, Mrs. Greenfield, acting on her beliefs as a Quaker, manumitted the child's parents and sent them to Liberia; she took Elizabeth with her to Philadelphia. The child stayed with Mrs. Greenfield until she was eight, then went to live with her own sister, Mary Parker. When she was in her late teens, she returned to Mrs. Greenfield as a companion.

The young woman's remarkable voice was noticed early by a neighbor—a Miss Price—who gave her musical instruction. The neighbor's father, Dr. Price, heard them practicing and decided that Mrs. Greenfield should know of her ward's gift. Elizabeth Greenfield was concerned that the older woman would disapprove of the secular music she was singing. However, Mrs. Greenfield encouraged the young singer's talent and, while still young, Elizabeth Greenfield began performing as a soloist at private parties. In 1844, Mrs. Greenfield died, leaving her companion an income of $100 a year for life. However, the will was contested, and Greenfield's inheritance was exhausted in lawyer's fees.

In about 1849, one of Philadelphia's leading musicians hired Greenfield to perform in Baltimore, where she advertised as a music teacher. The next stage of her life took place in Buffalo, New York, where she went either to hear Jenny Lind or to make contact with friends of Mrs. Greenfield's. She saved her money to make the journey and, on the boat, encountered Mrs. H. B. Potter. Potter, hearing her sing, invited Greenfield to her mansion. There she performed and was heard by a number of influential people, a group of whom sponsored her in a series of concerts for the Buffalo Music Association. It was this series that brought Greenfield to the attention of the press. She was an immediate sensation, receiving the nickname that remained with her throughout her career—"The Black Swan." Soon she was giving concerts in New York City, Boston, and Toronto. Within a few years she had sung in all of the free states.

Though her voice was universally praised, her experiences were not always pleasant. She was criticized for her lack of training by reviewers whose racist bias went undisguised. She sang in halls to which other African Americans were denied admittance. In New York, in 1853, she debuted at Metropolitan Hall, which held an audience of four thousand white patrons only. Because of a threat that the building would be burned if she appeared, police were stationed in the hall during the concert. After the concert, Greenfield apologized to her own people for their exclusion from the performance. She later gave a concert to benefit the Home of Aged Colored Persons and the Colored Orphan Asylum.

Greenfield then went to England to perform, but her arrangements fell through. So she took matters into her own hands again and sought out Harriet Beecher Stowe, who was in London at the time. Stowe listened to her sing and was amazed by Greenfield's range, which spanned more than three octaves. Stowe was interested enough in Greenfield's artistry to introduce her to the Duchess of Sutherland, who took her to Sir George Smart, the queen's musician. Smart was charmed, and presented Greenfield in a concert at Stafford House.

"The Black Swan," Elizabeth Taylor Greenfield, gave a command performance before Queen Victoria early in her career, astonishing Her Majesty with a range of more than three octaves. (SCHOMBURG CENTER)

This concert led to others, in London and in the provinces. Greenfield also studied extensively with Smart and attended concerts by other musicians. When the time came for her to return to the United States, Smart and the Duchess of Sutherland went to Queen Victoria, who arranged a command performance at Buckingham Palace on May 10, 1854. The queen gave Greenfield £20 for the performance, which helped to pay her way back to her own country.

Back in the United States, Greenfield went on tour again, including in her performance a well-known tenor, Thomas J. Bowers. The reception was again mixed. Certainly, Greenfield's remarkable range was something of a novelty. She amazed her audiences with vocal feats such as singing "Old Folks at Home" as a soprano then as a baritone. Still, the reviews make it clear that she had much more than novelty appeal. Critics praised her emotional power and the weight and sweetness of her voice. Audiences seem to have responded also to her intelligence and personality. She was frequently compared to Jenny Lind. If she was not the best black singer of the period—and many have said she was not—she was probably the most ambitious, and her accomplishments broke new ground for black musicians. She also organized a troupe of black musicians who performed in Washington, D.C., in 1862 and in Philadelphia in 1866.

In July of 1854, Greenfield returned to New York to perform then went to Philadelphia to live. She did not tour again until 1863. After that tour, she went back to teaching. She also sang for a variety of social causes, giving dozens of benefits for orphans, among others. She died in Philadelphia on March 31, 1876.

KATHLEEN THOMPSON

Grimké, Charlotte (1837–1914)

Antislavery poet, educator, civil rights advocate, and minister's wife Charlotte L. Forten Grimké was a member of the prominent, activist Forten-Purvis family of nineteenth-century Philadelphia. Forten joined the antislavery crusade while attending school in Salem, Massachusetts. On June 4, 1854, she recorded a distressing event in her diary. The previous week, a black newcomer to the city had been arrested and tried as a fugitive slave. The abolitionist community mounted

a vigorous defense, but to no avail. The unfortunate man was returned to the South in chains. Deeply affected by this human tragedy, Forten renewed her dedication to the emancipation cause. Referencing these events, she wrote, "yet they shall be fresh incentive to more earnest study, to aid me in fitting myself for laboring in a holy cause, for enabling me to do much toward changing the condition of my oppressed and suffering people."

Charlotte Forten's grandfather was James Forten, Sr., a wealthy Philadelphia sailmaker and abolitionist, and Charlotte's parents, Robert Bridges Forten and Mary Woods Forten, were both activists. Besides being a member of several antislavery organizations, Robert Forten worked with his brother-in-law, Robert Purvis, on the Philadelphia Vigilant Committee, one link in the slave assistance network. When she died in 1840, Mary Woods Forten was a member of the **Philadelphia Female Anti-Slavery Society**.

Sent to Salem, New England by her father to complete her education, Forten led a life centered around school and antislavery activities. Higginson Grammar School on Beckford Street provided a fertile learning ground for the budding abolitionist. She was the only nonwhite student of the 200 students enrolled in 1854. Mary Shepard, the school's principal, and her three assistants stressed intellectual development through critical analysis. The Higginson curriculum consisted of history, geography, drawing, and cartography. When she had completed her studies at Higginson, Charlotte enrolled in the Normal School at Salem. Besides her classroom studies, she read many books, including some classics by Shakespeare and Milton, and works by contemporary authors Margaret Fuller and William Wordsworth.

Charlotte Forten's antislavery labors were extensive. As a member of the Salem Female Anti-Slavery Society, she attended sewing circles whose members prepared items for the annual fund-raising bazaars. She frequently attended antislavery lectures in Salem and sometimes traveled to nearby Haverhill or Boston to hear speakers such as Ralph Waldo Emerson, Henry Ward Beecher, Theodore Parker, and U.S. Senator Charles Sumner. Although she found Sumner to be a gifted speaker, she disagreed with his reverence for a constitution that condoned slavery.

Forten met many famous people as a boarder at the home of black abolitionists John and Amy Remond. On May 31, 1854, she dined with *Liberator* editor William Lloyd Garrison, and his wife. The Garrisons extended an invitation to Charlotte Forten to visit them. On other occasions she met Wendell Phillips, the renowned antislavery orator, and antislavery activists Maria Weston Chapman and William Wells Brown.

During June 1856, dwindling finances threatened to curtail Forten's Normal School studies. She accepted a teaching position at Epes Grammar School for a salary of $200 per year. Forten remained at Epes for two years, before a recurring bout of tuberculosis forced her to resign and return to Philadelphia. Salem school officials promised to reassign her when her health permitted.

Charlotte Forten, like her aunt, **Sarah Forten Purvis,** was a gifted poet. When she was in Salem, her creative works began to appear in antislavery periodicals, including the *Liberator, National Anti-Slavery Standard*, and Bishop Daniel Payne's *Anglo African* magazine. Although the majority of her poems contained antislavery themes, she

Charlotte Forten Grimké was a prominent poet, educator, and civil rights advocate.

published works on a variety of subjects. Her poem "Wind among the Poplars" told the tragic story of young lovers. "Glimpses of New England" appeared in the *National Anti-Slavery Standard* in June 1858, and a choir sang her poem "Red, White, and Blue" at a ceremony in Boston honoring Crispus Attucks and other heroes of the Boston Massacre.

With the outbreak of the Civil War, Charlotte Forten looked for a way to hasten the end of slavery. The Port Royal Project in South Carolina gave her that opportunity. By spring 1862, Union forces had routed the Confederates from their stronghold on the South Carolina Sea Islands near Charleston. The planter class on those islands, most of whom were Confederate sympathizers, abandoned their homes and fled to the mainland. Thousands of slaves and a valuable cotton crop were left behind. Salmon Chase, Lincoln's secretary of the treasury, convinced the president that Northern teachers and agriculture superintendents should be sent to prepare the black population for citizenship. Forten applied for a teaching post. After some delay, on October 21, 1862, she received a note from James Miller McKim announcing her assignment with Philadelphia's Port Royal Commission. She was the first black teacher hired for the Sea Islands mission.

Charlotte Forten's two-year contribution to the project was substantial. She joined Laura M. Towne and Ellen Murray, two Philadelphia teachers, at a school held in the Central Baptist Church on St. Helena Island. The three women dedicated themselves to the enormous task at hand. From noon until three o'clock nearly one hundred students attended the school. Classes resumed in the evening when adults hurried from their daytime labors for tutoring in reading and spelling. Despite the hard work and long hours, Forten enjoyed her job. She hoped to inspire her students with lessons about black liberators and heroes, such as Haitian liberator Toussaint L'Ouverture. For their Christmas program in 1862, Forten taught the students a song written especially for them by New England poet John Greenleaf Whittier.

As an author, Charlotte Forten took the opportunity to record her Sea Islands experiences and observations for the Northern reading public. Her essays entitled "Life on the Sea Islands," published in the May and June 1864 issues of *Atlantic Monthly*, provided a rare glimpse of the newly freed black

people's character and fitness for citizenship. Many Northerners were skeptical that they could bridge the gap from slavery to freedom. Forten's work presented a firsthand account of a people who were eager to work, eager to learn, and eager to enjoy the rights and responsibilities of citizenship.

After the war, Forten held a variety of posts. During the late 1860s, as secretary of the Freedmen's Relief Association in Boston, she recruited teachers. From 1871 to 1872, she assisted black educator Richard T. Greener, who was the principal of Sumner High School in Washington, D.C. Then, on July 3, 1873, the *New National Era and Citizen* reported Forten's new position as a clerk at the U.S. Treasury Department. She was one of fifteen selected from almost 500 candidates.

On December 19, 1878, at the age of forty-one, Charlotte Forten wed Francis J. Grimké, a promising Presbyterian minister and graduate of Pennsylvania's Lincoln University and the Princeton Theological Seminary. The major tragedy of their thirty-six years of married life was the death of their infant daughter, Theodora Cornelia, in June 1880. By all accounts Charlotte Grimké enjoyed her duties as a minister's wife. From 1885 until 1889, her husband served as pastor of the Laura Street Presbyterian Church in Jacksonville, Florida. Charlotte Grimké taught a Sunday school class for girls and organized a women's missionary group. In January 1889, the couple returned to Washington, D.C., where Francis Grimké assumed the pastorship of the Fifteenth Street Presbyterian Church.

True to her family's activist legacy, Charlotte Forten Grimké was a perennial advocate of black civil rights. In October 1889, she responded to an *Evangelist* editorial entitled "Relations of Blacks and Whites: Is There a Color Line in New England?" Her response dismissed the editor's assertion that a color line had never existed. Charlotte recounted the harsh reality of segregated schools and separate public accommodations, in existence until the 1850s. Further, she rejected the editor's characterization of black men and women as merely agricultural laborers, bootblacks, and chimney sweepers. In support of her statements, Grimké cited a dozen black attorneys, including her brother-in-law, Archibald H. Grimké, who was practicing in the Boston area. She also listed other black professionals residing in New England. She reminded the editor that black Americans achieved in spite of overwhelming odds, and she rejected the notion that they wanted to force social integration. Above all else, she insisted, black people desired the rights of American citizenship and fair treatment from others in a Christian spirit.

JANICE SUMLER-EDMOND

H

Hemings, Sally (1773–c. 1835)

It is believed by some that Sally Hemings, a black American woman who lived and died as a slave, was the mistress of Thomas Jefferson and the mother of several children by him. Although not nearly enough is known about the specific facts of her life, what is known suggests a woman of considerable interest and character whether or not the legends that surround her are true.

Born in 1773, she was the daughter of Betty Hemings and John Wayles. Her mother was the daughter of "a full-blooded African" woman and an English ship captain; her father was both her mother's master and the father-in-law of Thomas Jefferson. When Wayles died the same year Sally was born, Hemings and her family became the property of Jefferson; thus she grew up in the household of her half-sister, Martha Wayles Jefferson. When Jefferson's daughter Maria joined him in 1787 on his diplomatic mission in France, Hemings attended her. Abigail Adams, who helped them travel from London to Paris, described the fourteen-year-old Sally as "quite a child" who nonetheless "seems fond of [Maria] and appears good natured." Upon returning to America, Hemings became a house servant at Monticello, where she bore five children, Harriet (1795–97), Beverley (b.1798), Harriet (b.1801), Madison (1805–77), and Eston (b.1805). These are the children supposedly fathered by Jefferson, but strong evidence points to their paternity by either Samuel Carr, Jefferson's nephew who lived nearby, or his brother, Peter. Sally Hemings seems to have figured at Monticello, however, more because of her abilities and character than because of the identity of her lover. Jefferson's *Farm Book* indicates that, at Monticello in 1796, Hemings had with her Edy, the daughter of Isabel, who was then employed elsewhere on the farm, and she seems to have cared briefly in 1799 for Thenia, the daughter of Abram and Doll, who similarly were working elsewhere. Sally's caring nature seems to have made her a significant presence in the life of the black people at Monticello even as it made an impression on her white cousins.

Various descendants of Betty Hemings became free over the years, but as Jefferson's finances became more troubled the contradictions of chattel slavery asserted themselves. When Jefferson died on July 4, 1826, his will freed Sally's sons Madison and Eston; Harriet and Beverley apparently had been permitted to run away four years earlier. Sally Hemings was not freed at this time, partly because she was no longer Jefferson's property but that of his granddaughter, Ellen Randolph Coolidge, and partly because under Virginia law at the time she would have had to leave the state if freed. Surviving family correspondence from the decade after 1826 reveals genuine concern for her and for respecting her wishes about where and how she would live. She seems to have spent her last years with her son Eston, who had been permitted to stay in the neighborhood of Monticello, although there is no record of her formal emancipation. Trapped in the economic wreckage of the Jefferson family, her life ended in 1835 or 1836 as it began, in slavery.

The accusations that Sally Hemings was Jefferson's concubine were first made in 1802 by James T. Callender, a sensationalistic journalist and disappointed office-seeker. They found wide circulation in the mudslinging political campaign of 1804, and subsequently entered the fabric of American folklore. William Wells Brown's novel *Clotel, or the President's Daughter* (1853) fictionalized the tale in the interest of the abolition movement, and Barbara Chase-Riboud's prize-winning novel *Sally Hemings* (1979) reinvented Hemings against the background of a new black consciousness and an emerging feminism. Fawn Brodie's 1974 biography of Jefferson attempted to assert the relationship as historical fact, but most professional historians fault her analysis of the evidence and find little convincing proof that such a relationship existed. If stories like these have made Sally Heming's place in American history, they should not be allowed to obscure either the intelligent, caring woman behind them or the situation in which she lived.

FRANK SHUFFELTON

Hinard, Eufrosina   (b. 1777)

While no one knows for sure what Eufrosina Hinard thought of slavery, her actions as a slaveholder challenge any easy assumptions about her views. Born in New Orleans in 1777, she was the offspring of both slavery and freedom, the descendant of a black slave woman and a free white man. Because her mother had been freed, Hinard was free, never personally witnessing the exploitation of slavery. Instead, Hinard understood slavery from what she learned from her mother and from her experiences as a slaveholder. What brings her views about the institution of slavery into question is the extraordinary way in which she balanced slavery and its antithesis, emancipation.

In 1791, when Hinard was fourteen years old, she, like so many other free women of color in the frontier Spanish port of New Orleans, was *placéed* (committed) to a man, in her case the Spaniard Don Nicolás Vidal, *auditor de guerra*, the military legal counselor to the governor. Hinard's arrangement was not unusual for women of her caste, especially in the Spanish colonies. There, as in the French colonies, interracial marriage was against the law; thus *plaçage* and *concubinato*, both forms of de facto marriage, were regularly practiced. Both offered some political, legal, economic, and social protection to the women involved, and to their offspring.

Eufrosina bore two quadroon daughters, Carolina (1793) and Merced (1795). When Vidal died in 1806 in Spanish Pensacola, where he had taken his family after Louisiana was ceded to the United States with the Louisiana Purchase in 1803, he left his estate to Hinard and the two daughters. It was after Vidal's death that Hinard's abilities as a businesswoman and slaveholder became evident, and she combined her astute business sense and her view of slavery in seemingly antagonistic ways.

Like other urban slaveholders, Hinard rented out the slaves she owned or allowed them to live out, bringing a portion of their profits to her. While the Spanish governed Louisiana and the Floridas, they offered slaves the right to purchase their freedom, and several thousand urban slaves were able to accumulate enough money to buy themselves out of slavery. When Spanish Louisiana and Florida were ceded to the United States and joined the Southern states, slaves lost that right. In fact, as the antebellum period progressed, freedom became more and more difficult to acquire. State after state clamped down on manumission, leaving few avenues to freedom.

Eufrosina Hinard, however, had lived much of her life as a Spanish subject and by Spanish tradition freedom was a natural right. Slavery, in that view, was an unfortunate condition. All slaves had the right to purchase themselves, if they could pay their estimated value. Yet by the time Hinard became a slave owner, a slave's right to purchase his or her own freedom had been annulled. That, however, did not prevent Hinard from continuing the practice. Throughout the antebellum period, she regularly bought slaves and allowed them to pay her their purchase price, plus interest. Then she freed them. Thus, while Hinard can understandably be viewed as a slaveholder, her method of slaveholding actively challenged the assumptions behind the Southern institution that defined slavery as a natural condition and the slave as having no rights.

VIRGINIA GOULD

Hooks, Julia Britton (1852–1942)

Julia Hooks was one of the pioneer black clubwomen in Memphis, Tennessee. Through various organizations and institutions, she worked to help alleviate the social ills that befell the increasingly segregated and destitute black Americans who migrated from rural Tennessee, Mississippi, Arkansas, and Alabama during the post-Reconstruction era. Because of her tireless efforts, she is fondly remembered as "The Angel of Beale Street."

Julia Amanda Morehead Britton was born free in Frankfort, Kentucky, in 1852. Julia's mother, Laura Marshall, had been freed by her mistress, Elizabeth Marshall, in 1848, and she married a free carpenter named Henry Britton the same year. Julia inherited musical talent from her mother and received professional training in classical music. Julia's parents enrolled her in the interracial program in Berea College in 1869, and from 1870 to 1872, Julia Britton was listed as the faculty instructor of instrumental music, making her one of the first black professors to teach white students in Kentucky. In 1872, Julia moved to Greenville, Mississippi, to marry Sam Werles, a public school teacher. Both Julia and Sam taught school, but Sam died suddenly in the yellow fever epidemic of 1873. Eventually, Julia accepted a position within the Memphis Public School system in 1876. Four years later she married Charles Hooks, who had been born a slave in Memphis circa 1849.

In 1883, Julia Hooks and her close friend Anna Church (the wife of Robert Church, one of the country's first black millionaires) started the Liszt-Mullard Club. This was probably the first black organization in the city entirely devoted to music. The club promoted classical music and raised money to provide scholarships for aspiring musicians. Several years later Julia established the Hooks School of Music, an integrated institution that fostered some well-known pupils: W. C. Handy (the father of the blues); Sidney Woodward (one of the first black concert artists to tour

Europe); and Nell Hunter (known for her work on Broadway in the Pulitzer Prize–winning play, *The Green Pastures*).

Julia Hooks was also committed to the education of black children. She taught at several public schools and served as principal, but was always dissatisfied with the poor quality of education parceled out to the underprivileged. Julia's position was that separate would never be equal because the idea was based on the superiority of one race over another. Children in black Memphis were shortchanged due to poorly prepared teachers, lack of books and supplies, overcrowded classrooms, low standards and attendance, and inferior shelter, food, and clothing. Sometimes there were over sixty children in a classroom, and many were recent migrants who had never attended school. In 1892, Julia Hooks opened her own private kindergarten and elementary facility, the Hooks Cottage School.

A few years before, in 1887, Julia Hooks had written an article on character building, the responsibility of government toward its neglected citizens, and the necessity of instilling morality in children. Entitled "The Duty of the Hour," Hook's essay was so popular that she was asked to give public readings at numerous churches, functions, and organizations throughout the black community. "Duty of the Hour" was published in the 1895 edition of the *African-American Encyclopedia*.

Social services were another of Julia Hook's concerns. She was especially interested in the plight of black orphans and old people, since there were no orphanages or homes for them in Memphis. Hooks decided that combining the two would be a good idea, and she established and became one of the charter members of the Colored Old Folks and Orphans Home Club in 1891. The members purchased twenty-five acres and erected shelters for orphans and elderly women. Julia Hooks gave concerts to help raise money to pay off the debt, which was discharged in three years.

Because of her social service work, Hooks was selected to serve as an officer of the court when the city established a black juvenile court in 1902. She and husband Charles, who became a truant officer, supervised the court's detention home, which was built next to their residence. One of the inmates shot and killed Charles a year later. Julia Hooks remained committed to the institution, sometimes being called to advise in cases involving black youth. Her compassion, gentleness, and calm manner won her the trust and cooperation of both young and adult inmates.

Julia Hooks remained active for over fifty years in club work and social services, until her death at the age of ninety in 1942. She and Charles Hooks had two sons, Henry and Robert. They became photographers and founded the Hooks Brother's Photographers Studio on Beale Street, the first of its kind in black Memphis, and they photographed decades of black Memphis history. Julia and Charles Hook's most famous descendent is the Reverend Benjamin L. Hooks, who served as the city's first black judge since Reconstruction. In 1977, he became the executive director of the National Association for the Advancement of Colored People—a fitting tribute to grandmother Julia who sixty years earlier had been one of the charter members of the NAACP's Memphis branch.

EARNESTINE JENKINS

Hyers, Anna Madan (1853?–1930s) and Emma Louise (1855? –c. 1899)

The first black repertory theater in the United States was formed by two women in their twenties in the year 1875. Acclaimed singers, the Hyers Sisters turned the racist

Emma Hyers (pictured here) and her sister Anna, who were billed as the Hyers Sisters, were the first black women to gain success on the American stage. They toured nationally in the 1870s and early 1880s, appearing in musical plays dealing with the black experience. (MOORLAND-SPINGARN)

limitations on their concert career into the foundation of the black theater in America.

Anna and Emma Hyers were born in Sacramento in the 1850s. Their parents were both musicians and provided the children with their early training. However, both girls showed such remarkable promise that they were soon studying with professional teachers, including Hugo Sank and the Italian opera singer Josephine D'Ormy.

In April of 1867, when they were in their early teens, the Hyers Sisters made their debut at the Metropolitan Theater in Sacramento. Anna, a soprano, and Emma, a contralto, received excellent reviews.

After several more years of study, the sisters began touring the country, along with their father, Sam Hyers, a tenor; baritone Joseph LeCount; and an accompanist. They sang operatic arias, duos, trios, and quartets. The reviewer for the *San Francisco Chronicle* states that "Miss [Anna] Madah has a pure, sweet soprano voice, very true, even, and flexible, of remarkable compass and smoothness. . . . Miss [Emma} Louise is a natural wonder . . ."

In 1872, the Hyers Sisters sang at the World Peace Jubilee in Boston. They apparently gave a brilliant performance, and their reputation grew. Indeed, reviews were enthusiastic almost everywhere they performed.

Of course, there were limitations on their careers. No opera company, for example, was going to hire two black divas, or even one. So the Hyers Sisters, with their father as manager, worked around the problem and made theatrical history. They formed a professional black repertory company—the first and, at that time, the only one—and began producing musical plays. Their first, written especially for them, was *Out of Bondage*. It was described as the story of a man's journey from slavery to "education and refinement."

Over the next few years, the Hyers Sisters produced and starred in five musical plays. They were successful with audiences and critics alike. In 1883, they briefly disbanded their company and re-formed as part of the Callendar Consolidated Spectacular Minstrel Festival. After an engagement at the Grand Opera House in New York, the show toured the country. The owners of the show, white show business entrepreneurs Charles and Gustave Frohman, intended to create a huge Coloured Opera Troupe, but their plans fell through. In 1886, the Hyers were again producing on their own.

In the early 1890s, the Hyers Sisters apparently disbanded their company for good. No notices of their performing together appear after 1893. Emma appeared in a production of *Uncle Tom's Cabin* in 1894 and died before the end of the century.

Anna joined John Isham's famed *Octoroons* company in 1894. She sang her concert repertoire in the finale of the show, "Thirty Minutes Around the Operas." She also toured with the M. B. Curtis All-Star Afro-American Minstrels in Australia starting in 1899. After her return to the United States, she appeared with John Isham until 1902, when she retired

Pictured above is Emma's sister Anna. The Hyers Sisters were exceptional also because they dared to deviate from the stereotypes of the era. (MOORLAND-SPINGARN)

from the stage. She married a Dr. Fletcher and settled in her hometown of Sacramento. She died there some time in the 1930s.

KATHLEEN THOMPSON

J

Jackson, Rebecca Cox (1795–1871)

Rebecca Cox Jackson was a charismatic itinerant preacher, the founder of a religious communal family in Philadelphia, and a religious visionary writer. Though an important example of black female religious leadership and spirituality in the nineteenth century, she was virtually unknown after her death until the rediscovery and publication of her manuscript writings in 1981.

Jackson was born into a free black family in Horntown, Pennsylvania, near Philadelphia. She lived at different times in her childhood with her maternal grandmother, and with her mother, Jane Cox, who died when Rebecca was thirteen. In 1830, she married Samuel S. Jackson, but apparently remained childless. She and her husband lived in the household of her older brother, Joseph Cox, a tanner and local preacher of the Bethel African Methodist Episcopal (AME) Church in Philadelphia. Jackson cared for her brother's four children while earning her own living as a seamstress.

As the result of the powerful religious awakening experience in a thunderstorm in 1830 with which her autobiography begins, Jackson became active in the early Holiness movement. She moved from leading praying bands to public preaching, stirring up controversy within AME Church circles not only as a woman preacher, but also because she had received the revelation that celibacy was necessary for a holy life. She criticized the churches, including the AME Church and its leaders, for "carnality."

Jackson insisted on being guided entirely by the dictates of her inner voice, and this ultimately led to her separation from her husband, brother, and church.

After a period of itinerant preaching in the late 1830s and early 1840s, Jackson joined the United Society of Believers in Christ's Second Appearing (the Shakers), at Watervliet, New York. She was attracted by the Shaker's religious celibacy, their emphasis on spiritualistic experience, and their dual-gender concept of deity. With her younger disciple and lifelong companion, Rebecca Perot, Rebecca Jackson lived at Watervliet from June 1847 until July 1851. However, she was increasingly disappointed by the predominantly white Shaker community's failure to take the gospel of their founder, Ann Lee, to the African-American community. Jackson left Watervliet in 1851, on an unauthorized mission to Philadelphia, where she and Perot experimented with seance-style spiritualism. In 1857, she and Perot returned to Watervliet for a brief second residence, and Jackson won the right to found and head a new Shaker "outfamily" in Philadelphia. This predominantly black, female Shaker family survived her death in 1871 by at least a quarter of a century.

Rebecca Jackson's major legacy is her remarkable spiritual autobiography, *Gifts of Power*, which describes her spiritual journey as a woman with a divine calling.

Jackson records in vivid detail a wide variety of visionary experiences, including mysterious prophetic dreams and supernatural gifts. Her visionary writing has received recognition as spiritual literature of great power. Alice Walker has described Jackson's autobiography as "an extraordinary document" which "tells us much about the spirituality of human beings, especially of the interior spiritual resources of our mothers." In her review of Jackson's writings, however, Walker questioned the editor's speculation that Jackson's relationship with Perot, in the modern age, might have been interpreted as lesbian. In this context, Walker first coined the term "womanism" to distinguish a specifically black feminist cultural tradition that includes women's love for other women but is not separatist.

JEAN McMAHON HUMEZ

Jacobs, Harriet Ann (1813–1897)

Harriet Ann Jacobs is now known as the author of *Incidents in the Life of a Slave Girl: Written by Herself* (1861), the most important slave narrative by an African-American woman. Jacobs is also important because of the role she played as a relief worker among black Civil War refugees in Alexandria, Virginia, and Savannah, Georgia. Throughout most of the twentieth century, Jacob's autobiography was thought to be a novel by a white writer, and her relief work was unknown. With the 1987 publication of an annotated edition of her book, however, Jacobs became established as the author of the most comprehensive antebellum autobiography by an African-American woman.

Harriet Ann Jacobs was born into slavery in Edenton, North Carolina, in 1813. Her mother was Delilah, daughter of Molly Horniblow and slave of Margaret Horniblow; her father was Daniel, a carpenter, probably a son of the white Henry Jacobs and slave of Andrew Knox, a doctor. *Incidents* is a first-person pseudonymous account of a slave woman's sexual oppression and of her struggle for freedom. Narrated by Jacobs as "Linda Brent," the book is a remarkably accurate (although incomplete) rendering of Jacob's life up to her emancipation in 1853. It describes her experiences as a slave and fugitive in the South, and as a fugitive in the North. Narrator Linda Brent credits her family, and especially her grandmother (who had gained her freedom and established a bakery in the town), with sustaining her and her younger brother, John S. Jacobs, in their youthful efforts to achieve a sense of selfhood despite their slave status.

When Jacobs was six years old, her mother died, and she was taken into the home of her mistress, who taught her to sew and to read, skills she later used to support herself and to protest against slavery. But when in 1825 Jacob's mistress died, the slave girl was not freed, as she had expected. Instead, her mistres's will bequeathed her, along with a "bureau & work table & their contents," to a three-year-old niece, and Jacobs was sent to live in the Edenton home of the little girl's father, Dr. James Norcom ("Dr. Flint" in *Incidents*). As the slave girl approached adolescence, the middle-aged Norcom subjected her to unrelenting sexual harassment and, when she was sixteen, threatened her with concubinage. To stop him, Jacobs became sexually involved with a neighboring white attorney, young Samuel Tredwell Sawyer ("Mr. Sands"). Their alliance produced two children:

Joseph (c. 1829–?), called "Benny," and Louisa Matilda (1833–1917), called "Little Ellen" in the narrative. When Jacobs was twenty-one, Norcom told her if she did not agree to become his concubine, he would send her away to one of his plantations. Jacobs again rejected his sexual demands and was taken to a plantation. After she learned that Norcom also planned to send her children out to the country, fearing that once they became plantation slaves they would never be free, she decided to act.

In June 1835, Jacobs escaped. She reasoned that if she was missing, Norcom would be willing to sell her and the children and that their father would buy and free them all. Joseph and Louisa were indeed bought by Sawyer, who permitted them to continue living in town with Jacob's grandmother. Jacobs was hidden by neighbors, both black and white, but with Norcom searching for her, she was unable to escape from Edenton. As the summer wore on, her grandmother and uncle built her a hiding place in a tiny crawlspace above a porch in their home. For almost seven years, Jacobs hid in this space, which, she wrote, measured seven feet wide, nine feet long, and—at its tallest—three feet high.

Finally, in 1842, she escaped and was reunited with her children, who had been sent North. In New York City, Jacobs found work as a domestic in the family of litterateur Nathaniel Parker Willis. In 1849, she moved to Rochester to join her brother, who had also become a fugitive from slavery. John S. Jacobs was now an antislavery lecturer and activist, and through him, Harriet Jacobs became part of the Rochester abolitionist circle surrounding Frederick Douglas's newspaper the *North Star*. After the passage of the 1850 Fugitive Slave Law,

she left Rochester for New York, where her North Carolina masters tried to seize her and her children on the streets of Manhattan and Brooklyn. Determined not to be sent back into slavery or to bow to the slave system by permitting herself to be bought, Jacobs fled to Massachusetts. In 1852, however, without her knowledge, Cornelia Grinnell Willis arranged for her and her children to be bought from Norcom and Sawyer. Jacobs and her children were free.

Amid conflicting emotions—determination to aid the antislavery cause, humiliation at being purchased, and a deep impulse perhaps prompted by the death of her beloved grandmother in Edenton—Jacobs decided to make public the story of her sexual abuse in slavery. A few years earlier, she had whispered her history to Amy Post, her Rochester Quaker abolitionist-feminist friend, and Post had urged her to write a book informing Northern women about the sexual abuse of women slaves. Now Jacobs was ready. Harriet Beecher Stowe's newly published *Uncle Tom's Cabin* (1852) had become a runaway best-seller, and Jacob's first thought was to try to enlist Stowe to write her story. When she learned that Stowe planned to incorporate her life story into *The Key to Uncle Tom's Cabin* (1853), however, Jacobs decided instead to write her story herself. After practicing her writing skills in letters she sent to the *New York Tribune*, she began her book. Five years later, it was finished. Soliciting letters of introduction to British abolitionists from Boston antislavery leaders, Jacobs sailed to England to sell her manuscript to a publisher. She returned home unsuccessful. Finally, with the help of African-American abolitionist William C. Nell and white abolitionist Lydia Maria Child, early in

1861 Jacobs brought the book out herself. *Incidents in the Life of a Slave Girl: Written by Herself* was published for the author, with an introduction by L. Maria Child, who was identified as editor on the title page. Although Jacob's authorship was later forgotten, she was from the first identified as "Linda Brent." Reviewed in the abolitionist and African-American press, *Incidents* made Jacobs a minor celebrity among its audience of antislavery women.

Within months, however, the nation was at war, and in the crisis, Jacobs launched a second public career. Using her new celebrity, she approached Northern antislavery women for money and supplies for the "contrabands"—black refugees who crowded behind the Union lines in Washington, D.C., and Alexandria, Virginia (which had been occupied by the army). In 1863, with the support of Quaker groups and the newly formed New England Freedmen's Aid Society, Harriet Jacobs and her daughter Louisa went to Alexandria. There they provided emergency health care and established the Jacobs Free School, a black-owned and black-taught institution for the children of the refugees.

Throughout the war years, Jacobs and her daughter reported on their Southern relief efforts in the Northern press and in England, where in 1862 her book had been published as *The Deeper Wrong: Incidents in the Life of a Slave Girl, Written by Herself*. In May 1864, Jacobs was named a member of the Executive Committee of the Women's National Loyal League, an antislavery feminist group mounting a mass petition campaign to urge Congress to pass a constitutional amendment to end chattel slavery. In July 1865, the mother-daughter team left Alexandria, and in 1866 they moved to Savannah, where they again worked to provide educational and medical facilities for freedpeople. The following year, Louisa joined Susan B. Anthony and Charles Lenox Remond to campaign for the Equal Rights Association—a group of radical feminists and abolitionists who worked for the inclusion of the enfranchisement of African Americans and women in the New York State constitution.

In 1868, Harriet and Louisa Jacobs went to London to raise money for an orphanage and home for the aged in the black Savannah community. Aided by British supporters of Garrisonian abolitionism, they raised £100 sterling for the Savannah project. Despite their success, however, they recommended to their New York Quaker sponsors that the building not be built. The Ku Klux Klan was riding and burning; it would not tolerate the establishment of new black institutions.

In the face of the increasing violence in the South, Jacobs and her daughter retreated to Massachusetts. In Boston, Jacobs was briefly employed as clerk of the fledgling New England Women's Club, perhaps with the patronage of her old employer and friend Cornelia Grinnell Willis and her New England Freedmen's Aid Society colleague Ednah Dow Cheney, both club members. As the new decade began, Jacobs settled in Cambridge, where for several years she ran a boardinghouse for Harvard students and faculty.

When Harriet and Louisa Jacobs later moved to Washington, D.C., Harriet continued to work among destitute freedpeople, and Louisa was employed in the newly established "colored schools," then at **Howard University**. They did not return to the South, and in 1892 Jacobs sold her grandmother's house and lot in Edenton, property that her family had managed to arrange for her to inherit, despite her earlier status as a fugitive. When in 1896 the **National Association of Colored Women** held organizing meetings in Washington, D.C., Louisa Jacobs apparently attended. The following spring, Harriet Jacobs died at her Washington home. She is buried in the Mount Auburn Cemetery, Cambridge.

Harriet Jacobs experienced life before the Civil War as a slave in the South, as a fugitive in the South and in the North, and as an abolitionist activist and slave narrator in the North. She served as a relief worker among black refugees in the South during the Civil War and Reconstruction and as a public commentator on the condition of these people. Later she was involved as an adjunct to the post-Civil War club movement among white women and she witnessed the birth of the black women's club movement. No other woman is known to have possessed this range of experience.

JEAN FAGAN YELLIN

Johnson, Ann Battles (b. 1815) and Katherine Johnson

Ann Battles was born into slavery in Concordia Parish, Louisiana, in 1815. Her mother, Harriet Battles, struggled for years to secure her own freedom and that of her daughter, finally achieving it in Cincinnati in 1829, when Ann was fourteen. Even though their freedom redefined their lives, offering them opportunities that they could only have imagined as slaves, it did not distinguish them from the hundreds of thousands of other free women of color who lived in the hostile environment of the South.

What distinguishes Ann Battles Johnson and her daughter, Katherine Johnson, from

their neighbors is the collection of letters and the diary that they left to their descendants. Perhaps the Johnsons knew that their experiences as free women of color in a society that practiced slavery were significant. Perhaps they did not. Either way, they accumulated and jealously protected the letters that their family members regularly sent. Most of the letters were from Ann Johnson's nieces in New Orleans—Emma, Octavia, and Lavinia Miller. Katherine Johnson left her own contribution by writing and preserving a diary.

The letters and the diary are significant because none of the authors stepped outside the bounds that circumscribed the lives of Southern women, slave or free. The documents are invaluable because few free women of color were allowed the education necessary to correspond with their families and friends. Only those free women of color who lived in the predominantly Catholic-Creole Lower South were regularly educated in the skills of reading and writing, and only the Johnson collection offers an extensive set of writings.

The letters written by the Miller women describe the experiences of free women of color of urban New Orleans. They also include glimpses into the lives of their aunt, Ann Battles Johnson, who devoted herself to her husband and children, and of family members and friends scattered up and down the Mississippi River. The community was united by color and condition, by its freedoms despite the conventions of the dominant culture. The letters also tell the story of women, in Natchez and New Orleans, who were freed slaves who owned slaves, who were accomplished musicians or seamstresses, but who struggled to make ends meet. Most poignantly, these women turned to each other for comfort and support because, as the letters suggest, they lived in an uneasy truce with their white neighbors.

Katherine Johnson's diary was written later than the letters and describes the life of a young woman who devoted herself to her community by becoming a schoolteacher. Her diary begins during the Civil War and continues, sporadically, for ten years. It offers the reader an invaluable glimpse of the dilemmas faced by the small community of free people of color who lost their elite status with the war.

VIRGINIA GOULD

Jones, Sissieretta (1868–1933)

Sissieretta Jones once summarized her love of singing by comparing her life to the life of flowers. "The flowers absorb the sunshine because it is their nature. I give out melody because God filled my soul with it." Distinguished by over ten years of solo performances at locations ranging from the White House (President Harrison) to Covent Garden, England; by her travels to the West Indies and South America; by enthusiastic reviews from the black and white press alike; by over eighteen years of travel in America as a prima donna with the Black Patti Troubadours (later the Black Patti Musical Comedy Company) with one of the most difficult schedules on the road, Sissieretta Jones became a major black concert and theatrical pioneer on the American stage. She was hailed as America's leading prima donna. She was nicknamed the Black Patti by the *New York Clipper*, a theatrical journal, after a writer heard Sissieretta in a private concert-audition at Wallack's Thea-

ter, July 15, 1888, and compared her to Italian singer Adelina Patti.

Born in Portsmouth, Virginia, in 1868 to Henrietta Beale and Malachi Joyner, Sissieretta Jone's unique talent was identified by Northern visitors who persuaded her father to move to Providence, Rhode Island. In this new environment, Sissieretta, fondly called "Sissy" and "Tilly" by her classmates, became well known at school events for her sweet and bell-like voice that could be heard above all the rest.

Known as the Black Patti, Sissieretta Jones formed her own company when she found herself limited by racism. The Black Patti Troubadours, who performed an eclectic mix that ranged from grand opera to ragtime, toured the country successfully for almost twenty years. (MOORLAND-SPINGARN)

After voice study with Ada Baroness La-combe at the Academy of Music, she married David Richard Jones, who suggested that she continue her voice study at Boston Conservatory. Here, for approximately two years, 1886–88, she studied and broadened her contacts with other artists, such as Flora Batson, the leading star of the Bergen Star Company. It was this company that first featured Jones, billed as "the rising soprano from New England," in a New York City concert that brought her to the attention of concert managers Abbey, Schoffel, and Grau, who scheduled her for a Wallack Theater debut on July 15, 1888. Henry Abbey, manager for Adelina Patti, attended this performance and recommended a tour to the West Indies with the Tennessee Jubilee Singers. This tour gave birth to Sissieretta Jone's professional concert career.

Engagements in the famous African Jubilee in Madison Square Garden, a career managed by Major Pond for the 1892–94 seasons, and performances across America (including appearances at the Pittsburgh, Buffalo, and Toronto Expositions) followed. Reviews of Jone's performances, although sometimes tinged with the racial myths of the day, were positive. For instance, John van Cleve, a respected Boston-trained musician and critic, defined her style of singing and her particular attributes as being of "high and genuine ability both as concerns the gift of nature and the supplementary additions of art." Jones was possibly the first black performer to appear at Carnegie Concert Hall. She performed with Antonín Dvovrák and the National Conservatory of Music in the United States, and at the Wintergarten in Berlin and at Covent Garden, England.

Frustrated by the conditions of performance on the serious concert stage, and disturbed by the mistreatment of black people by the Metropolitan Opera, Jones surrounded herself with approximately forty black performers and formed the Black Patti Troubadours. Managed by Rudolph Voelckel and John J. Nolan, the company opened its first season on July 25, 1896. Initially adopting the format of a loose skit (as in *A Rag-time Frolic at Ras-bury Park* (1898–99) with comedy, dancing, and acrobatics, the company featured an operatic kaleidoscope and highlighted Sissieretta and a chorus in excerpts from such works as *Cavalleria Rusticana*, *Chimes of Normandy*, and *Faust*. As the shows became more organized, a definite plot and musical comedy appeared. Jones began to appear in the storyline rather than exclusively in the kaleidoscope.

With shows such as *A Trip to Africa* (1909–10), *In the Jungles* (1911–12), *Captain Jasper* (1912–13), and *Lucky Sam from Alabam'* (1914–15), the Black Patti company appeared in the new black-owned theaters (such as the Howard in Washington, D.C.) and its future course and popularity seemed assured. However, an illness prevented Jone's full participation in the 1913–14 season, and her return in 1914–15 was cut short after a production in Church's Auditorium in Memphis, Tennessee, when the company disbanded.

With the close of the Black Patti company, Jones gave a performance at the end of 1915 at the Grand Theater in Chicago, which was followed by her last performance, at the Lafayette Theater in New York City in October 1915. Although Jones promised her audiences that she would return, she went into total retirement, quietly living with her ill mother until her mother died. Sissieretta

Jones died on June 24, 1933. To those who worked with her, she struggled to establish racial pride and self-esteem in young performers during a most depressing and difficult period in American history.

WILLIA E. DAUGHTRY

Joseph-Gaudet, Frances (1861–1934)

Frances Joseph-Gaudet was born in a log cabin in Holmesville, Pike County, Mississippi. A seamstress by profession, she became known throughout the country at the turn of the century for her work in reforming prisons and the juvenile court system and for founding the Gaudet Normal and Industrial School for black youth in New Orleans, Louisiana, in 1902.

The young Frances moved to New Orleans from Mississippi when she was eight years old. She attended public schools in uptown New Orleans then enrolled at Straight University, but was unable to complete her studies because she and her brother were needed at home to help support the younger children. Married at twenty-three, she lived happily with her husband for ten years until alcohol, "the curse of America," caused the Josephs to seek a legal separation.

Following her separation in 1894, she began working for prison reform. She visited prisons for weekly prayer meetings for the next eight years and was dismayed by the plight of young black boys who were housed with inveterate criminals. The Prison Reform Association supported her efforts to improve the prisons and the conditions of the indigent insane, and she founded the city's first juvenile court.

As president of the Louisiana Negro chapter of the Women's Christian Temperance Union (WCTU), Joseph was a delegate to the International WCTU Convention in Edinburgh in 1900. For five months she toured England and Europe, speaking in Ireland, Paris, and London about the welfare of poor children, and visiting prisons and juvenile detention homes. Shortly after her return to New Orleans, she bought 105 acres of farmland on Gentilly Avenue to build a school devoted to saving homeless Negro children and teaching them a craft by which they could make a living.

In founding the Colored Industrial and Normal School (later called Gaudet School) in 1902, Joseph had the support of the *Times-Democrat* and of Ida A. Richardson, wife of Tobias G. Richardson, dean of the Louisiana State University School of Medicine. The first secretary of the board was Adolphe P. Gaudet, whom Joseph later married.

Because much of the support for the school had come from members of the Episcopal Church, Joseph-Gaudet decided to offer the school to the Episcopal Diocese in 1919 for a long-lasting sponsorship. She continued as principal for a short while, but, becoming increasingly blind, she felt compelled to resign. She moved to Chicago to live with relatives but returned to New Orleans several times to see the progress of the school before her death on December 24, 1934. At the 1935 Episcopal convention, a Memorial Minute was adopted in tribute to Joseph-Gaudet "in which her unselfish service in behalf of her own people was gratefully acknowledged."

VIOLET HARRINGTON BRYAN

K

Keckley, Elizabeth (1818–1907)

Few events are more likely to stir up controversy in the nation's capital than the publication of the personal memoirs of a first lady's confidante. This was as true in 1868 as it is today. One of the first, and still

Few events are more likely to stir up controversy in the nation's capital than the publication of the personal memoirs of a confidante of a First Lady. One of the first, and still one of the most controversial, of all the "serve-and-tell" books was Behind the Scenes *by Elizabeth Keckley, which revealed the often prickly opinions of Mary Todd Lincoln.* (MOORLAND-SPINGARN)

one of the most controversial, of all the "serve-and-tell" books was *Behind the Scenes: or Thirty Years a Slave and Four Years in the White House*. This book revealed the often prickly opinions of Mary Todd Lincoln and information about the Lincoln's family life that many who idolized the president did not want to know.

There is a continuing argument about who actually wrote the words and sentences of this startling publication, but there is no disagreement about whose story it tells. Elizabeth Keckley was Mary Todd Lincoln's dressmaker and close friend for a span of seven years that included the Civil War and the death of President Abraham Lincoln. That friendship ended with the publication of *Behind the Scenes*.

Elizabeth Keckley was born Elizabeth Hobbs in 1818 at Dinwiddie Court House in Virginia. She was a slave and the daughter of slaves. Her owners, the Burwell family, sold her while she was in her teens to a North Carolina slave owner by whom she had a son. She was repurchased by one of the Burwell daughters, Anne Burwell Garland, shortly thereafter and taken to St. Louis. There she began her career as a dressmaker, helping to support her owners and their five daughters. Against her better judgment, she married James Keckley, who claimed to be a free man, but who turned out to be a slave and a bad husband. The two soon separated.

Keckley was so popular with her dressmaking customers that several of them offered to lend her the money to buy her freedom and that of her son, George. On November 15, 1855, at the age of thirty-seven, Keckley paid Mrs. Garland $1,200 for her freedom. Her dressmaking business thrived, and she soon paid off her loan. She also learned to read and write and, in 1860, left St. Louis for Baltimore. Six months later, she went to Washington, D.C., where she rented an apartment and began to attract an elite group of customers, including the wife of Jefferson Davis.

The Lincolns had been in Washington, D.C., a mere two weeks when Mary Todd Lincoln heard of and sent for Keckley. The first gown she designed for the first lady met with approval, as did Keckley's quiet, good-natured temperament. Keckley began to make all of Mary Todd Lincoln's clothes and became her traveling companion and friend. During this time, George Keckley was killed in action while fighting for the Union.

In 1862, Keckley helped to found the Contraband Relief Association, an organization of African-American women formed to provide assistance to former slaves who had come to the District of Columbia. Mary Todd Lincoln donated $200 to the effort. Keckley also garnered financial support from Wendell Phillips and other prominent white abolitionists and philanthropists as well as the great Frederick Douglass and other prominent African Americans. She even received donations of goods from England.

On April 5, 1865, Mary Todd Lincoln and Keckley left Washington on the steamer *Monohasset* for City Point. They met President Lincoln the next day, on board the steamer *River Queen*, and continued by special train to Petersburg. On the morning of April 14, Mary Todd Lincoln told Keckley that she was going to the theater in the evening with the president. At 11:00 that night, Keckley was awakened and given the news of the president's assassination. She spent the night torn by grief and concern. In the morning, she was called to her friend's side and remained with her in the days that followed.

After Lincoln's assassination, his wife turned to Keckley for comfort, and though she could no longer afford to keep the dressmaker with her, the two remained friends. When Mary Todd Lincoln, believing herself to be in serious financial trouble, decided to sell part of her White House wardrobe, Keckley met her in New York to help her organize the auction. Keckley turned to her own friends to find help for Lincoln, and, at her urging, Frederick Douglass agreed to lecture to raise money for the president's widow.

Then *Behind the Scenes* was published. Keckley insisted that her purpose was to present a sympathetic picture of the former first lady, but the book caused a permanent rift between the two women. Keckley's business also suffered. Many African Americans believed she had betrayed their honored and beloved hero, President Lincoln. The book, however, is considered by scholars to be a valuable source of information about the Lincolns.

The controversy about whether Keckley wrote *Behind the Scenes* herself has never centered on the accuracy of the observations in the book. Indeed, it contains forty letters from Mary Todd Lincoln to Elizabeth Keckley. However, there are those who have argued that a greater degree of education and skill than Keckley possessed might have been necessary to produce the book. At any rate, Keckley's importance in history does not depend on whether hers was the hand that held the pen that wrote the words. It derives from her position in the Lincoln household and her participation in the events surrounding the Civil War.

During the last years of Keckley's life, she lived on a small pension that she received as the mother of a fallen Union soldier. She died in 1907 of a paralytic stroke at the Home for Destitute Women and Children, an institution which she had helped found.

KATHLEEN THOMPSON

L

Laney, Lucy Craft (1854–1933)

"To woman has been committed the responsibility of making the laws of society, making environments for children. She has the privilege and authority, God-given, to help develop into a noble man or woman the young life committed to her care. There is no nobler work entrusted to the hands of mortals." This conviction, expressed by Lucy Craft Laney in 1897, reflected the beliefs and principles of one of the most important African-American female educators in the late-nineteenth-century South.

Early in her development Laney concluded that women's most profound power derived from their roles as mothers and wives. She saw a relationship between the progress of the race and the need to defend, preserve, and strengthen the moral integrity of black women. Laney was convinced that women molded the character of the nation, that highly moral, educated black women were a prerequisite for the uplift of the race, and that the first line of defense was the home. In Laney's view, "The home [was] the nearest approach on earth to heaven. The chief joy of home [was the] mother." These convictions not only shaped Lucy Craft Laney's character and inspired her choice of a career but also provided the basic ideas to which she devoted her life's work. Laney's respect for the home, the major role of women in sustaining it, and the significance of the home and family in the struggle to uplift the black race were instilled in her during her youth.

Born in Macon, Georgia, on April 13, 1854, Lucy was the seventh of ten children of David and Louisa Laney. Her father, who had succeeded in purchasing his freedom and that of his wife, was a carpenter by trade. A deeply religious man, David Laney served as a preacher among his people before the Civil War and on May 13, 1866, was ordained as a Presbyterian minister. During the following year, he cofounded the John Knox Presbytery, the first all-black Presbyterian Synod in the United States, which was received into the Northern Assembly in 1868. David Laney was a renowned religious and community leader in Georgia. He retired in the early 1890s and died in 1902.

Louisa, Lucy's mother, was purchased by the Campbell family of Macon from a group of nomad Indians when she was a small child. Mr. Campbell bought the little girl at the urging of his daughter, to whom Louisa became a personal maid. A cute and likeable child, Louisa and the Campbell's daughter developed an amicable relationship. Louisa not only mastered the skills necessary to perform her duties, but also, with the assistance of her mistress, learned to read and write. When Louisa was about fifteen years old, she married David Laney and, in spite of her small frame and frail body, gave birth to ten healthy children, four boys and six girls, one of whom was Lucy Craft.

Lucy C. Laney spent her childhood in Macon, Georgia, where she was reared in a large, loving, nourishing, close-knit, Christian family that stressed sharing, responsibility, sacrifice, and education. She received her first formal education at the Lewis School, an institution opened by missionary teachers in 1865, and from which she was graduated in 1869. When the American Missionary Association opened a black college in Atlanta, Georgia, Lewis was one of the schools asked to send its best and brightest students for advanced education. Lucy C. Laney was one of the twenty-seven women among the first eighty-nine students admitted to Atlanta University in fall 1869.

Lucy and a fellow Lewis graduate, William S. Scarborough, quickly earned the reputation of being the most intelligent students at the university. In 1873, Laney and three other women in the "Higher Normal Course" became the first students to receive degrees from Atlanta University.

Lucy C. Laney began her teaching career in Milledgeville, Georgia, but between 1873 and 1877 she also taught at schools in Macon and Savannah. When illness necessitated a more healthful climate, she moved to Augusta where she secured a position as a grammar school teacher in the public school system. During her initial tenure in Augusta (1877–80), Laney played a major role in the successful fight for Georgia's first black public high school. She was also instrumental in the selection of Richard R. Wright as the institution's first principal.

Laney returned to Savannah in 1880, but a few years later moved back to Augusta and opened a private school for black children. Haines Normal and Industrial Institute, as the school was later named, was opened in a rented hall at Christ Presbyterian Church on January 6, 1886. The idea for the school was rooted in Lucy C. Laney's convictions about the need for educated women in the struggle to uplift the race, and was prompted by her concern about the increasing number of young black "children out of school without the care of parents, [who were] left to grow up idle and ignorant." The school was chartered by the state of Georgia in 1886 and the same year Laney gained the distinction of being the only black woman at the head of a major school affiliated with the Presbyterian Church.

Although Lucy C. Laney never married or had a family of her own, she loved children, and devoted her career to improving their chances in life. Through self-sacrifice, devotion, faith, and hard work Lucy Craft Laney developed Haines Institute into one of the best secondary schools in the South. In the course of accomplishing this feat she earned the title "mother of the children of the people." Fired with boundless zeal for the elevation of her race and a keen sense of the welfare of women and of the larger society, Laney's activities were not confined to her school. She was a member of the **National Association of Colored Women**, the Southeastern Federation of Women's Clubs, the Georgia State Teachers Association, and the National YWCA, and she chaired the Colored Section of the Interracial Commission of Augusta. Lucy Craft Laney was the first woman to be awarded honorary degrees from Atlanta University (1898) and Lincoln University (1904). She was similarly honored by South Carolina State College (1925) and **Howard University** (1930). Although she was never a recipient, Laney was nominated for the prestigious William E. Harmon Award for Distinguished Achievement among Negroes in 1928, 1929, and 1930.

After a lingering illness, on October 24, 1933, Lucy C. Laney died of nephritis and hypertension. Two days later, funeral services were held in the Chapel of Haines Institute and she was buried on the campus of the school.

JUNE O. PATTON

Lange, Elizabeth Clovis (1784–1882)

Elizabeth Clovis Lange was the founder and first "Superior-general" of the Oblate Sisters of Providence, the first black Roman Catholic order to operate in the United States. Mother Mary Elizabeth, as she was known, was a towering figure in nineteenth-century educational circles around Baltimore, Maryland, for over fifty years.

Elizabeth was born in the French colony Saint-Domingue (Haiti), to Clovis and Annette Lange in 1784. Because of the Haitian revolution, she migrated to eastern Cuba, where she lived near the city of Santiago. She came to the United States in 1817 and settled in Baltimore in 1827.

Soon after arriving in Baltimore, she used her inheritance to open the first school for the city's French-speaking immigrants, in spite of strong attempts to discourage black education in antebellum Maryland. Elizabeth's persistent service to her church and help to the educationally deprived won approbation from Rome under Pope Gregory XVI to organize the Oblate Sisters of Providence.

Although she ran primarily an educational order she became involved in many community programs to aid the needy. During the Civil War, she also became local superior of Saint Benedict's School in Baltimore and later spearheaded the establishment of other schools in Baltimore, Philadelphia, and New Orleans. During 1880, she began the order's first mission school in St. Louis, Missouri. By the time she died, the influence of the Oblate order had extended across the United States, the Caribbean, and Central America. More than 100 years after her death there are attempts to make her the first African-American female to be canonized by the Roman Catholic Church.

GLENN O. PHILLIPS

Laveau, Marie (c. 1790–1881)

Marie Laveau, the Voodoo Queen of New Orleans, was perhaps the most powerful black woman in nineteenth-century America. Even as thousands of her contemporaries, black and white, slave and free, feared her and the Voodoo she practiced, they regularly turned to her for her mystical powers. Her followers believed that she could cure their ills with her *gris-gris*, that she could bring them luck with her charms, amulets, or *mascots*, and that she could see into the future. It has been said that slaves who hoped to escape bondage sought her blessings and charms for safe passage, that ladies sought her advice on love, and that local politicians wore her amulets of bone and wood for luck. Certainly, there can be little doubt that Laveau had considerable power and influence over the population of New Orleans. Her power was not so much mystical as it was a product of her common sense, her ability to organize, and her considerable sphere of influence.

Born in New Orleans in the last decade of the eighteenth century, Marie Laveau was a free woman of color, a quadroon. She married Jacques Paris, a carpenter and a free man of color, in 1819. Laveau did not stay with Paris; instead, she left him and began calling herself the widow Paris long before her husband died. During this interval, Laveau lived with Christophe Glapion, a free man of color from Saint-Domingue (Haiti), with whom she reputedly had fifteen children. Besides her duties as a wife and mother, Laveau was a hairdresser and cook for the city jail. Both trades placed her in a position to know the private and public lives of the black and white population where she collected the bits of news and gossip that served as the foundation of her powers of influence and manipulation.

Most certainly, Laveau's power was derived from her intimate knowledge of life in the city. It was the particular expression that her knowledge and influence took, Voodoo, that instilled respect and fear in her followers. Like most other free women of color of French descent in New Orleans, Laveau was Catholic. She also shared a common African heritage with much of the community, where she, perhaps more than any other person in the city, represented the retention of African culture and religious beliefs. African religious beliefs, influenced by Catholicism and expressed as the practice of Voodoo, inspired her neighbors, friends and foes alike, to at once fear and revere her.

Marie Laveau lived into her early nineties, dying in 1881, having passed her influence and knowledge to her daughter. The second Marie Laveau, who was born in 1827, became the more notable of the two women, serving as the high priestess of the Voodoo cult that is most often portrayed in the popular literature of the city.

VIRGINIA GOULD

Lee, Jarena (b. 1783)

Jarena Lee, the first female known to petition the African Methodist Episcopal

Initially denied permission to preach because she was a woman, Jarena Lee persisted. Bishop Richard Allen of the African Methodist Episcopal Church granted her request and publicly praised her preaching. (MOORLAND-SPINGARN)

(AME) Church for authority to preach, was seminal in her gospel labors. She was born February 11, 1783, at Cape May, New Jersey, and is recorded to have made a first request to preach in 1809 at Bethel African Methodist Church of Philadelphia. The denial of this request did not stop Lee from preaching, and neither did her family life.

She married Reverend Joseph Lee, an AME pastor, in 1811 and moved to Snow Hill, New Jersey. In the sixth year of marriage, Joseph Lee died, and Jarena was left with two children and a commitment "to preach his gospel to the fallen sons and daughters of Adam's race."

Jarena Lee returned to Philadelphia and renewed her request to preach. Reverend Richard Allen, who at Lee's first request could find no precedent in Methodist discipline for women preaching, was now bishop of the newly organized African Methodist Episcopal Church. Lee asked "to be permitted the liberty of holding prayer meetings in my own hired house, and of exhorting as I found liberty." Bishop Allen granted the request and was affirmed in the decision when Lee was moved to speak when Reverend Richard Williams, the assigned preacher for Bethel Church, appeared to lose the spirit. She spoke so well, linking the text to her life, that Bishop Allen publicly proclaimed her gifts.

Lee went on to preach throughout the Northeastern region. Although she often traveled alone, her autobiography reports constant companionship among African-American evangelical women. Because Lee was an itinerant preacher and because she carried out her ministry with and among other "sisters in Christ," she was a pathfinder for future preaching women, particularly women of the AME Church. The constant and successful preaching efforts of AME women eventually forced the denomination to create gender-specific positions where no organizational authority for women had previously existed.

JUALYNNE E. DODSON

Logan, Adella Hunt (1863–1915)

"My busy life has been without romantic event," Adella Hunt Logan said of herself in 1902, but others might disagree. She was born in Sparta, Georgia, in 1863, the daughter of a free mulatto woman and a white planter—the fourth of their eight children. During her childhood, she lived on Hunt's Hill, an enclave where the town's more comfortably situated African-American population resided.

Adella attended Bass Academy in her hometown and became a certified teacher at sixteen. She acquired a scholarship to Atlanta University, and in 1881 she completed

In the early years of Tuskegee Institute, Adella Hunt Logan filled a number of positions, including serving for a time as "Lady Principal." This family photograph, which includes her husband, Warren, and six of their nine children, was taken in Tuskegee, Alabama, in 1913; Logan is third from the left. (PHOTO BY ARTHUR BEDOU; COLLECTION OF ADELE LOGAN ALEXANDER)

the normal course there—four-year programs were closed to women. The school later awarded her an honorary M.A. for her continuing work in education.

She taught for several years in an American Missionary School and in 1883 declined a teaching opportunity at her alma mater, choosing instead to go to Alabama's new Tuskegee Institute. During the early years at Tuskegee, Hunt filled a number of positions. She taught English and social sciences, became the institute's first librarian, and was "Lady Principal" for a short time. She also met Warren Logan, a schoolmate and old friend of Booker T. Washington. Warren Logan became the treasurer of Tuskegee Institute and served on its board of trustees.

These two educators married in 1888. The impoverished new school could not support two-salary families; since Adella's work was considered less critical, she subordinated her career to her husband's. In 1890 she gave birth to the first of nine children; the last was born in 1909 when she was forty-six.

Adella Hunt Logan taught only intermittently between difficult pregnancies and was limited as well by domestic demands and official responsibilities as the wife of Tuskegee's second-ranking official. Teaching remained her greatest passion, however, and she was the creative force behind Tuskegee's model school and teacher's training facility.

She immersed herself in activities of the Tuskegee Women's Club, a chapter of the **National Association of Colored Women** (NACW), as well. Logan's most important work centered around the club's efforts on behalf of local farm women and their children. She advocated health care for all and education for every child.

Logan's other major interest was woman's suffrage. At the turn of the century, most white Alabamans vehemently opposed votes for women, but Logan led regular forums about suffrage at Tuskegee and encouraged students to debate and participate in demonstrations of participatory democracy. She lectured at NACW conferences as well and served briefly as that group's national director of both suffrage and rural affairs. She also wrote about suffrage in the *Colored American* and the *Crisis*.

Because of her predominantly white ancestry, Adella Hunt Logan looked white. When the National American Woman Suffrage Association (NAWSA) held conventions in the segregated South, she attended without identifying herself as "colored." Subsequently, she brought back information from those meetings to share with colleagues in the African-American community. For a decade she was the only life member of the NAWSA from the state of Alabama. She also contributed articles about NACW activities to that organization's newspaper.

Logan became swept up in the ideological feud between Booker T. Washington and W. E. B. DuBois over the direction of the black community, but she managed to maintain her philosophical alliance with DuBois even while remaining a personal friend, professional associate, and next-door neighbor to Washington.

A combination of events, including defeats for the suffrage movement and tensions in her marriage, led to an emotional collapse in September 1915, when Adella Hunt Logan was sent to a Michigan sanitarium. A few weeks later, however, news of Booker T. Washington's precipitously declining health summoned her home. After her friend's death, Logan never recovered. On December 12, as visiting dignitaries assembled at Tuskegee to attend a memorial service for Washington, Logan jumped to her death from the top floor of one of the school's buildings.

ADELE LOGAN ALEXANDER

M

Mason, Biddy (Bridget) (1818–1891)

Biddy (Bridget) Mason, an illiterate slave and plantation-trained midwife, walked across the United States from Mississippi to California to become a powerful force in the economic, educational, spiritual, and health-care developments of the nascent black community of Los Angeles.

Born a slave in Hancock County, Mississippi, on August 15, 1818, Biddy's parents remain unknown. However, records indicate that she was of mixed blood, black and three kinds of Indian—Choctaw, Seminole, and Geegi. Biddy was owned in turn by three families who operated plantations: the Smithsons of South Carolina, the Bankses of Georgia, and the Crosby family of Mississippi. Biddy Mason's childhood was spent in Mississippi where she was trained to assist the house servants and midwives in the Smithson household. When his cousin Rebecca married Robert Marion Smith in 1836, John Smithson made her a present of Mason, along with three other slaves—two house servants, Hannah and Ella, and Buck, a blacksmith and horse trainer. Mason managed the plantation's business affairs and cared for the sickly Rebecca. Robert Smith became the father of Mason's three daughters, Ellen, Ann, and Harriet. He also was father to nine children by Hannah and six children by his wife.

Around 1844, Robert Smith was converted to Mormonism by Elder John Brown. By March 1848, the Smith clan had joined the Crosbys, Bankses, and Smithsons in the third Mormon migration into Indian territory. Biddy Mason, Hannah, and forty other slaves accompanied the Mormons on this migration. They were promised their freedom at the completion of this journey if they chose to accompany the family.

During this trip to Utah, Mason herded the cattle, cared for her newborn daughter, Harriet, and made camp at the end of the day. She also made the first meal of the day and broke up camp. Because hers was the last wagon, she literally ate the dust of the entire wagon train.

They lived in Utah for three years. In 1851, Brigham Young requested volunteers to establish a settlement in Southern California. After camping at Cajon Pass for three months, they moved into San Bernardino. During this time, Mason came into contact with the black community of Los Angeles.

In December 1855, Charles Owens notified his father, Robert Owens, that Smith was planning to remove Biddy and her three daughters to Texas. Lizzy Flake Rowan, a friend to Mason, joined Robert Owens in a petition to Judge Benjamin Hayes that resulted in freedom papers for Biddy Mason and thirteen other of Smith's slaves. Hayes asked Sheriff Burnside to place Mason and her three daughters in his protective custody. This lawsuit set a precedent regarding the legal rights of black settlers in the American West.

Freedom was officially achieved on January 21, 1856, ending Biddy Mason's long and arduous quest for freedom for herself and her children. She became a nurse and midwife to Dr. John S. Griffin, serving members of the Los Angeles, San Bernardino, San Diego, and Santa Barbara communities. She saved her wages of $2.50 per day to purchase her homestead at Spring Street. Mason was a founding member of the First African Methodist Episcopal Church in 1872, and she established a nursery and day-care center for the children of black working parents. Mason also visited and nursed the sick and insane in the hospitals and in jail. She was always available to assist persons in need regardless of color and creed.

Biddy Mason died on January 15, 1891, and was mourned by the community that she had served faithfully for over forty years. She was a compassionate woman who endeared herself to those with whom she came in contact.

BOBI JACKSON

Mason, Lena Doolin (b. 1864)

Lena Doolin Mason is one of only a handful of nineteenth-century preaching women for whom we have visual images. She was born in the Soldier's Barracks on Hampshire Street in Quincy, Illinois, on May 8, 1864. Her mother, Relda Doolin, had taken refuge in the barracks after escaping from slavery, and her father, Vaughn Poole Doolin, was fighting in the Civil War. Lena was the fifth of ten children and one of eight girls. She attended Douglass High School in Hannibal, Missouri, as well as Knott's School in Chicago.

At the age of seven, Lena experienced her first call to preach, and in January 1872 she joined the African Methodist Episcopal Church of Hannibal, Missouri, under the pastorate of Reverend John Turner. At the age of twelve, she was again called to preach. On March 9, 1883, Lena married George Mason. The couple had four sons and two daughters, but only Bertha May is known to have survived to adulthood.

Lena Doolin Mason actively began her ministry at the age of twenty-three and for the first three years she preached exclusively to white congregations. She traveled and preached in almost every state and was especially acclaimed during her five months in Minneapolis, Minnesota. Mason is credited with having influenced some 1,617 persons to convert to Christianity.

JUALYNNE E. DODSON

Matthews, Victoria Earle (1861–1907)

Victoria Earle Matthews was "a Salvation Army field officer, a College Settlement worker, a missionary, a teacher, a preacher, and a Sister of Mercy, all in one." Matthews, as described by a New York City reporter who was her contemporary, dedicated her life to helping others. She volunteered for settlement activities, social welfare work, and club organizations with relentless zeal. Matthews was resourceful, assertive, and had great foresight.

Matthews was born on May 27, 1861, in Fort Valley, Georgia, one of nine children born to Caroline Smith. Her mother, a native of Virginia, escaped from slavery to New York during the Civil War, but returned to Georgia for her children after emancipation. Victoria, her mother, and the family arrived in New York City around 1873, after spending three years in Richmond and Norfolk.

Although she was born into slavery and had little formal education, Victoria Earle Matthews became a journalist, lecturer, social reformer, and pioneer in travelers' aid work at the turn of the century. (SCHOMBURG CENTER

Matthews received very little formal education. She attended Grammar School 48 in New York City until poverty and the illness of a family member forced her to leave. She began working as a domestic, but continued to read and attend special lectures. In 1879, at the age of eighteen, she married William Matthews, a coachman and native of Petersburg, Virginia. During the early years of her marriage, Matthews wrote short stories and essays for *Waverly* magazine and other publications.

In 1893, under the pen name "Victoria Earle," she published *Aunt Lindy*, her most ambitious work. Matthews did freelance writing for the *New York Times*, the *New*

York Herald, and the *Brooklyn Eagle*. She wrote articles for the leading black newspapers, the Boston *Advocate*, *Washington Bee*, *Richmond Planet*, and *Cleveland Gazette*. She edited *Black Speeches, Addresses, and Talks of Booker T. Washington* (1898).

A journalist with the *New York Age*, Matthews was sympathetic to the antilynching crusader and writer **Ida B. Wells.** Matthews helped organize a testimonial for Wells on October 5, 1892, at Lyric Hall in New York City that brought together black women from Boston, Philadelphia, and New York. This event inspired the founding of the Woman's Loyal Union of New York City and Brooklyn two months later. Matthews was a founder and the first president of the women's club.

Matthews attended the first national conference of black women in July 1895. She presented a stunning address on "The Value of Race Literature," praising the creative ability of black men and women and their contributions to race literature and race building. The national conference sparked the founding of the National Federation of Afro-American Women (NFAAW). Matthews was appointed to the executive board and to the editorial staff of the *Woman's Era*, the official journal of the NFAAW.

In July 1896, the National Colored Women's League of Washington and the Federation of Afro-American Women held their conventions in Washington, D.C. Seven women from the two national organizations, including Matthews, formed a joint committee to consider uniting. Their recommendations led the two women's organizations to join together as the **National Association of Colored Women (NACW).** **Mary Church Terrell** was elected president of the NACW. Matthews became the first national organizer of the NACW and the New York State organizer for the Northeastern Federation of Women's Clubs.

In December 1895, Matthews attended the Congress of Colored Women of the United States in Atlanta. Black clubwomen from twenty-five states attended the women's congress. Immediately after the congress, she toured the South. She visited the red-light districts and employment agencies in New Orleans and other Southern cities. Following her investigations, Matthews returned to New York determined to continue her "uplift" and improvement work there.

Victoria Matthew's concern for social welfare work in the black community increased after the death of her son and only child, Larmartine, at the age of sixteen. At this time, she began to focus on issues related to the well-being of children and young women. She began to visit local families and held mother's meetings in the various homes.

The **White Rose Mission**, established by Matthews, opened on February 11, 1897. It was founded with the purpose of "establishing and maintaining a Christian, non-sectarian Home for Colored Girls and Women, where they may be trained in the principles of practical self-help and right living." It offered a social center for community women and children as well as shelter and protection for young women who came from the South in search of employment. Matthews organized a group of women from different religious denominations to assist in operating her program.

With the desire to do practical, useful work, Matthews began to lecture. With a talent for dramatic and forceful speeches, she often spoke before black audiences on the political and social responsibilities of self-improvement. She encouraged respect

for black women, their work, and accomplishments. Matthews was invited to represent Black American women at the annual convention of the Society of Christian Endeavor in San Francisco. On July 11, 1897, in her address "The Awakening of the Afro-American Woman," she stated that it was the responsibility of the Christian womanhood of the country to join in "elevating the head, the heart, and the soul of Afro-American womanhood."

Matthews voiced concern about black women who came to the North seeking employment. Employment agents went into the rural districts of the South with convincing stories of the "North" and of "New York," and pressured women into signing contracts. These unfortunate young women were then at the mercy of the agencies that had financed their trip to the North.

A pioneer in traveler's aid work, Matthews and her assistants met the boats at the Old Dominion pier and helped the inexperienced young women from the South. Matthews, as superintendent of the White Rose Mission, established a series of social services from Norfolk to New York. In 1905, she organized the White Rose Traveler's Aid Society. White Rose agents watched the docks to prevent black women from the South from being victimized. The appointed agents were Dorothy Boyd in New York and Hattie Proctor in Norfolk.

Matthews established a special library of books by and about black people at the White Rose Home for Working Girls. Many of the books were used in her teachings on "Race History." As her health gradually failed, her duties as superintendent of the White Rose Home were assumed by her assistants, including Frances Reynolds Keyser.

Matthews maintained her Brooklyn residence at 33 Poplar Street and her membership at St. Philips Episcopal Church. A plaque outside the brownstone distinguishes it as "The White Rose Home" and a large photograph of Victoria Earle Matthews, which dominates the entry hall, are memorials to her inspirational and dedicated service. She died on March 10, 1907, of tuberculosis at the age of forty-five and was buried in the Maple Grove Cemetery, New York City.

FLORIS BARNETT CASH

McCoy, Mary Eleanora   (1846–1923)

Mary Eleanora Delaney Brownlow McCoy rose from humble beginnings to become a person of great influence in social improvement and philanthropic clubs and organizations in Michigan.

Born on January 7, 1846, in an Underground Railroad station in Lawrenceburg, Indiana, she was the daughter of Jacob C. Delaney and Eliza Ann (Montgomery) Delaney. Her formal education was limited to attending classes first at mission schools taught in private homes in Indiana and later at the Freedman's School in St. Louis, Missouri, in 1869. Moving to Michigan in the early 1870s, Mary met and later married Elijah McCoy on February 25, 1873, the second marriage for both. Elijah, born in 1843 in Colchester, Ontario, Canada, to former slaves who had also escaped on the Underground Railroad, studied mechanical engineering in Edinburgh, Scotland, for five years before looking for a job in the United States. Elijah's career as an inventor began when he was working as a railroad fireman on the Michigan Central Railroad. It was necessary to stop railroad trains after a certain amount of use to oil the moving parts. Elijah invented several types of self-lubricating devices that made it unnecessary to stop trains merely to oil them. His inventions led to the popular saying, "Is it the real McCoy?," which warned people to beware of imitations. Prolific as an inventor, Elijah received six patents for lubricating devices and one for an ironing table between 1872 and 1876 and another forty-four patents (thirty-six of which were for lubricators) between 1882 and 1926. Elijah organized the Elijah McCoy Manufacturing Company in Detroit in 1920 and died in October 1929.

The McCoys had moved to Detroit by 1882. In the 1890s, Mary McCoy became a leader in founding and administrating black women's clubs, earning her the title "Mother of Clubs." In 1895, Mary was one of the founders of the "In as Much Circle of King's Daughters and Sons Club," said to be the first black women's club in Michigan. She was also the only black woman to be a charter member of the prestigious Twentieth Century Club, started in 1894. In 1898, Mary was one of the cofounders of the Michigan State Association of Colored Women and eventually became its vice president. The Michigan association became a member of the **National Association of Colored Women**, widening its scope of activity. Mary called the first meeting, which led in 1898 to the establishment of the Phillis Wheatley Home for Aged Colored Women in Detroit, and later served as its vice president. She was also the major financial supporter of the McCoy Home for Colored Children, vice president of the Lydian Association of Detroit, and president of the Sojourner Truth Memorial Association, whose purpose was to erect a monument to

Truth, a former slave and powerful speaker for abolition and women's rights who lived in Battle Creek, Michigan, from the 1850s until her death in 1884, and to establish University of Michigan scholarships in Truth's name.

McCoy was a charter member of the Detroit chapter of the National Association for the Advancement of Colored People in the 1910s, a member of the Order of the Eastern Star, Prince Hall Affiliate, and at the Bethel African Methodist Episcopal Church she was a member of the Willing Workers and the King's Daughters clubs. One of the early black supporters of the Democratic party, McCoy also campaigned for women's right to vote in all elections. Consequently, she was chosen as flag bearer from Michigan in a women's suffrage parade held as part of the inaugural ceremonies for President Woodrow Wilson in 1913. Governor Ferris of Michigan appointed McCoy to the socially prestigious Michigan Commission for the Half-Century Exposition of Freedmen's Progress to be held in Chicago in 1915. As a member of the commission, Mary was a "Field Agent, Eastern Michigan," charged with finding materials to be put on display at the Chicago exposition and information to be listed, with photographs, in the companion book, the *Michigan Manual of Freedmen's Progress.* Both Mary and Elijah McCoy are prominently referred to in the book, and Elijah's work was on display in Chicago. In early 1920, Mary and Elijah were in a traffic accident, and Mary was seriously injured. Her health declined, and she died in early 1923.

DE WITT S. DYKES, JR.

Menken, Adah Isaacs (1835–1868)

What would make a dirty Colorado gold miner of the 1860s drop his pick, slick down his hair, and go to the theater to watch an adaptation of Lord Byron's poem "Mazeppa"? Adah Isaacs Menken in a body stocking charging onto the stage strapped to a horse. This actress knew how to draw a crowd.

Menken loved to wrap herself and her life in mystery, but she was probably Creole, born in 1835 in Chartrain, Louisiana, to Auguste Theodore, a storekeeper referred to as a "free man of color," and his wife Marie Theodore, a native of Bordeaux, France. Her father died shortly after her birth, and her mother later married a man named Josephs. In 1856, twenty-one-year-old Adah married Alexander Isaac Menken, a Jewish musician from Cincinnati. After he suffered serious financial setbacks, she went on the stage to support them. She made her theater debut under the name Adah Isaacs Menken in 1857 as Pauline in *The Lady of Lyons.* She was well received in spite of her inexperience and average acting ability, probably because she had a good voice, a pretty face, a remarkable figure, and stage presence. Managed by her husband, she traveled around the South and the Midwest.

Menken and her husband separated in July 1859, shortly after her New York debut. Thinking that she was divorced, she quietly married a boxer named John Carmel Heenan in September. When her secret marriage was revealed, Alexander Menken claimed there had been no divorce. Heenan left for England, and Adah Menken was left pregnant and alone. Her child died shortly after birth.

Scandal surrounded Menken, and she decided to exploit it. She discovered the role of the Tartar youth in *Mazeppa.* During the

Victorian era, boy's roles, in which actresses wore tights, were the theater's cheesecake. *Mazeppa* offered the additional lure of a boffo ending when the naked youth—Menken wore neck-to-toe tights—was strapped to a horse that walked up a narrow runway through the crowd to the stage. From its opening on June 3, 1861, until her death, Menken had a guaranteed crowd pleaser. She took the show west. Her third husband, journalist Robert Henry Newell, went with her to San Francisco, where her first run in that city brought in $9,000. Her western tour thrilled miners and literary lights equally, her considerable skills as a poet making it respectable for people such as Bret Harte and Joaquin Miller to admire her.

After divorcing Newell, Menken took *Mazeppa* to England, where she caused a terrific scandal and received $500 a performance, making her the highest-paid actress on record at the time. She was adopted by the British literati and had a romantic relationship with the poet Algernon Swinburne. She was married once more, in 1866, to James Paul Barkley; the marriage lasted three days, and a son was born three months later. Then Menken hit Paris. When she wasn't delighting audiences, she was scandalizing the city by posing for photographs embracing Dumas *père*.

After Paris, Menken's career began to slide. Six weeks after her last performance, at Sadler's Wells on May 30, 1868, her health failed. She died, probably of tuberculosis complicated by peritonitis, in August. A volume of her poetry published posthumously received some attention, and she is listed in many literary reference works as a poet and keeper of salons. Yet Adah Menken's place in history is more truly marked by the image of the "naked lady" riding her horse across the

American frontier in defiance of Queen Victoria and all her kind.

KATHLEEN THOMPSON

Merritt, Emma Frances   (1860–1933)

Emma Merritt's contributions as teacher and administrator in the Washington, D.C., public schools changed the face of education for black Americans around the country. That she was able to carve out a career in education in Washington, D.C., in the 1870s was a remarkable feat in itself for a young black woman. At the same time, her accomplishments were impressive for any educator of any race, gender, or period in history.

Emma Frances Grayson Merritt was born on January 11, 1860, in Dumfries (Cherry Hill), Prince William County, Virginia. She was one of seven children of John Merritt, a black man, and Sophia Cook Merritt, a Cherokee woman. When Emma was three years old, the Merritt family moved to Washington, D.C., where she attended the black public schools that had been funded by Congress in 1864.

The first school Merritt attended was a part of the Ebenezer African Methodist Episcopal Church, which was publicly subsidized as a school. She graduated from high school and became a teacher at the age of fifteen. In 1883, after eight years of teaching in grammar school, Merritt entered **Howard University**. There she studied under both James M. Gregory and Wiley Lane. In 1887, she became principal of the Banneker Elementary School. She also continued her own education. From 1887 to 1890, she studied at Columbian University (now George Washington University) then went back to Howard in 1889 to focus on mathematics. In 1890, she took over as principal of Garnet

School and established the first kindergarten for African-American students, an astounding move at a time when kindergartens were almost unheard of in the general population.

In 1898, Merritt became director of primary instruction and in 1927 supervising principal of all black schools in Washington, D.C. She remained in the latter position until her retirement in 1930. Throughout her career, she was an innovator. She developed a primary department for black students and modernized instruction in that department, organized "demonstration and observation" schools to improve teaching methods, classified students in homogeneous learning groups, established excursions and field trips, and introduced silent reading into the schools—all in the first quarter of the twentieth century.

Her innovations carried far beyond the District of Columbia, in part because she corresponded with former students who were teaching in the rural South and kept them apprised of new ideas in education. She also lectured on her methods at a variety of institutions, including the State College in Delaware, Howard University, Cheyney Institute in Pennsylvania, Manassas Industrial School and Hampton Institute in Virginia, the Normal School in Baltimore (now Coppin State College), West Virginia State College, and Dallas Institute in Texas. While she made such major contributions to education, she was herself continuing to be educated. She spent some time between 1898 and 1901 at the Cook County Normal School in Chicago studying mathematics and child psychology. She also completed a course of study at the Phoebe Hearst (Kindergarten) Training School in Washington, D.C., and at the Berlitz School of Languages.

Merritt's educational genius was widely recognized in her own time. The District of Columbia superintendent of schools, F. W. Ballou, praised her highly and asked his board of education to establish two laboratory schools in which her methods could be used and observed. In 1925, Howard University awarded her an honorary Master of Arts degree.

Merritt was also active in community affairs. She organized and presided over the Teacher's Benefit and Annuity Association of Washington, D.C., and the Prudence Crandall Association for needy children. From 1930 to 1933, she was president of the District of Columbia branch of the National Association for the Advancement of Colored People. She was also a founding member of the **National Association of Colored Women**.

Emma Merritt died on June 8, 1933. Eleven years later, an elementary school was named in her honor in the District of Columbia.

GERRI BATES

Mitchell, Nellie B. (1845–1924)

> My motto is excelsior. I am resolved to give myself up wholly to the study of music, and endeavor, in spite of obstacles, to become an accomplished artist.
>
> —Nellie B. Mitchell, c. 1865

The worth of an artist can often be measured by the impact she or he has on the local level. It is at this level that the most enduring impressions are made, for the true artist in full bloom has often been well planted and tilled in home soil. Nellie B. Mitchell was a concert singer, educator, and arts function organizer whose presence was known and felt in and around New England. Her vocal talents, charm, and grace won her admiration and praise from seasoned critics and local audiences alike.

Born in Dover, New Hampshire, in 1845, Nellie B. Mitchell was devoted to music from an early age until her death, in Boston in 1924, at the age of seventy-nine. As a child she studied voice in Dover and began her career as a church soloist in local churches in Dover, New Hampshire, Haverhill, Massachusetts, and Boston between 1865 and 1886. She trained at both the Boston and the New England conservatories of music as well as the School of Vocal Arts in Boston, from which she received a performance diploma in 1879. In 1874, she made her New York singing debut in Steinway Hall; she made an appearance in Philadelphia in 1882.

Many performances followed. In 1885, Mitchell did a concert tour of the South, and in 1886 she formed her own touring company to travel around New England. Critics mentioned her attractive voice as well as her charm as an artist. "Miss Nellie Brown showed a particularly well-modulated voice, trained study, and appreciative method, which served her well in the pleasant rendering given by her so graciously and unaffectedly," said the Boston *Traveller* in 1874. "This lady is fortunate in her exceedingly sweet and well-trained voice, which, in conjunction with her fine personal appearance and stage manners, rendered her reception unusually enthusiastic," said the Boston *Globe* in 1874.

During the later years of her career, between 1890 until her death in 1924, she devoted her time to teaching and organizing and attending concerts and arts events. Mitchell organized the "Centennial Musical Festival" to benefit Boston's young people,

and for the festival she organized and conducted fifty young girls in the performance of the operetta *Laila, the Fairy Queen*. This concert was given May 16–17, 1876, and repeated in Haverhill, December 13, 1876. She was the primary organizer and financier of a Boston concert performed on March 21, 1918, with other prominent Boston artists. Among the concert patrons and sponsors were William Dupree, James Monroe Trotter, and Mme. Mamie Flowers. Sponsored by the Shamut Congregational Church in Boston, the concert was a benefit for the great black prima donna of the time, Madame Selika.

Nellie B. Mitchell spent her later summers teaching at the Hedding Chautauqua summer school in East Epping, New Hampshire. In addition to starting her own singing company, she was also a founding member of the Chaminade Club. This club was organized by black women in order to study light classical music, notated spirituals, and the accomplishments of women artists. Also during this time, Mitchell was an active member of the music teacher's national association.

Although Nellie B. Mitchell certainly became an artist of national reputation (to the extent that a black artist during her lifetime could be so recognized), her most enduring impact has been in her native New England.

WILLIAM C. BANFIELD

Mossell, Gertrude (1855–1948)

Through her books, articles, and newspaper columns, Gertrude Mossell wrote about her political and social ideology, reflecting the views of a feminist and social reformer in the late nineteenth and early twentieth centuries. She encouraged women to go into professions such as medicine and journalism, and she dismissed the notion that a woman had to choose either to have a family or a career. Mossell and other black women leaders of her era combined roles as activists and professionals with those of wife and mother. Taken together, her views would not be seriously considered by most African Americans for at least another generation.

Gertrude E. H. Bustill Mossell, educator, journalist, and feminist, was born in Philadelphia, Pennsylvania, on July 3, 1855. She died at the age of ninety-two at Frederick Douglass Memorial Hospital in Philadelphia, the city where she spent most of her life, on January 21, 1948. She had been ill for about three months.

Her parents, Charles H. and Emily (Robinson) Bustill, were among the free-black elite of nineteenth-century Philadelphia. The prominent Bustill family included generations of achievers, including Gertrude's great-grandfather, the former slave Cyril Bustill (1732–1806), who earned his freedom and served on George Washington's staff as a baker during the American Revolution. One of Cyril's daughters, Grace Bustill Douglass (1782–1842), was an abolitionist and a member and officer of the **Philadelphia Female Anti-Slavery Society**, as was her daughter, **Sarah Mapps Douglass** (1806–82), who also married a Douglass. Sarah was not only an abolitionist but a feminist and noted educator. Perhaps the most illustrious member of the Bustill family was Gertrude's cousin, the actor and political activist Paul Bustill Robeson (1898–1976), who became a Rhodes scholar after graduating from Rutgers University.

Gertrude Bustill and her elder sister (who later became Mrs. William D. Robertson) were raised as Quakers, as were many of the Bustills. Both women later followed the lead of several family members and joined the Presbyterian church. They were educated in Philadelphia "colored" schools.

After completing her studies at Roberts Vaux Grammar School, Gertrude Bustill taught school for seven years at various places, including Camden, New Jersey, and Frankford, Delaware. As was the custom, her marriage to physician Nathan F. Mossell of Lockport, Pennsylvania, probably in the early 1880s, ended her formal teaching career. She returned to live in Philadelphia, where she raised two daughters, Mazie and Florence. A few years after her marriage, however, Gertrude Mossell resumed her writing and developed a career as a journalist, educating the public about women's rights and social reform movements.

Mossell's career goal emerged from her exceptional ability as a writer who came from a family of political activists and feminists. Reverend Benjamin Tucker Tanner discovered her writing potential, probably in the late 1860s, as a guest at the closing exercises of the Roberts Vaux Grammar School, where he heard Bustill read her essay "Influence." He invited her to submit it for publication to the periodical he edited, the *Christian Recorder*. As a result of this first literary success, Gertrude Mossell began an outstanding literary career, writing essays and columns for numerous newspapers and periodicals and eventually writing two books, *The Work of the Afro-American Woman* (1894) and *Little Dansie's One Day at Sabbath School* (1902).

Mossell developed a national reputation as a journalist writing for African-American newspapers. Her articles and columns appeared in the *AME Church Review*, the (New York) *Freeman*, and the (Indianapolis)

World. In Philadelphia, she wrote for leading papers with syndicated columns in the *Echo*, the Philadelphia *Times*, the *Independent*, and the *Press Republican*. In addition, Mossell assisted in editing the *Lincoln Alumni Magazine*, the journal of her husband's alma mater.

African-American women journalists were few and far between during the 1880s when Mossell wrote the column "Our Woman's Department," which appeared in the first issue of T. Thomas Fortune's New York *Freeman*, in December 1885. Mossell titled her first column "Woman Suffrage," and wrote that her column would "be devoted to the interest of women" and that she would "promote true womanhood, especially that of the African race." Mossell encouraged her readers to read books and periodicals to educate themselves about the issues of woman suffrage. She hoped that those who thought unfavorably about votes for women would be convinced to change their opinions with new awareness. Married women, Mossell argued, supported woman suffrage. Her words indicated a significant political awareness and sophistication shared by only a few outspoken black woman suffragists in the 1880s.

Mossell's column appeared every other week throughout 1886, and in it she promoted career development in business and the professions. She called for the training of women in skills that would prepare them for businesses such as the restaurant industry. As for literary and journalistic careers, Mossell introduced her readers to role models such as **Frances Ellen Watkins Harper**, **Josephine Turpin**, and **Charlotte Ray**, to essayists such as **Mary Ann Shadd Cary**, and to journalists such as **Ida B. Wells-Barnett**, Clarissa Thompson, and Mattie Horton, using her column to promote women and encourage them to seek their rights.

Gertrude Mossell believed that all types of African-American women needed to ally themselves in order to help one another in a process that she and others of her era called "racial uplift." Although she was known as a product of Philadelphia's black elite, Mossell looked beyond the lines of status when she called for women of color to come together to work on behalf of their race.

ROSALYN TERBORG-PENN

N

Napier, Nettie Langston (1861–1938)

Nettie Langston Napier worked hard as the president of the Day Homes Club and as a member of the **National Association of Colored Women** (NACW) to help meet the needs of families who faced discrimination and economic hardship. Although her own life was free of economic deprivation, Napier was a generous philanthropist dedicated to improving life for all black people.

Born on June 17, 1861, in Oberlin, Ohio, Nettie DeElla Langston was the daughter of Caroline M. (Wall) Langston and John Mercer Langston. John Langston was the son of white plantation owner Ralph Quarles and his mistress, a woman of Indian and African-American descent. He went on to become a prominent lawyer and founder and head of **Howard University's** law school. He is considered by many to have been one of the first great black orators, second only to Frederick Douglass. Both of Nettie Langston's parents were educated at **Oberlin College**.

When Nettie was nine years old, the family moved from Oberlin to Washington, D.C., where she attended public schools and then Howard University. After one year at Howard, she transferred to her hometown in order to complete her education in music, attending the Oberlin conservatory from 1876 to 1878. In 1878, she married James Carroll Napier. The couple probably lived in Nashville, Tennessee, where James Napier had grown up, before moving to Washington, D.C., in 1910. The Napiers had one adopted daughter, Carrie Langston Napier.

In Washington, the Napiers lived in the historic Hillside Cottage located at Fourth and Bryant streets near Howard University. The couple moved within an elite social circle. Booker T. Washington was a close friend, and he would make their home his headquarters whenever he was in the city. James Napier rose within his profession, the law, and, as a Republican, became prominent within political circles at the local and national levels. Nettie Langston Napier was considered a dedicated wife and mother and an elegant, stately hostess. In 1913, however, following James Napier's resignation from his two-year office in the Register of the Treasury in protest against President Woodrow Wilson's policy on segregation, the couple returned to Nashville.

In Nashville, James Napier dedicated himself to the One Cent Savings Bank (later Citizen's Savings Bank) in which he was an investor, while Nettie Napier focused on community concerns. As in many other cities, numerous children in Nashville were left unattended at home while their parents were at work. Napier believed these children needed food, health care, and training, and in order to accomplish these tasks she proposed the establishment of the Day Homes Club, a black women's organization designed to help meet the needs of poor communities in a manner similar to that of the Phyllis Wheatley Club, which was associated with the City Federation of Colored Women's Clubs.

The club was formed in 1907, with Napier as its president. It was housed at 618 Fourth Avenue South, later known as Porter Homestead. On January 14, 1907, a meeting of interested women supporters framed a constitution; elected officers; appointed Josie E. Wells, a specialist in diseases of women and children, as physician-in-charge; and decided to seek a woman superintendent for the home as well as vice presidents for the city's wards. The following month, Napier convened a large meeting of black women to debate the day home concept in Nashville and to generate interest in her organization. After a general discussion of contemporary issues involving women, such as temperance and education, Napier delivered the key item on the agenda, her presentation on neglected children.

Initially, only daytime hours were set for the home, but it soon became apparent that because of irregular work hours, arrangements would have to be made to keep some children overnight; thus, some ten to twelve children became boarders. Although there was a pressing need for the home, and even though the local newspapers were more than sympathetic, within eighteen months the home was in financial trouble. Food and clothing were badly needed. The club needed more members in order to receive adequate funding. Napier said in an article published in *The Globe* on October 30, 1908, that although the club was trying desperately to raise enough money to keep the home running, it would be forced to close it if further contributions did not arrive. It should have been possible to secure funding for the home, but enough contributions were not forthcoming. The exact date—and the exact cause—of the home's closure have yet to be established.

Napier's community efforts did not stop with the failure of this venture, however. Having been instrumental in bringing the NACW to Nashville in 1897, she attended their meeting in Buffalo in 1901 and was thereafter an active member of the organization. She held various positions in the NACW national body, including auditor and national treasurer. She served on many of the organization's most important committees and was president of the Douglass Memorial Fund. Napier also was chairperson of the executive committees of the New Idea Club and the City Federation. Her work as head of the Committee of Colored Women assisted the Red Cross campaign during World War I.

Nettie Langston Napier died on September 27, 1938, at her home in Nashville. She is buried in Nashville's Greenwood Cemetery.

FENELLA MACFARLANE

P

Patterson, Mary Jane (1840–1894)

The 1860 census lists Mary Jane Patterson as one of fourteen residents in her parent's household in Oberlin, Ohio. Two years later she graduated from **Oberlin College**, becoming the first black woman to receive a B.A. degree from an established American college. Patterson devoted the rest of her life to the education of black children.

Born in Raleigh, North Carolina, in 1840, Patterson was the oldest of Henry and Emeline Patterson's seven children. In 1856, she and her family moved to Oberlin, Ohio, where they joined a growing community of free black families who worked to send their children to the college. Henry Patterson worked as a master mason, and for many years the family boarded large numbers of black students in their home. Eventually, four Patterson children graduated from Oberlin College. All became teachers.

Mary Jane Patterson's first known teaching appointment was in 1865, when she became an assistant to Fanny Jackson in the Female Department of the **Institute for Colored Youth** in Philadelphia. In 1869, when Jackson was promoted to principal, Patterson accepted a teaching position in Washington, D.C., at the newly organized Preparatory High School for Colored Youth—later known as Dunbar High School. She served as the school's first black principal, from 1871–72, and was reappointed from 1873–84. During her administration, the name "Preparatory High School" was dropped, high school commencements were initiated, and a teacher-training department was added to the school. Patterson's commitment to thoroughness as well as her "forceful" and "vivacious" personality helped her establish the school's high intellectual standards.

Patterson also devoted time and money to other black institutions in Washington, D.C., especially to industrial schools for young black women, as well as to the Home for Aged and Infirm Colored People. She never married, nor did her two Oberlin-educated sisters (Chanie and Emeline), who later joined her and taught in District schools.

Mary Jane Patterson died in Washington, D.C., September 24, 1894, at the age of fifty-four. Her pioneering educational attainments and her achievements as a leading black educator influenced generations of black students.

MARLENE DEAHL MERRILL

Peake, Mary Smith Kelsey (1823–1862)

Mary Smith Kelsey was born in Norfolk, Virginia, the daughter of a light-skinned free black woman and a white European, to whom Virginia law forbade marriage. She was educated in Alexandria, Virginia, living with an aunt until she returned to Norfolk at the age of sixteen. In 1847, her mother married Thomas Walker, and Mary moved with the couple to Hampton, Virginia, where she worked as a seamstress. She was already deeply committed to Christianity and active in charity, founding an organization called Daughters of Benevolence sometime between 1847 and 1851. She also began illegally teaching both slaves and free black Americans to read. In 1851, she married Thomas Peake; the couple were part of Hampton's antebellum black elite. Her daughter, Daisy, was born about 1856.

At the start of the Civil War, her teaching was given official sanction by Union officers at Fort Monroe, and she became one of the first teachers in the South to be supported by the American Missionary Association. By early 1862, she was teaching over fifty children in her day school as well as twenty adults in the evenings. Deeply religious herself, she taught the Bible and singing, reading, writing, and simple mathematics, and she founded a Sunday school for children. She died of tuberculosis in February 1862.

MARILYN DELL BRADY

Pettey, Sarah E. C. Dudley (1869–1906)

Sarah Dudley Pettey initiated the Woman's Column in the *Star of Zion*, the weekly newspaper of the African Methodist Episcopal (AME) Zion Church. She began writing the column in 1896, during a period in which she toured the United States, speaking on behalf of woman suffrage and African-American political rights. Pettey championed equal opportunity for women in the AME Zion Church hierarchy, and her husband, Bishop Charles Calvin Pettey, ordained the first woman elder in that denomination in 1897. In her column, Pettey argued for full political participation for black Americans in the South and for the right of African-American men and women

to pursue a classical education and to participate in the industrialization of the New South. Her article "What Role Is the Educated Negro Woman to Play in the Uplifting of Her Race?" appeared in D. W. Culp's *Twentieth-Century Negro Literature* (1902).

Sarah Dudley was born in New Bern, North Carolina, in 1869, the daughter of a state representative. She graduated with honors from Scotia Seminary in Concord, North Carolina, in 1883. After graduation she taught at New Bern's grade school and at the state Normal School located there. Six years later she married Charles Calvin Pettey, a North Carolina native who had graduated from Biddle Memorial Institute in Charlotte. In addition to Pettey's two daughters, the couple had five children. Bishop Pettey supported his wife's journalistic career and her suffrage activism. Sarah Dudley Pettey served as a national officer in the AME Zion Woman's Home and Foreign Missionary Society from 1892–1900, during which time she and her husband traveled widely in the United States and Europe. Widowed at the age of thirty-one, Pettey died in 1906 after a short illness. She was thirty-seven.

GLENDA ELIZABETH GILMORE

Philadelphia Female Anti-Slavery Society

For thirty-six years, from 1833 until 1870, the members of the Philadelphia Female Anti-Slavery Society labored in the crusade against slavery and discrimination. Besides being champions of black emancipation, the members of the society pursued their work as a pioneering interracial group steadfastly dedicated to racial and sexual equality. Black women played significant roles in charting the society's progressive philosophical agenda over those years.

The society had a modest beginning, when on December 9, 1833, an interracial group of twenty-one women met at Catherine McDurmot's schoolroom in Philadelphia. The constitution they adopted set forth their firm belief that slavery and prejudice against color were contrary to both the laws of God and the ideals stated in the Declaration of Independence. Opposed to the use of physical force or political affiliations, the society employed a moral suasion strategy to meet its goals.

Of the forty-two women who became the society's charter members, nine were black. Lucretia Mott, Esther Moore, Rebecca Buffum, and other white abolitionists were joined by their black colleagues, namely Charlotte Forten and her three daughters, Harriet D. Purvis, Sarah Louisa **Forten**, and Margaretta **Forten**. Grace Douglass, Mary Woods, Lydia White, Margaret Bowser, and Sarah McCrummel also signed the charter, while **Sarah Mapps Douglass**, Grace Douglas's daughter, joined the organization shortly thereafter. In subsequent years, other black women, including Anna Woods, Debrah Coates, Hannah Coates, Amerlia M. Bogle, and Amy Matalida Cassey, became members.

The black member's activism characterized the organization. The society's powerful board of managers, which set policy and allocated finances, typically had one or two black members. During 1836, Sarah Forten and Sarah McCrummel served on the twelve-member board. In 1837, Sarah Forten and Grace Douglass joined their white colleagues, Lucretia Mott and three others, to form a six-member board of managers. Black members helped coordinate the

society's annual fairs to raise funds for the emancipation cause. From 1866 to 1868, Harriet Purvis and her daughter, Hattie Purvis, Jr., worked on the fairs. The society also actively supported black education in Philadelphia by visiting schools and distributing books to students. For nine consecutive years, from 1840 to 1849, the society's education committee, which included several black members, allocated $120 annually to finance a school taught by Sarah Mapps Douglass. Additional funds were spent in January 1847 to purchase a stove for the school.

Other activities involving the society's black members included raising money to build an antislavery hall, distributing antislavery literature and periodicals, and spearheading petition campaigns to abolish slavery in the District of Columbia. In 1857, **Sarah Parker Remond**, a black abolitionist from Boston, reported to the society on her antislavery work in Ohio. Harriet Purvis introduced Remond to the society. The women also worked with Robert Purvis and other black Americans of the Philadelphia Vigilant Committee by donating money to clothe, feed, and transport slaves fleeing the South.

Thus, with the close of the Civil War and the ratification of the post-Civil War constitutional amendments, members of the society determined that their work was finished. Resolutions offered at the final meeting of the society, on March 21, 1870, celebrated the occasion. "Whereas," began the resolution offered by Margaretta Forten, "the object for which this Association was organized is thus accomplished, therefore resolved, that the Philadelphia Female Anti-Slavery Society, grateful for the part allotted to it in this great work, rejoicing in the

victory which has concluded the long conflict between slavery and Freedom in
America, does hereby disband." The women
of the society had much to celebrate. As a
model of racial equality and cooperative
sisterhood for almost four decades, the society's members could rejoice that their efforts
to achieve black emancipation had been successful.

JANICE SUMLER-EDMOND

Plato, Ann   (1820?–?)

The first black woman to publish a book of
essays in the United States was born and died
in obscurity. But her need to express her
thoughts and feelings pushed through the
limitations of her position and guaranteed
her a place in history.

Ann Plato was born in Hartford, Connecticut, probably in about 1820. As a very
young women, she became a teacher. She
was a devout Congregationalist in a community where that was the principal
denomination. From the information available in her poetry, she had a brother named
Henry who died when she was just a child.

Ann Plato's book, *Essays: Including Biographies and Miscellaneous Pieces in Prose
and Poetry*, was published in 1841. She was
only about twenty years old at the time.
Some of the pieces in the book were written
when she was fourteen or fifteen.

There are sixteen essays in the book, dealing with death and the changing of the
seasons, as well as with religion, benevolence, employment, and education. They are
not particularly original or elegantly written, but they are of enormous importance
historically. This was only the second book
ever published by an African-American
woman. And the first, a book of poems by

Phillis Wheatley, had been published almost
seventy years before.

There are also four short biographies in
the book. They detail the lives of young,
middle-class black women who died young.
Her subjects—Louisa Sebury, Julia Ann Pell,
Eliza Loomis Sherman, and Elizabeth
Low—led sheltered lives, but they lived in
the shadow of their enslaved sisters and
brothers.

Finally, there are twenty poems in the
volume. It is in the poetry that most of what
we know about Ann Plato is revealed. Apart
from the death of her brother, we learn
about her teaching and about her church
membership, and what she thought about
these things. Eleven of the poems are about
death. Even in the romantic, death-obsessed
nineteenth century, that is a high proportion.

In a way, it is good that we know so little
about this young writer. Like the soldier
buried in the Tomb of the Unknown Soldier
in Washington, D. C., she could be any
young black woman of her time. The details
are unimportant. The act of expression is
everything.

KATHLEEN THOMPSON

Prince, Lucy Terry   (c. 1730–1821)

Lucy Terry Prince led a remarkable life as
advocate, devoted mother, wife, and poet.
Since documentation of her early life is
sketchy, biographers speculate that Lucy
Terry was born in Africa, enslaved there,
and brought to Bristol, Rhode Island, where
at about age five she was bought by
Ebenezer Wells. Records show that Wells
had her baptized in his home in Deerfield,
Massachusetts, on June 15, 1735, and that
he apparently taught her to read and write.

Lucy Terry remained in slavery until 1756 when she married Abijah Prince, who bought her freedom from Wells.

Lucy Terry Prince is perhaps best known for her rhymed poem "Bars Fight," which has been called the most accurate account of an Indian raid that occurred on August 25, 1746, in that part of Deerfield known as "The Bars." Although Prince's poem was not published until 1855 (in Josiah Gilbert Holland's *History of Western Massachusetts*), it was written over a century earlier in the year of the raid and almost certainly makes Prince the first black poet in America.

"Bars Fight" is Prince's single poem, but it is not the only accomplishment in her long, full life. She was twenty-six when she married Abijah, who was twenty-five years her senior and by all accounts an extraordinary man. Abijah had served four years in the militia during the French and Indian War (1744–48), and perhaps because of this military service (no one knows for certain) was granted his freedom and three parcels of land in Northfield, Massachusetts. The Princes paid taxes in Northfield but remained in Deerfield until they moved in the 1760s to a hundred-acre lot in Guilford, Massachusetts, that had been left to Abijah by an employer, Deacon Samuel Field. Later, Abijah became one of the fifty-five original grantees and founders of the town of Sunderland, Vermont, where he owned another one-hundred-acre farm.

It was while they lived in Guilford that Lucy Prince first demonstrated a willingness to defend her rights in a public debate. In 1785, white neighbors, the Noyeses, threatened the Prince's lives and property, tearing down fences and burning haystacks. Lucy appealed in person to Governor Thomas Chittenden and his council for protection from these assaults, and on June 7, 1785, the council ordered the selectmen of the town to defend the Princes.

Between 1757 and 1769, Lucy and Abijah had six children: Caesar (January 14, 1757), Durexa (June 1, 1758), Drucella (August 7, 1760), Festus (December 12, 1763), Tatnai (September 2, 1765), and Abijah, Jr. (June 12, 1769). The two oldest sons, Caesar and Festus, enlisted in the militia during the American Revolution. Although Festus was only fifteen at the time, he falsified his age and served for three years as an artilleryman. After the war he married a white woman and settled on a farm in Sunderland. Not much is known of the other children except that Durexa acquired a reputation as a poet, and Tatnai became a shopkeeper in Salem, New York.

We do know that the education of her youngest child, Abijah, Jr., was the impetus for another of Prince's appeals to public authority, when she tried, unsuccessfully, to gain her son's admission to Williams College. On that occasion Prince spoke for three hours before the college trustees, recounting her family's military contributions, quoting the law and the Bible, and reminding her audience of what she considered her friendship with the late Colonel Ephraim Williams, whose property bequeathal had established the Free School that became Williams College in October 1793. Despite her efforts, however, Prince's son was not admitted.

A short time later, Prince once again engaged in public debate to establish her rights by pleading a property dispute case before the U.S. Supreme Court. Her neighbor, Colonel Eli Bronson, had claimed part of the Sunderland lot that Abijah had been granted by King George III. The town could not settle the matter and the lawsuit eventually reached the Supreme Court. Prince was represented by Isaac Tichnor, who later be-came governor of Vermont, but it was she who presented the argument before the court with Justice Samuel Chase of Balti-more presiding. Bronson's attorneys, prominent jurist Stephen R. Bradley and Royall Tyler, the poet and later chief justice of Vermont, faced a formidable adversary in Lucy Prince. Although there is no surviving record of the case, George Sheldon, a nine-teenth-century historian, writes that the court ruled in her favor and Justice Chase declared her argument exceptional, "better than he had heard from any lawyer at the Vermont bar."

In 1803, at age seventy-three, Prince moved to Sunderland. Abijah had died nine years earlier and was buried at Bennington, some eighteen miles from Sunderland. As evidence of her fortitude and strength, Prince made an annual visit by horseback to her husband's grave until 1821, the year of her death. The August 21, 1821, obituary that appeared in the *Franklin Herald* of Greenfield, Massachusetts, is a fitting sum-mary of Lucy Prince's life: "In this remarkable woman there was an assemblage of qualities rarely to be found among her sex. Her volubility was exceeded by none, and in general the fluency of her speech captivated all around her, and was not des-titute of instruction and edification. She was much respected among her acquaintance, who treated her with a degree of deference."

BARS FIGHT

August 'twas the twenty-fifth,
Seventeen hundred forty-six
The Indians did in ambush lay,
Some very valient men to slay,
The names of whom I'll not leave out.

Samuel Allen like a hero fout,
And though he was so brave and bold,
His face no more shall we behold.
Eleazer Hawks was killed outright,
Before he had time to fight,—
Before he did the Indians see,
Was shot and killed immediately.
Oliver Amsden he was slain,
Which caused his friends much grief
    and pain.
Simeon Amsden they found dead,
Not many rods distant from his head.
Adonijah Gillett we do hear
Did lose his life which was so dear.
John Sadley fled across the water,
And thus escaped the dreadful slaughter.
Eunice Allen see the Indians coming,
And hopes to save herself by running,
And had not her petticoats stopped her,
The awful creatures had not catched her,
Nor tommy hawked her on her head,
And left her on the ground for dead.
Young Samuel Allen, Oh lack-a-day!
Was taken and carried to Canada.

JAN FURMAN

Prince, Nancy Gardner (1799–c. 1856)

The preface to the second edition of Nancy Prince's autobiography, *A Narrative of the Life and Travels of Mrs. Nancy Prince* (1853), is brief, yet it reflects the essential nature of her character: she was a coura-geous, resilient, fervently religious reformer who chose different paths from the ones that most women were expected to follow during the era of slavery, as mounting tensions led to the Civil War. Prince had traveled to Europe; she had lived and worked in Russia (1824–33) and Jamaica (1840–41; 1842), bridging cultural and geographical gaps in her fight against slavery, her evangelical work, and her advocacy for women's rights.

Nancy Gardner was born in 1799 in Newburyport, Massachusetts, to free parents. Her maternal grandfather, Tobias Wornton, a slave, fought at Bunker Hill; her maternal grandmother was a Native American captured by the English. Prince's father, Thomas Gardner—a black seaman who survived at sea better than on land—died when she was three months old. Gardner's stepfather, Money Vose, entertained her with stories of his escape from slavery. After his death, Gardner's mother suffered a mental collapse and Gardner essentially took over the parenting role for six children. The family experienced dire poverty and homelessness, forcing Gardner, on one occasion, to rescue her sister from a brothel.

After marrying Nero Prince, a seaman, a founding member of the Prince Hall Freemasons, and a servant in Russia's imperial court in 1824, Prince traveled through Europe en route to Russia. Her narrative relates romantic and harrowing adventures in Russia, where Prince boarded children, operated a sewing business, and became involved in religious affairs.

Prince went to Jamaica in 1840 and 1842, believing she could help convert and educate Jamaica's emancipated slaves. Identifying with their struggles, she felt vindicated against apologists of slavery when she saw that newly freed Jamaicans could prosper. However, because of widespread violence between former slaves and masters, corruption within the ranks of evangelists, and their alleged abuse of her (she stated that they attempted to rob her), Prince made a perilous journey home.

Little is known of Prince after the 1856 edition of her narrative, but the aspects of her life that are omitted from the narrative—perhaps for her own protection—are just as revealing. These include her 1841 letter to William Lloyd Garrison protesting racist treatment aboard a steamboat, her leadership in attacking a slaveholder tracking a runaway (1847), and her participation in the 1854 National Woman's Rights Convention.

AUSTRALIA TARVER

R

Ray, Henrietta (1808–1836)

Henrietta Green Regulus Ray was an activist among free African Americans in New York City during the 1820s and 1830s. She was one of many urban women whose access to education and property propelled them into benevolent, self-help, and community uplift work in the antebellum years.

Little is known of Henrietta Green's early life, except that she was a native New Yorker, lived in the home of African-American newspaper editor Samuel E. Cornish for three years, acquired a basic education, and pursued a "useful trade." Sometime before 1828, she married Laurent (Lawrence) D. Regulus, the shoemaker son of Dominique Regulus, a French merchant residing in both St. Thomas (Virgin Islands) and New York, and an Afro-Caribbean woman named Delaydo. Regulus died in 1828, leaving Henrietta a house in which she lived with her second husband, Charles B. Ray, after their 1834 marriage. Charles Ray was a young Massachusetts native who, driven from a theological seminary by racial prejudice, had moved to New York City in 1832 where he opened a boot and shoe store. Later he became a well-known New York minister, newspaper editor, political activist, and community leader. The Rays had one child, Matilda, born in January 1836, who at the age of six months died of tuberculosis, the same ailment that killed her mother.

From 1828 until her death on October 27, 1836, Henrietta Regulus Ray played an active part in forming and running free black women's educational and self-help organizations. After participating in establishing the African Dorcas Association, a group devoted to providing clothing to children attending the African Free School, she became the Association's assistant secretary in 1828. Six years later, she became the first president of the New York Female Literary Society (sometimes referred to as the Colored Ladie's Literary Society), "formed for the purpose of acquiring literary and scientific knowledge" and dedicated both to women's self-help and self-improvement and to racial uplift. Like African-American women's literary societies in other Northern cities, the Female Literary Society combined educational activities with abolitionist concerns, raising funds to assist runaway slaves and donating money to support a petition campaign aimed at ending slavery in Washington, D.C.

In her brief life, Henrietta Regulus Ray exemplified the experiences of members of northern free black women's organizations: creating multifaceted groups, combining benevolence with reform, and associating individual improvement with the advancement of the race. Her husband and his second wife, Charlotte Burroughs, honored her by naming one of their seven children for her, Henrietta Cordelia Ray, whose career as a student at New York University and as a poet perhaps fulfilled some of the aspirations of the woman for whom she was named.

ANNE BOYLAN

Remond, Sarah Parker (1826–1894)

"I appeal on behalf of four millions of men, women, and children who are chattels in the Southern States of America. Not because they are identical with my race and color, though I am proud of that identity, but because they are men and women. The sum of sixteen hundred millions of dollars is invested in their bones, sinews, and flesh—is this not sufficient reason why all the friends of humanity should not endeavor with all their might and power, to overturn the vile systems of slavery." Sarah Parker Remond, a lady of no ordinary character, made this statement during a lecture on slavery in Warrington, England, in 1859. A free person of color, she was touring Britain hoping to impress on the British people the evils of slavery in the United States and to implore them to endorse propositions protesting this evil as a blot on the civilized world.

Sarah Parker Remond was born in Salem, Massachusetts, on June 6, 1826, one of eight children of John and Nancy Lenox Remond. She received a limited education in the primary schools and was primarily self-educated by reading newspapers, books, and pamphlets she borrowed from friends or purchased from the Anti-Slavery Society depositories, which sold many titles at cheap prices.

Raised in a family that included many abolitionists, from childhood Remond learned of the horrors of slavery and witnessed many incidents involving the Underground Railroad. Her home was a haven for black and white abolitionists. She regularly attended antislavery lectures in Salem and Boston. Charles Lenox Remond, her older brother, was a well-known antislavery lecturer in the United States and Great Britain. Along with household duties, cooking and sewing, Nancy Remond taught her daughters to seek liberty in a lawful manner and that being black was no crime.

Sarah Remond determined early in life to fight the prejudice she constantly faced because of her color. In May 1853, she was denied a seat, for which she had a ticket, to attend a performance of the opera *Don Pasquale* at the Howard Athenaeum in Boston. Remond was forcibly ejected from the theater and pushed down the stairs, and suffered an injury as a result of this abuse. She sued the managers of the theater and won her suit. The small award of $500 she received was unsatisfactory compensation

Sarah Parker Remond's commitment to the cause of abolition took her to England in 1859. She gave more than forty-five speeches from 1859 to 1861 to British audiences, enlisting their aid in the antislavery movement. (COURTESY, ESSEX INSTITUTE, SALEM, MASSACHUSETTS)

for her injury and embarrassment. Her object, however, was not to make money from the case but to defend a right.

In 1856, Remond accompanied her brother Charles on his antislavery lecture tour in New York State. She spoke briefly at some of the meetings, and gained confidence in her ability to lecture. She addressed several antislavery meetings in New York, Massachusetts, Ohio, Michigan, and Pennsylvania between 1856 and 1858. Sarah and her brother faced prejudice on many occasions. Some boarding houses and hotels refused to accept them, and special accommodations had to be found in private homes.

On December 28, 1858, Sarah Parker Remond left Boston in the steamer *Arabia* for Liverpool to enlist the aid of the English people in the American antislavery movement. Accompanied by Samuel May, Jr., she arrived in Liverpool on January 12, 1859, after a frightening trip. The ship had been covered with ice and snow. It rolled and tossed so much that many passengers were sick, including Remond, who regained her strength after a few days of recuperation at the home of William Robson in Warrington.

At Tuckerman Institute on January 21, 1859, Remond gave her first antislavery lecture on the free soil of Britain. Without notes, she eloquently spoke of the inhuman treatment of slaves in the United States. Her shocking stories of atrocities brought tears to the eyes of many listeners.

Between 1859 and 1861, Remond gave over forty-five lectures in eighteen cities and towns in England, three cities in Scotland, and four cities in Ireland. Everywhere the press reported her speeches and the reactions of her audiences. In spite of a heavy lecture schedule, Remond, desirous of furthering her education, attended classes at Bedford College for Ladies,

later a part of the University of London, from October 1859 to mid-1861. She studied history, elocution, music, English literature, French, and Latin.

At the end of the Civil War, Remond lectured on behalf of freedpeople. She was an active member of the London Emancipation Society and the Freedmen's Aid Association in London. These organizations solicited funds and clothing for ex-slaves.

In 1865, she published a letter in the *Daily News* protesting attacks on black people in the London press after an insurrection in Jamaica. One lecture she delivered in London, "The Freeman or the Emancipated Negro of the Southern States of the United States," was published in *The Freedman* (London) in 1867.

Remond visited Rome and Florence on several occasions while living in England. In 1866, she left London and entered the Santa Maria Nuova Hospital in Florence, Italy, as a medical student. She received a diploma certifying her for professional medical practice in 1871. She practiced medicine in Florence, Italy, for more than twenty years. In Florence, on April 25, 1877, Sarah Parker Remond married Lazzaro Pintor, a native of Sardinia.

This remarkable woman from a unique African-American family died on December 13, 1894. She was buried in the Protestant Cemetery in Rome.

DOROTHY PORTER WESLEY

Richards, Fannie M. (1841–1922)

Educator and clubwoman Fannie M. Richards was the first black person to teach in Detroit's public schools.

Richards was born on October 1, 1841, in Fredericksburg, Virginia. She was one of fourteen children of Maria Louise Moore, a free woman of color born in Toronto, and

Adolphe Richards, a British-educated Hispanic with some African ancestry. All of the children received the best private education available, even as Virginia tightened restrictions on black education. The Richardses risked expulsion from the state for educating their children.

When her husband died in 1851, Maria Richards moved the family to Detroit to escape the increasingly hostile atmosphere in Virginia. Detroit had gained a reputation as a center of antislavery activity and had many black settlers. The Richards family soon took its place among the Cultured 40, the educated, white-collar segment of the black community. Fannie's brother John was a barber who was active politically; he became known as Detroit's most eloquent orator.

Richards was educated in the segregated public schools of Detroit and decided to go into teaching. However, no normal school or university in the area would accept black students at that time, so Richards moved to Toronto to study. After graduating from Toronto Normal School in 1863, she returned to Detroit and founded a private school for black children. There was, at the time, only one public school for Detroit's black students.

When Richards learned that a second public school for black children was to open, she applied for a teaching position. She was hired over several other applicants and became the first black teacher in Detroit's public schools. Four years later, she joined with a group of liberal citizens to sue the Detroit Board of Education over its refusal to comply with a Michigan Supreme Court order to integrate the state's schools. She provided funds for the suit and probably served as an advisor to the man who led it, future Michigan governor John Bagley.

Two years later, because of the court ruling in this action, Richards became the first black teacher of white students in Detroit. For the next forty-four years she taught a wide variety of students at Everett School and developed a reputation as an outstanding teacher. She introduced the kindergarten concept to Detroit schools at a time when only Boston and New York had experimented with the idea.

Richards was also a clubwoman, active in charitable pursuits. She helped to found Detroit's Phyllis Wheatley Home for Aged Colored Ladies in 1897 and served as its first president.

Fannie M. Richards died in Detroit on February 13, 1922.

JOHN REID

Ridley, Florida Ruffin (1861–1943)

Florida Ruffin Ridley had for her role model a mother who had achieved distinction in her own right. Born in 1861 in Boston, Massachusetts, Florida Ruffin was the daughter of George Lewis Ruffin and **Josephine St. Pierre Ruffin**, one of the black community's leading clubwomen. She was educated at Boston Teachers College and Boston University and then taught in the Boston public schools. She married Ulysses A. Ridley and had two children. Like her mother, Ridley had a multifaceted career as clubwoman and community activist.

Ridley was active in her community throughout her life. However, it is her work with her mother for which she is primarily remembered. In 1893, along with **Maria Baldwin**, Ruffin and Ridley founded the Woman's Era Club, which was open to women of all races, and Ridley's report to the first meeting is a matter of record. She talked about an antilynching leaflet published by the club, which indicates that the aims of the organization were not primarily social. Ridley spent three years, at one point, working with a kindergarten in Atlanta, Georgia, that was partially supported by the Woman's Era Club.

In 1895, Ridley was one of the organizers of the first national conference of black women. Out of this Boston conference, which was attended by delegates from sixteen states and the District of Columbia, came the National Federation of Afro-American Women, of which Ridley was recording secretary. She was editor of its official magazine, the *Woman's Era*, until 1900. She was also active in the suffrage movement and was a member of the Brookline Equal Suffrage Association from 1894 to 1898.

During World War I, Ridley became deeply involved in activities supporting American soldiers. From 1917 to 1919, she served as executive secretary of the Soldiers Comfort Unit, which evolved into the League of Women for Community Service. She served as executive secretary of the league until 1925. At the same time, she was a member of the board of directors of the Robert Gould Shaw Settlement House. When the Cooperative Committee of Social Agencies was formed to coordinate the services of that house, the Harriet Tubman House, and the Boston Urban League, Ridley returned to her role as editor and took responsibility for its journal, the *Social Service News*.

Florida Ruffin Ridley died in March 1943 in Toledo, Ohio, where she had gone to live with her daughter. She was eighty-two years old.

KATHLEEN THOMPSON

The Rollin Sisters

During the Reconstruction period, the five Rollin sisters were well known socially and politically among the people of Columbia, the South Carolina capital. The sisters were Frances Anne (1845–1901), Charlotte, known as Lottie (b. 1849), Kate (1851–76), Louisa (b. 1858), and Florence (b. 1861). They have been celebrated for their cultural and political influence within the black and white Radical Reconstruction government in South Carolina.

The Rollin family was one of the elite South Carolina families of color descended from emigrants who fled the Haitian Revolution in the late eighteenth century. William and Margaretta Rollin were married in 1844, and they lived in an elegant mansion on American Street in Charleston. William was a fair-skinned mulatto who operated a successful lumberyard and transported lumber by ship between the port of Charleston and South Carolina coastal plantations. He and Margaretta sent all their daughters to private Catholic parish schools for free "colored" people in Charleston then North to Boston and Philadelphia for secondary education. Both of these urban centers had large, free-black networks. Frances, Lottie, Louisa, and Kate attended school in Philadelphia. Lottie and Kate also enrolled at Dr. Dio Lewi's Family School for Young Ladies in Boston.

After the Civil War, the family moved to Columbia. Of the five sisters, Frances, Lottie, and Louisa were the most active in Reconstruction politics. Kate's bad health prevented her from participating as fully as her sisters. She died in 1876, at the age of twenty-five. Kate was said to have been engaged to marry a white South Carolina senator from Colleton County. Little else is known about her.

Of the three political activists, the youngest was Louisa. Like her sisters, Louisa was a feminist and woman suffragist. She addressed the South Carolina House of Representatives in 1869 to urge support for universal suffrage.

Lottie Rollin was well known in South Carolina and in the American Woman Suffrage Association (AWSA). In 1870, she was elected secretary of the South Carolina Woman's Rights Association, an affiliate of the AWSA. In 1871, Lottie led a meeting at the state capital to promote woman suffrage. By 1872, she was elected by her state organization to represent South Carolina as an ex-officio member of the executive committee for AWSA, which met in New York City.

Frances Rollin, who became the wife of William J. Whipper, appears to have been the only sister who married. Through her descendants, more information about her has survived than about her siblings. Frances was a feminist, an educator, and a civil rights activist. She kept company with the leading black abolitionist women in Philadelphia during the antebellum period, including **Sarah M. Douglass** and Charlotte Forten.

Like Charlotte Forten, Frances kept a diary, written during her 1868 sojourn in Boston, the same year she published the biography of the abolitionist and emigrationist Martin R. Delany. She published the book, *The Life and Times of Martin Robison Delany*, under the name Frank A. Rollin. Delany wanted a competent and sympathetic author to write about his life but felt the public would not take the book seriously if the author was known to be female.

Frances Rollin had met Delany when he was a Freedmen's Bureau agent in Charleston and she was teaching with the bureau in the Sea Islands. It was with the help of the bureau that Frances sued the captain of a Sea Islands steamer for refusing to honor her first-class ticket because she was black. Frances won the suit, and the captain was fined.

After completing her book on Delany in 1868, Frances began working for William James Whipper as a law clerk in his Columbia law office. He was born free in Philadelphia, the nephew of black abolitionist William Whipper. In an attempt to escape the racial prejudice in the United States, Whipper's parents took him to Chatham, Canada, to live in a black settlement. During the Civil War, he returned to the states, joined the Union Army, and settled in South Carolina. Whipper served in the state constitutional convention and became a state senator and later a judge. He was a supporter of women's rights, and he married the talented Frances Rollin shortly after he hired her in 1868.

After marriage, Frances taught at Avery Institute, a well-respected black postsecondary education institution in the 1870s and 1880s. She also began a family. Frances and William Whipper conceived five children. The three who survived grew to be successful adults. Their only son, Leigh Whipper, became a well-known stage and screen actor in the 1940s and 1950s.

The oldest surviving Whipper was Winifred. She taught in the "colored" schools at the turn of the century in the District of Columbia. The youngest surviving daughter, Ionia Rollin Whipper, attended **Howard University** Medical College in the 1890s. She did so with the help of her mother, who by then had separated from William Whipper. Frances wrote Whitefield McKinlay, Washington realtor and political ally of

Booker T. Washington, asking for a loan to help pay for Ionia's tuition. France's investment in her daughter was worthwhile: Ionia Whipper became a gynecologist and the founder of the Whipper Home for Unwed Mothers, the only facility of the kind that accepted black girls in the racially segregated nation's capital.

Frances Anne Rollin Whipper died in 1901, shortly after her daughter completed medical school but not before she saw Ionia provide services to the black middle-class Washington, D.C. community that they had adopted. There appear to be no extant records of what happened to Lottie and Louisa Rollin after the Reconstruction era. They both were living in Columbia during the 1880s after their parents separated, and Margaretta moved in with Frances when William Rollin died. The sisters lost most of their wealth and property at the end of the century, as did many black Americans during the depressions of the 1890s and the political setbacks resulting from the conservative Democratic backlash that drove out the radical Republicans following Reconstruction. Nonetheless, the Rollin sisters remain part of the legacy and social history remembered from the era when black Americans significantly influenced the politics of South Carolina.

ROSALYN TERBORG-PENN

Ruffin, Josephine St. Pierre (1842–1924)

Josephine St. Pierre Ruffin was a women's club activist, journalist, and suffragist. She was born in Boston in 1842 to John St. Pierre, a man of African, French, and Indian ancestry, and Eliza Matilda (Menhenick) St. Pierre, a native of Cornwall, England. Her education began in Salem and finished in Boston after its schools were integrated. At sixteen she married George Lewis Ruffin (1834–86), and the couple promptly moved to England to spare themselves and their future family the trials of American racism.

At the outbreak of the Civil War, however, they returned to the United States to help with efforts to abolish slavery. Josephine Ruffin recruited for the colored Fifty-fourth and Fifty-fifth Massachusetts regiments and worked for the U.S. Sanitation Commission. She also became very active in women's clubs and in professional and charitable organizations such as the Associated Charities of Boston, the Massachusetts State Federation of Women's Clubs, and the Boston Kansas Relief Association for black migrants. Through her work for the black weekly paper the *Courant*, she became a member of the New England Women's Press Association.

In February 1893, Ruffin founded the **New Era Club** with her daughter, Florida, who joined her mother in much of her work, and **Maria Baldwin**, a Boston school principal. Its aims were to organize a number of kindergartens in Boston and one in Georgia and to keep the women's clubs in touch with each other with regular reports. Ruffin served as editor of the club's monthly journal, the *Woman's Era*, the first newspaper published by black women. As president of the club, Ruffin became a member of the Massachusetts State Federation of Women's Clubs.

Ruffin participated in two nineteenth-century traditions: black women's alliance with white abolitionists and suffragists, and black women's separation into their own service-oriented clubs. African-American women began organizing antislavery and literary societies in the 1830s and joined white women in the suffrage movement that began in the 1840s. Antislavery work, in particular, introduced white women and free Northern black Americans to activism and trained them for future agitation in other areas.

Ruffin helped found both colored and integrated organizations, such as the Massachusetts School Suffrage Association, and she became friends with such prominent activists as Julia Ward Howe and Lucy Stone. As the reaction against integration stiffened in the late nineteenth century, however, Ruffin and other black women stopped trying to join white organizations and formed their own.

Ruffin was at the center of a well-publicized incident. In 1900, the General Federation of Women's Clubs held its biennial meeting in Milwaukee. Ruffin was eligible to attend through her membership in the Massachusetts Federation of Women's Clubs, and because she was the New Era Club's president, she was automatically a vice president of the general federation. She was also an alternate delegate for the meeting through her membership in another predominantly white organization, the New England Women's Press Association. Ruffin insisted, however, on going as the president of the New Era Club. When the executive board discovered that all of the club's members were black women, they would not accept Ruffin's credentials or seat her as a vice president. Someone even tried to snatch her badge on the convention floor, but Ruffin resisted. She also refused the attempt to refund her registration fee. The policy that she was acceptable only as a delegate from a white club was typical of a number of national organizations, such as the

When racists moved to oust her from the biennial meeting of the General Federation of Women's Clubs, Josephine St. Pierre Ruffin refused to compromise. "It was an opportunity which I did not seek," she said in a historic explanation of her courageous actions, "but which I did not shirk."
(SCHOMBURG CENTER)

Women's Christian Temperance Union and the Young Women's Christian Association.

The Massachusetts delegation sent a letter of protest to the executive board. Delegates from Iowa, Utah, and a majority of the delegates from Northern states sided with them, but the Southern delegates, led by president Rebecca Lowe, skillfully used parliamentary procedures to keep the issue from discussion in an open meeting. Ironically, Lowe herself had done a great deal of work to establish kindergartens for black children.

Ruffin regarded the matter calmly, reporting that "I did not feel angry. It was an issue clearly set before the women of the country. It was an opportunity which I did not seek, but which I did not shirk." The president of the Massachusetts general federation opined that

Ruffin had "demonstrated the splendid possibilities of her race."

During the controversy, a letter of support for Ruffin was written to the *Woman's Journal*, a feminist newspaper. The writer decried "American women's desire to inflict shame and humiliation upon other women," then warned that "it is a most dangerous policy to alienate from the common national interest so large a body as is constituted by the colored population of the United States. . . . The Negro has hitherto been intensely American in his feelings and ambitions," and white people should not recklessly seek to "denationalize him." The many undesirable results, according to the writer, might include "weakening our strength in case of war."

One of Ruffin's greatest accomplishments came in response to an inflammatory letter concerning black women's character. In 1895, the president of the Missouri Press Association, James W. Jacks, wrote to Florence Belgarnie, an Englishwoman who served as secretary of the Antislavery Society of England. Belgarnie had become sympathetic to the struggles of black Americans through the work of **Ida B. Wells**. Jack's letter accused black women of having "no sense of virtue and of being altogether without character," as well as being "prostitutes, thieves, and liars." This was no isolated charge. The defense of their moral character was a recurring, important issue for black women. The ability of white men to coerce black women into sexual relations, both during slavery and afterward, paradoxically led to a stereotype of black women as being of easy virtue.

Copies of Jack's letter were circulated among clubs across the country. Ruffin responded with a manifesto titled "A Call: Let Us Confer Together." Extending her invitation "to all colored women of America, members of any society or not," Ruffin proposed the first national convention of black women, to carry out what she called "our right and our bounden duty . . . to teach an ignorant and suspicious world that our aims and interests are identical with those of all good aspiring women." This and other goals must be achieved, she wrote, "for the sake of thousands of self-sacrificing young women, teaching and preaching in lonely southern backwoods, for the noble army of mothers . . . whose intelligence is only limited by their opportunity to get at books, for the sake of the fine cultured women who have carried off the honors in school here and often abroad."

She proposed to spread the message "not by noisy protestations of what we are not, but by a dignified showing of what we are and hope to become." She emphasized that "We are not drawing the color line. . . . We are not alienating or withdrawing, we are only coming to the front, willing to join any others in the same work."

Ruffin maintained that the conference could provide mutual encouragement and inspiration as well as the chance to discuss black people's special interests. She also was interested in general questions of the day—temperance, morality, higher education, hygiene, and the home. Most important, she believed, was the chance to offer help to black women who lacked "opportunity, not only to do more, but to be more." Ruffin was irked that too many Americans "glibly" described black women as, "for the most part, ignorant and immoral, some exceptions of course, but these don't count." Ruffin argued that "because all refutation has only been tried by individual work, the charge has never been crushed."

The conference's resolutions included working to end discrimination against black labor and championing homemaking and purchasing homes. The participants called for the abolition of segregated transportation and the convict lease system, and they proposed measures to be taken against the destruction of black people's rights that had resulted from the withdrawal of federal troops from the South. They also commended the Republican Party for condemning lynching in its platform and voiced regret that the Democrats did not.

One hundred women from twenty clubs in ten states attended the conference and formed the National Federation of Afro-American Women. It ultimately united thirty-six clubs in twelve states. The federation merged in 1896 with the Colored Women's League to form the **National Association of Colored Women**, of which Ruffin became the first vice president.

In some ways, black and white women's clubs were similar: they were primarily middle class with mostly Protestant members, and they emphasized education, material progress, and the importance of the home and a woman's influence in it. The clubs differed, however, in that the gap between the upper class and others was not as great for black Americans as it was within white society. Black clubwomen were more likely to see their heritage and future as tied to those of the less fortunate. The motto of the National Association of Colored Women made this clear: "Lifting as We Climb."

The charitable aims of black clubs also tended to be direct and specific: providing an individual with money for an education, granting money to a school district, and generally addressing the needs of the aged, the poor, the sick, and the young. Club-

woman Fannie Barrier Williams observed that "among white women the club is the onward movement of the already uplifted. Among colored women the club is the effort of the few competent in behalf of the many incompetent." Because black women were largely excluded from major national organizations except in certain areas, such as New England, and from labor unions, including the black National Labor Union, local clubs took on a greater significance.

Ruffin was able to pursue her philanthropic callings because of the financial position that she and her family enjoyed. Her husband was born into a prominent black family that had moved from Richmond to Boston. On the young couple's return from England in 1858, George Ruffin worked as a barber—a common occupation among the African-American middle class—until he graduated from Harvard Law School in 1869. Later he became a state legislator, a Boston city councilman, and, in 1883, Boston's first black municipal judge. Of their three sons, one became a lawyer, another an inventor and manufacturer, and the third an organist; their daughter taught in Boston's public schools. Josephine Ruffin provided convincing evidence against those who argued that black women who were college graduates might not be fit to manage households and rear children.

In 1889, Ruffin gave a speech, "An Open Letter to the Educational League of Georgia," that demonstrated both the diplomacy that black leaders often had to employ when dealing with white people and the boldness of this particular woman. She complimented the group of Southern white women on undertaking "the moral training of the colored children of Georgia" but chastised them nonetheless:

One of the saddest things about the sad condition of affairs in the South has been the utter indifference which Southern women, who were guarded with unheard of fidelity during the [Civil] war, have manifested to the mental and moral welfare of the children of their faithful slaves, who, in the language of Henry Grady, placed a black mass of loyalty between them and dishonor. This was a rare opportunity for you to have shown your gratitude to your slaves and your interest in their future welfare.

These words possess an intriguing subtext; they mine the Confederacy's lost-cause romance of the faithful slave in order to invoke the notion of paternalism that the Old South used to defend slavery as not merely a benign institution but a benevolent one. Ruffin took her audience to task, especially for persecuting Northern teachers "simply because they were doing your work," which she said Southern women were too bitter or too poor to do. Speaking of the antilynching campaign, she called on Southern women "to join in this great altruistic movement of the age and endeavor to lift up the degraded and ignorant, rather than to exterminate them. . . . If you had done your duty to them at the close of the war," she argued, "you would not now be confronted with a condition which you feel it necessary to check, in obedience to that great first law of nature—self-protection." She argued that these women should dismiss any critics, since "the South has suffered too much already from that kind of false pride to let it longer keep her recreant to the spirit of the age." Clearly, black leaders of the late nineteenth century had to maintain a delicate balance as they tried to help create a New South.

After the New Era Club disbanded in 1903, Ruffin helped found the Association for the Promotion of Child Training in the South, the Boston branch of the National Association for the Advancement of Colored People, and the League of Women for Community Service, adding to the long list of organizations with which she had been affiliated. She also served in the New England Women's Club and organized funding for the Mount Coffee School in Liberia.

Two weeks before Ruffin's death, she attended the annual meeting of the League of Women for Community Service, where she cast her vote and waited until 1:00 A.M. for the outcome. She died of nephritis at the age of eighty-one and was buried in Cambridge at the Mount Auburn Cemetery.

ELIZABETH FORTSON ARROYO

S

Scott, Minnie Taylor (1872–1914)

Clubwoman Minnie Taylor Scott of Indiana represents many women of her era—second generation out of slavery, member of an extended family of achievers, and a hard worker dedicated to racial uplift. She also represents African-American women who have kept the family legacy and passed it down to others. The major source of information about her life comes from her family Bible, which was maintained and passed from her grandmother, Marie Woods, to other generations of women in the family.

Scott's mother, Emma Woods Taylor, maintained a list of all of the women in her family, beginning with her mother, Marie Woods, a mulatto slave from North Carolina. Both Emma and her husband, William Taylor, were born into slavery. Like many North Carolina freedpeople, they migrated to the Midwest after emancipation, where they settled in Indianapolis, Indiana. Their daughter, Minnie, was born on October 25, 1872, and named for one of her mother's sisters. Their son, Marshall Woods Taylor, was born in 1878. By the time he was twenty-one, he had become nationally acclaimed as a cyclist, nicknamed Major. In 1899, he won the U.S. and World sprint championships. Racial prejudice, however, drove Major Taylor to become an expatriate who took his celebrated skill to Europe and Australia. In 1982, the city of his birth honored him by naming its first cycling arena the Major Taylor Velodrome.

Minnie Taylor decided to take a different path by staying in her home state to work with other women of color who assisted their own people. She married William Aaron Scott, whose parents had been freed by their North Carolina master before emancipation and sent by ox cart to the Midwest. The Scotts also settled in Indianapolis, where several of their descendants achieved success in education, business, and the arts. One son, Rufus, became a vaudeville actor and performed with Bert Williams. Another son, Edward, went to college and became a teacher. His son, William Edouard Scott, became a celebrated artist whose works can be found in the Indiana Museum of Art, the Tuskegee University Museum, and the DuSable Museum in Chicago.

Minnie Scott lived in one of the houses on the Scott family compound with an extended family of achievers. Her two children, Aaron and Emma, were encouraged to become professionals at a time when black families paid dearly for higher education. Nonetheless, Aaron became a pharmacist and the owner of a drugstore in Indianapolis, and Emma became a teacher. Their grandmother, Emma Taylor, cared for them during most of their lives as Minnie Scott traveled throughout the state and the country organizing other black women to uplift their communities.

She began in Indianapolis during the 1890s while her children were small. Minnie

Scott was one of the early presidents of the Alpha Home in Indianapolis. The home was founded in 1886 by the former slave Elizabeth Goff as a refuge for impoverished and homeless former slave women. By 1887, the home had opened its doors to former slave men also. Although Marion County, Indiana, allocated funds to assist the home, the meager amount was never enough. As a result, black Indianapolis clubwomen like Minnie Scott regularly raised funds to support it. Throughout the 1890s and 1900s, the Alpha Home picnic in July and the Emancipation picnic in August raised funds for the home.

As a pioneer in the Indiana women's club movement, Minnie T. Scott functioned on the state and national levels. She was the second president of the Indiana State Federation of Colored Women's Clubs, serving from 1907 until her sudden death in 1914. As president, she represented the women of her state on the national level in the **National Association of Colored Women** (NACW) conventions. The year of Scott's death, Minnie M. Scott of Toledo, Ohio, became prominent in the NACW leadership. As a result, the activities of the two women are sometimes confused, and Minnie T. is listed in NACW as the person from Toledo.

Minnie T. Scott's untimely death at the age of forty-two left a void for her family and the women she served. Her daughter, Emma, was still in high school, and her son, Aaron, was in college. Minnie Scott's legacy and extended family continued as her mother, her husband, and his relatives kept the family together. Consequently, the children were able to complete college. Family members say that Minnie Scott died of overwork and the pressures of being a leader in the women's club movement. Similar rea-sons have been given for the early demise of many other black women leaders who labored to uplift their race.

ROSALYN TERBORG-PENN

Selika, Marie Smith   (c. 1849–1937)

Marie Smith Selika, concert and operatic soprano, was one of the small group of internationally recognized black women singers during the second half of the nineteenth century. Selika, like her contemporaries, studied with European voice teachers and entrusted her career to a series of concert managers.

Marie Smith Williams adopted the stage name "Selika," the name of the leading female character in Meyerbeer's opera *L'Africaine*. The black press reported that Selika performed this role in a stage production at the Academy of Music in Philadelphia. She was often referred to as the "Queen of Staccato" for her sensational singing of E. W. Mulder's "Polka Staccato."

Little information is available on Selika prior to 1875, except that she was born c. 1849 in Natchez, Mississippi, and soon after the family moved to Cincinnati, Ohio. She studied voice as a child under the patronage of a wealthy white family who arranged for her lessons with a professional teacher. Between 1873 and 1876, she moved to San Francisco where she continued her voice studies with Signora G. Bianchi and made her West Coast debut in 1876. She met her husband, Sampson Williams, in Chicago, where both studied with Antonio Farini, who taught the so-called Italian method.

Selika first appeared in Philadelphia on November 21, 1878, accompanied by Thomas A. Beckett at the Academy of Mu-

Musical history was made on October 12, 1896, when Marie Selika joined Sissieretta Jones and Flora Batson on the stage of New York City's Carnegie Hall. The three leading black singers of their time thrilled a rapt audience. (SCHOMBURG CENTER)

sic. The following year she appeared at Steinway Hall in New York. From 1882 to 1885, Selika and her husband toured Europe, performing in Paris, Russia, Germany, and England, and giving a command performance for Queen Victoria at St. James' Hall in October 1883. She performed at the Musée du Nord in Brussels and sang Weber's *Der Freischütz* in Germany. The press reported

that the European trips provided excellent musical experiences for Selika and Sampson Williams.

From 1885 to 1891, the Williamses toured the United States giving benefit recitals and making church appearances, sometimes with other artists. After a second European tour in 1891, Selika and her husband, now called "Signor Velosko," sang in the West Indies. Selika performed at the Chicago World's Fair in 1893 and soon after the couple settled in Cleveland, Ohio. On October 12, 1896, Selika, **Sissieretta Jones**, and **Flora Batson**—the three leading black singers of the period—sang together at New York City's Carnegie Hall.

After her husband's death in 1911 and with her career in decline, Selika accepted a teaching position at the Martin-Smith Music School in New York City. A testimonial concert in her honor was given in 1919 at which she performed. She was active as a private teacher until her death on May 19, 1937, in New York City.

Selika reigned for almost three decades as a queen of song in the United States and Europe. She was the first concert coloratura in African-American music culture. As a tribute to her vocal excellence, Frederick G. Carnes wrote *Selika, A Grand Vocal Waltz of Magic*, which included staccato passages, trills, and vocal cadenzas.

ELLISTINE P. LEWIS

Simpson, Georgiana (1866–1944)

In 1921, at the age of fifty-five, Georgiana Simpson became the first black American woman to earn a Ph.D. Georgiana Simpson was born and raised in the District of Columbia. She attended Washington, D.C., public schools and graduated from the normal school under the leadership of **Dr. Lucy Moten.** In 1885, at the age of nineteen, Simpson became an elementary school teacher.

Simpson studied German language and literature in Germany then returned to Washington, D.C., to teach German at Dunbar High School (formerly the M Street School). Throughout her teaching career, Simpson attended summer sessions at the University of Chicago and Harvard University. During this period she received her B.A. degree in German from the University of Chicago.

Simpson was awarded a Ph.D. in German from the University of Chicago in 1921. (Two other black women received Ph.D.s in 1921: Sadie Tanner Mossell [Alexander] and Eva Dykes, but in order of actual receipt, Simpson's was awarded first.) After completing her Ph.D., Simpson undertook postdoctoral study in French language and literature. A dedicated and hard-working scholar, Simpson edited Grangon La Coste's *Toussaint L'Ouverture* in 1924. This text is frequently used by college French instructors.

Simpson left Dunbar High School in 1931, accepting a professorship at **Howard University**. A beloved and respected teacher and scholar, Simpson retired from Howard University in 1939. She died in 1944. In 1976, she received a posthumous achievement award from the National Association of Black Professional Women.

CATHERINE JOHNSON

When, in 1921, Georgiana Simpson became the second black American woman to earn a Ph.D., she was fifty-five years old. At sixty-five, she became a professor at Howard University. (MOORLAND-SPINGARN)

Slew, Jenny (b.c. 1719)

It is commonly assumed that women did not appear as advocates before American courts until the late nineteenth century when they were allowed to enter the legal profession. However, in 1766 John Adams, later to become the second president of the United States, wrote in his diary: "5 Wednesday. Attended Court: heard the trial of an action for trespass, brought by a mulatto woman, for damages, for restraining her of her liberty. This is called suing for liberty; the first action that ever I knew of the sort, though I have heard there have been many." The mulatto woman was forty-six-year-old Jenny Slew, who in 1765 filed suit in the Massachusetts colony, claiming she had been unlawfully kidnapped and enslaved in 1762. As Adam's diary entry points out, there are records of freedom suits as early as the seventeenth century in the states of

Maryland and Virginia. However, it is diffi-cult to find many of these cases without searching through mountains of court rec-ords. The evidence of advocacy by African Americans, and African-American women in particular, remains undiscovered unless noted in the few newspapers of the era or in the personal diaries of prominent individu-als like Adams.

Slew was able to sue on her own behalf, although enslaved, because at the time Mas-sachusetts was one of the few states that permitted slaves, considered property, not persons, under the law, to bring civil suits. She initially lost in the lower court, but prevailed a year and a half later in a higher court.

At both trials the defendant challenged Jenny Slew's legal capacity to sue, saying that she could not sue in her own name because she had been married several times to slaves (presumably black men), thus she had no legal identity separate from her hus-band. However, a 1706 state law prohibited interracial marriages, so there was some question whether a marriage between a free mulatto and black slave was valid. There also was some question about the legality of marriages between enslaved individuals. The Superior Court, without explanation, refused to dismiss Slew's claim. Perhaps the explanation lies in the court's resolution of Slew's substantive claim, namely that Jenny Slew was born free because her mother was white. Counsel for Slew argued that the legal status of an individual followed the mother, so it did not matter whether Slew's father, a black man, was free or slave. The Superior Court judges were divided on this point and as a result Jenny Slew was awarded her freedom, four pounds, and court costs.

TAUNYA LOVELL BANKS

Smith, Lucie Wilmot (b. 1861)

Lucie Wilmot Smith was a professional jour-nalist and an articulate, outspoken defender of women's rights. Unfortunately, little is known about her life.

Lucie Wilmot Smith was born in Lex-ington, Kentucky, on November 16, 1861. Her mother was Margaret Smith, but her father is unknown. She probably was born into slavery, but this is far from certain. At age sixteen, Smith was supporting both her-self and her mother by working as a teacher. Smith later graduated from the normal (edu-cation) school at the state university in Louisville in 1877.

Acclaimed nineteenth-century journalist Lucie Wilmot Smith was an ardent supporter of woman's suffrage and black civil rights. (MOORLAND-SPINGARN)

After working as a teacher, Smith became private secretary to the educator William J. Simmons, a position she held until 1884, when, at his suggestion, she began to write the children's column of the *American Baptist*. She enjoyed the work and soon moved on to direct the publication of *Our Women and Children*, established in Louisville in 1888. Smith edited the "Women and Women's Work" department, a section that came to reflect her strong interest in women's suffrage and struggle for equality. Smith also was a frequent contributor to the *Baptist Journal*, published in St. Louis by Reverend R. H. Coles; *The Journalist*, a black newspaper published in New York City; and the acclaimed *Indianapolis Freeman*, the country's first, and at that time only, illustrated paper for a specifically black readership. Her articles were reprinted in many papers, including the *Boston Advocate* and the *Freeman*. Smith also held a faculty position at the University of Louisville.

Lucie Wilmot Smith was a member of the Afro-American Press Convention, several religious societies, and other national bodies. Unfortunately, almost nothing is known about her life after 1891. From what is known about her, however, it is clear that she was both a determined advocate of women's rights and suffrage as well as a highly successful journalist.

FENELLA MACFARLANE

Sprague, Rosetta Douglass (1839–1906)

In describing the relationship of her parents, Frederick and Anna Murray Douglass, Rosetta Douglass Sprague explained: "As is the condition of most wives her identity became so merged with that of her husband's that few of their earlier friends in the North really knew and appreciated the full value of the woman who presided over the Douglass home for forty-five years." While Sprague was concerned about the plight of African Americans, she made her greatest historical contribution by making visible the personal life of her parents. Her famous speech, "Anna Murray Douglass—My Mother as I Recall Her," delivered at the founding meeting of the NACW, recaptured her mother's marital role in the life of her father, Frederick Douglass. From Rosetta's recollections, bits and pieces of her own life can be reconstructed as well.

Rosetta Douglass Sprague, the older daughter of Frederick and Anna Murray Douglass, and her offspring were social activists committed to their spouses and to the causes of the African-American community. **Anna Murray Douglass** was a role model for this social consciousness and activism in her antislavery activities in Lynn, Massachusetts. A participant in the 1896 founding of the National Association of Colored Women, Rosetta Douglass Sprague, and later her daughters Fredericka and Rosabelle, utilized civic, club-related, and educational activities as avenues for improving the legal and social circumstances of the African-American community during the late nineteenth and early twentieth centuries.

Rosetta was born in June 1839, in the two-room Douglass home overlooking Buzzards Bay on Elm Street in New Bedford, Massachusetts. Her three brothers, Lewis, Frederick, Jr., and Charles, were also born in New Bedford. When Rosetta was around six years old, her father, Frederick Douglass, moved his family to a cottage he had purchased in Lynn, Massachusetts. Annie, Rosetta's younger sister, was born in Lynn.

Douglass later moved his family to Rochester, New York.

Because of racial segregation and differential treatment in the schools of Rochester, New York, Rosetta Douglass was educated in business-related skills at the Oberlin College Academy. Her first secure teaching position was in Salem, Massachusetts, where she taught until she married Nathaniel Sprague in 1863. The couple moved back to Rochester to start their family. The Spragues had seven children, six daughters and one son: Annie Rosine, Harriet Bailey, Alice Louise, Estelle Irene, Fredericka Douglass, Herbert Douglass, and Rosabelle Mary.

The Spragues lived in Rochester until Nathaniel was imprisoned for removing the contents from letters on his job in the Rochester post office. Nathaniel Sprague was an uneducated ex-slave who had difficulty keeping jobs and Frederick Douglass had helped him get the job in the post office. After he was released from jail, he joined Rosetta in Washington, D.C., where she had relocated with their children to obtain work after liquidating her personal property to cover the couple's debts. She was supporting the children by working as a government clerk in the Register of Deeds Office with her father. She remained in Washington, D.C., until her death in 1906.

WILMA PEEBLES-WILKINS

Stanley, Sara G. (1837–1918)

Sara Stanley, freeborn in an era when millions of black men and women were enslaved, was a pioneer integrationist in higher education, both as an antebellum college student and as a teacher.

Stanley's parents, John Stuart and Frances Griffith Stanley, ran a private school for free black children in New Bern, North Carolina, before the Civil War. Not surprisingly, therefore, she had an excellent early education. In fact, when she went to Ohio to study at **Oberlin College** in the early 1850s, Stanley was so well prepared that she did not have to take the preparatory courses that were required for many white and black students.

The Stanleys left North Carolina in the mid-1850s, as freedpeople were suffering heightened persecution and were immigrating North. The family settled in Cleveland. Sara Stanley left college before receiving her degree to teach school and became involved in the abolitionist movement prior to the Civil War. A speech she gave to the Ladies Antislavery Society in Delaware, Ohio, in 1856, one of the earliest by a black American woman, was later published as an antislavery tract.

In 1864, Stanley volunteered to teach freedpeople through the interracial, Protestant-based American Missionary Association (AMA). She taught in Norfolk, Virginia; St. Louis, Missouri; Louisville, Kentucky; and Mobile, Alabama, from 1864–70. Although she was born free, she identified with the freedpeople through "ties of consanguinity and love . . . socially and politically they are 'my people'." However, she also considered herself the equal of her white co-workers, noting that "God is man, Christ clothed in the habiliments of flesh, the Son of God in the person of a Negro." Therefore, she insisted, unsuccessfully at the time, on equal housing for black teachers.

In addition to being a teacher, Stanley was an accomplished writer. The *Weekly African-American* published her critique of John

Greenleaf Whittier's poetry in its April 19, 1862, edition, and the same year she was named to the National Young Men's Literary Association, a black organization. In the 1860s, the AMA regularly published her reports. One report describes a visit to her classroom by a government official, who told the children that education made them different from whites. Stanley told him that the children knew better: that the difference was money stolen off the backs of black people over the years.

In 1868, Stanley, a mulatto, married Charles Woodward, a white Civil War veteran who managed the Freedmen's Bank in Mobile, where she continued to teach. (The 1870 census lists her as white.) The couple's only child died in infancy. They moved to the North in the late 1870s, and Sara is listed as a widow in 1885. She died in 1918, the place and exact date are unknown.

Sara Stanley, born free, highly educated, and able to pass as white in the racist climate of the late nineteenth century, chose not to pass but, instead, to teach freedpeople in the South in a tumultuous era.

ELLEN MACKENSIE LAWSON

Stewart, Maria W. (1803–1879)

"What if I am a woman?" intoned Maria W. Stewart during a speech in Boston on September 21, 1833. Throughout her brief oration she reminded her mixed audience of women and men that women, even in the ancient world, had been honored for their wisdom, prudence, religiosity, and achievements. Yet, her own people of color, she noted, had failed to accord her similar recognition.

Maria Stewart, born in Hartford, Connecticut, in 1803, had taken up public speaking as a means of supporting herself following her husband Jame's death. Her marriage in 1826 at the Reverend Thomas Paul's African Baptist Church marked her as a member of Boston's small black middle class; but she had been cheated of a comfortable inheritance by unscrupulous white Boston merchants. Before her public speaking tour (1832–33) she had published a short pamphlet, *Religion and the Pure Principles of Morality, the Sure Foundation on Which We Must Build* (1831). During her brief public speaking career she also published *Meditations from the Pen of Mrs. Maria W. Stewart* (1832). William Lloyd Garrison reported all four of her speeches in the pages of his *Liberator*, the best known abolitionist newspaper of the time. Thus, it was neither a stranger nor an outside agitator that sought to address the problems faced by black Boston and American blacks.

Stewart's speeches were not well received due to the gender politics of nineteenth-century America. She was, after all, the first American-born woman to break the taboo against women participating in public political dialogues, a taboo shared by black and white communities alike. Moreover, Stewart experienced opposition from within conservative black Boston political circles.

Although married in the African Baptist Church, there is reason to believe that Stewart at the time of her public speeches was more influenced by the individuals and activities of Reverend Samuel Snowden's African Methodist Episcopal Church. In 1829, one of its members, David Walker, had published his controversial *Walker's Appeal*. Prior to that, in 1826, the Massachusetts General Colored Association was founded. These two events laid the groundwork for Stewart's advocacy of black self-determination and economic independence from even well-meaning whites. All three developments were part of a burgeoning radicalism among young black Bostonians, and perhaps an implied criticism of Reverend Thomas Paul's tendency to work consistently but not exclusively with white allies.

Although rebuffed in her attempt at public political speaking, Stewart had a distinguished career as a public schoolteacher in New York City, Baltimore, and Washington, D.C. In 1878, when applying for a widow's pension from her second husband, Stewart was reunited with her old friend and publisher, William Lloyd Garrison. She subsequently published, at her own expense, an enlarged edition of *Meditations* (1879). Shortly after, she died, and on December 17, 1879, Maria W. Stewart was buried at Graceland Cemetery in Washington.

The emergence of black history and women's studies has reintroduced scholars to the life and work of Maria W. Stewart, but this pioneering black political activist still lacks a critical biographical assessment. Her life and her continuing obscurity illustrate the double pressures of racism and sexism on the lives of black women. Rather than being recognized as a significant advocate of black autonomy, she has been silenced for more than four decades. Stewart's speeches and writings issue a clear challenge to our contemporary world: black women's need for self-determination cannot be addressed if it is only an adjunct to black men's freedom.

HARRY A. REED

T

Talbert, Mary (1866–1923)

"Clear and insistent is the call to the women of my race today—the call to self-development and to unselfish service. We cannot turn a deaf ear to the cries of the neglected little children, the untrained youth, the aged and the poor." These words, spoken by Mary Burnett Talbert on the eve of the twentieth century, characterize the work to which she dedicated her life as educator, lecturer, and human rights advocate.

Born in the college town of Oberlin, Ohio, on September 17, 1866, Mary Burnett was able to build on the firm foundation that her parents, Cornelius and Caroline Nicholls Burnett, had laid for her and their other seven children. Initially members of the Episcopal Church, the Burnetts later changed their affiliation to the Congregational Church because of its active involvement in the abolition movement and its promotion of education for black youth. Cornelius Burnett, who was active in the politics of both, had engaged in Reconstruction politics in his native North Carolina. Burnett continued his affiliation with the Republican Party in Ohio and attended several state conventions as an elected delegate. In the heart of Oberlin's business district the Burnetts operated a restaurant, boardinghouse, and barbershop that catered primarily to students from **Oberlin College** (one of the earliest colleges to admit black people and women as students). From her family's affiliations and business enterprises,

Burnett learned that the constraints of race and gender could be circumvented. In Oberlin's unique social environment she also learned the importance of service to both church and community.

Mary Burnett attended the public schools of Oberlin, played the organ at the Methodist Church, and embraced her parent's belief in service to the community. After graduating from Oberlin High School at age sixteen, and aided by a benefactor, she attended Oberlin College, where her ideals regarding community involvement were further cemented. **Mary Church** (**Terrell**) and **Anna Julia Cooper**, who later became renowned for their reformist activities, also were students at the college, and **Hallie Q. Brown**, another important black activist, grew up in Oberlin during this period. These women undoubtedly knew each other, and their promotion of human rights later reunited them.

Mary Burnett followed a literary track at Oberlin and received an S.P. in 1886. (Recipients of this degree later were awarded a bachelor of arts, which Talbert received in 1896.) Some biographers contend that Talbert earned a Ph.D. from the University of Buffalo, but that university did not award doctorates in arts and sciences on a regular basis until the 1930s, so it cannot be confirmed that Talbert received a Ph.D. Students who took continuing education classes at the university were awarded certificates called doctorates, and it is possible that Mary B. Talbert received one of these.

In 1886, she assumed a teaching position at Bethel University in the segregated school system of Little Rock, Arkansas, where she taught history, mathematics, Latin, science, and geography. In Arkansas she experienced the impact of Jim Crow laws firsthand, but at the same time, the respectability accorded black teachers gave her high visibility, and she earned a national reputation. As a result, the superintendent of schools appointed her assistant principal of Bethel University, and she became the only woman ever to be selected for this position. It was the highest ever held by a woman in the state. Then, in 1887, she was named principal of Union High School in Little Rock.

Mary Burnett's sister, Henrietta, introduced her to her brother-in-law, William Herbert Talbert, a successful city clerk and realtor in Buffalo, New York. On September 8, 1891, they were married, and Mary Burnett ended her teaching career and moved to Buffalo. The following year she gave birth to their only child, Sarah May, who later attended the New England Conservatory of Music and became an accomplished pianist and composer.

In Buffalo, Talbert spent her time managing the extended Talbert household and working in the Michigan Avenue Baptist Church, which had been founded by the Talberts in the early nineteenth century and was known for its political activism. Unable to teach in the public schools of Buffalo because regulations barred married women from teaching, Talbert established classes at her church, where she trained more than 300 Sunday school teachers. She also joined forces with other black women in Buffalo and, in 1899, became a charter member of the Phyllis Wheatley Club, the first club in the city to become an affiliate of the Na-

A lifetime of dedication to human rights was recognized when Mary Burnett Talbert became the first woman to receive the NAACP's coveted Spingarn Medal. (MOOR-LAND-SPINGARN)

tional Association of Colored Women (NACW). The NACW was founded in Washington, D.C., in 1896, and served as an umbrella group for many clubs throughout the United States. The Phyllis Wheatley Club established a settlement house in Buffalo and, in 1910, during Talbert's presidency, invited the National Association for the Advancement of Colored People (NAACP) to begin organizing activities in the city. Also a charter member of the Empire Federation of Women's Clubs, founded in 1911, Talbert served as its second president, from 1912 to 1916.

Mary Talbert attracted the attention of NACW members in 1901 when she challenged the all-white board of commissioners of the Buffalo Pan American Exposition to appoint an African American and to include an exhibit on black American life. Also in 1901, she was reunited with her Oberlin community colleagues Mary Church Terrell, Anna Julia Cooper, and Hallie Q. Brown at NACW's second biennial conference held at her home in Buffalo. Talbert subsequently held several NACW administrative positions, including parliamentarian, recording secretary, chair of the executive committee, and vice president. Delegates elected her president in 1916, and she served two terms, ending in 1920.

Mary Talbert's administration was noteworthy for several reasons. First, during this time club members embarked on a national project to purchase and restore Anacostia, the District of Columbia home of Frederick Douglass, as a monument to a great statesman and to commemorate the contributions made by African Americans to the United States. At the Denver conference, in 1920, President Talbert announced that the NACW owned the building outright. Second, under Talbert the organization was recognized as a full member of the International Council of Women (ICW) when she became the first official NACW delegate to be seated at ICW's fifth quinquennial conference, held in Christiana, Norway, in 1920.

Talbert was one of the Americans who addressed the ICW delegates, representing more than thirty countries. She told them that "the greatness of nations is shown by their strict regard for human rights, rigid enforcement of the law without bias, and just administration of the affairs of life." She further noted that because white women

have greater opportunity, "they are duty bound to lift [their] voices against the ills that afflict [their] sisters of color, both in America and elsewhere." Talbert asked delegates "to appeal to your strong men to justify their claim as leaders of mankind . . . and [to] uphold law and order . . . till no individual or race shall feel the hoof of oppression upon them." While in Europe, Talbert traveled to several countries, lecturing on the conditions of black Americans, especially women and children. The press gave extensive coverage to her speeches.

During the post–World War I era, Talbert engaged in many activities to rebuild Europe and promote democracy, often under the aegis of the NACW and the NAACP. In 1919, as NACW representative, she served as YMCA secretary and Red Cross nurse in Romagne, France, where she offered classes for African-American soldiers. She led the Third Liberty Bond Drive among black clubwomen, which raised $5 million. She was also an appointee to the League of Nations committee on international relations. In 1921, as a member of an NAACP delegation of prominent black Americans, Talbert petitioned President Warren Harding to grant clemency to members of the African-American twenty-fourth regiment who had been falsely accused of inciting a race riot in Houston, Texas, in 1917. In 1922, Talbert joined other NACW members to found, in Washington, D.C., the International Council of Women of the Darker Races, which was committed to uniting women of color around the globe in order to present a united attack against oppression; she was a member of the organization's committee on education. She also contributed articles to *Woman's Voice* and the *Champion*.

Talbert was an NAACP vice president and board member from 1918 until her death in 1923. By organizing NAACP chapters in Louisiana and Texas, she strengthened the organization's influence in key Southern states. It has been alleged that Talbert influenced the NAACP to investigate the atrocities perpetrated by the United States against Haitian women and children in 1921. As national director of the NAACP's antilynching campaign, Talbert assiduously sought support for the bill that Leonidas Dyer introduced into Congress in 1921. Although the campaign failed to reach its financial goal, enough funds were raised to advertise the atrocities of lynching and to win greater white support for its elimination. Congress failed to ratify the Dyer bill, however, and in response, Talbert urged clubwomen to use their newly won right to vote to oppose those representatives who voted against it. This was to be Talbert's last major contribution to her people. In 1922, she became the first woman to be awarded the NAACP's coveted Spingarn Medal for her efforts to purchase the Douglass home and for her human rights activities.

After a lengthy illness, at the age of fifty-seven, Mary B. Talbert died of coronary thrombosis at her home in Buffalo, New York, on October 15, 1923. She is buried in Forest Lawn Cemetery.

LILLIAN S. WILLIAMS

Taylor, Susie (1848–1912)

Susie Baker King Taylor is the only black woman to write of her participation in the Civil War, and for these experiences—as teacher, laundress, and nurse—she is remembered.

A cursory reading of her memoir, however, reveals something as unique as Taylor's reminiscences. Through oral tradition, Taylor traces her maternal line back to a great-great-grandmother who, she believed, lived to be 120 years old. According to family tradition, five of this woman's sons served in the American Revolution, establishing the precedent for patriotism that Taylor would later follow. This female ancestor also must have been among the first African slaves brought to the colony of Georgia, which was founded in 1732. A daughter of this ancestor, Taylor's great-grandmother, was said to have given birth to twenty-five children, only one of whom was a son. One of her many daughters was Taylor's grandmother; born in 1820, she was responsible in part for Taylor's upbringing.

Taylor's mother was born in 1834, and Taylor herself, the first child, in 1848. These remarkable genealogies indicate that the matrilineal black family was in place early, possibly from the beginning of African migration into pre–Revolutionary War Georgia. None of the men in the line, including Taylor's own father, is remembered.

Taylor's mother, known only by the last name Baker, was a domestic slave. While Taylor was still quite small, her grandmother obtained permission to remove her from plantation life to freedom in Savannah, where the older woman eked out a living primarily by bartering chickens and eggs for goods. In Savannah Taylor was fortunate enough to come into contact with two white children who taught her to read and write, skills forbidden to blacks in the pre–Civil War South.

When the Civil War erupted, Taylor and her grandmother returned to the plantation, but soon thereafter Taylor departed for the Sea Islands of South Carolina with her maternal uncle and his family. Taylor was only fourteen at the time, but even in old age she vividly recalled her first sight of the Yankees who were then fighting to take over the coastal areas. Taylor was immediately pressed into service by Union forces, first as teacher to freed slave children (and some adults). Later, after marrying Sergeant Edward King of the first South Carolina

The remarkable memoirs of Susie King Taylor tell of her exploits during the Civil War when she learned to handle a musket, served as a nurse with Clara Barton, and lived through a nearly fatal injury to continue working with her regiment. (SCHOMBURG CENTER)

Volunteers, she worked as both laundress and nurse for the Union.

Most of her wartime activities were centered in South Carolina, moving up and down the coast to Florida and Georgia. Taylor learned how to handle a musket as well as bandage and care for the dying—both black and white. In 1863, Taylor worked with Clara Barton during the eight months Barton practiced nursing in the Sea Islands. In late 1864, Taylor nearly died as a result of a boating accident, but after a few weeks was back at work, remaining with her regiment until the fall of Charleston in February 1865.

After the war, Taylor's movements exemplified those of many freedpeople during Reconstruction. She and her husband first settled in Savannah, where she opened a school. In 1866, on King's death, Taylor moved to rural Georgia. Finding that country life did not agree with her, however, she returned to Savannah and opened a night school for freedpeople where she taught until 1872. Then, using her husband's military pension, she traded her poorly paid career in education for service as a laundress and cook for a wealthy white family in Savannah.

When the family journeyed to New England on summer holiday, Taylor accompanied them and soon after moved to Boston. There she married Russell Taylor and became involved in civic activities as a founding member of the Corps 67 Women's Relief Corps. She was elected president of the organization in 1893.

In 1898, when her son lay dying in Louisiana, Taylor ventured to the South one last time. To her surprise, the winds of freedom had turned into the chains of segregation. She even witnessed a hanging in Mississippi. In old age she chose to overlook the devastation of the post-Reconstruction era and harkened back instead to 1861's "wonderful revolution"—the phrase she used in the closing words of her brief memoir.

PATRICIA W. ROMERO

Tituba (fl. 1690s)

Tituba, a slave indicted for witchcraft during the Salem witch trials in 1692, is one of the least known historical figures, despite the fact that the accusations made against her served as the catalyst for the trials. Before the hysteria about witchcraft in Salem Village came to an end, nineteen persons were hanged for witchcraft, and a man was crushed to death for refusing to testify as to his own guilt or innocence.

Tituba and her husband, John Indian, were slaves who belonged to Reverend Samuel Parris. They were not Indian but were given that last name because they came from Barbados, one of the islands of the West Indies. Parris, an impoverished, quarrelsome man, had been a trader in Barbados. After his business failed, however, he decided to return to Boston and to the ministry. He had studied theology at Harvard University, but had not completed work for his degree. Before he left Barbados with his ailing wife, his six-year-old daughter, Betsey, and his wife's nine-year-old niece, Abigail Williams, Parris purchased Tituba and John. The slaves would look after his household but, more importantly, would be hired out, thus assuring him of a small income.

In 1689, Parris finally received an offer from a church in Salem Village, a tiny community outside Salem. Once established in the parsonage, Parris hired out John to a tavern keeper and Tituba to a weaver. An expert weaver, Tituba supplied the woven goods used by the Parris family; she also managed the household, took care of Parris' invalid wife, and looked after the children.

During the long, cold winters, Tituba entertained the children with stories about Barbados, evoking the warmth and beauty of the island, telling stories of animals that could talk and of magic spells, and reading their palms. Gradually, the parsonage became a meeting place for bound girls who were eager to hear Tituba's stories of a livelier, more colorful world.

Meanwhile, in keeping rooms and taverns all over the Massachusetts Bay Colony, witchcraft had become a favorite—and frightening—topic of conversation. Some of the girls listening to Tituba's stories, including Parris' daughter and niece, became hysterical, performing strange antics, crying out, and barking like dogs. Some of the girls accused Tituba; Sarah Good, a tramp; and Sarah Osborne, a sick old woman, of having bewitched them. In 1692, these three women became the first persons to be accused of practicing witchcraft in Salem Village. Tituba was beaten and abused by Parris until she confessed to being a witch. Then she was indicted for the practice of witchcraft and was jailed in Boston for thirteen months.

Prisoners were charged for food and shelter during their imprisonment, and by law had to reimburse the jailer before they could be released. Parris refused to pay Tituba's fees because she insisted she was not, and never had been, a witch and would state so publicly if given the opportunity. Finally, she was sold to someone else. There is no further record of Tituba, a black woman who was the unwitting catalyst of the most famous of the seventeenth-century witchcraft trials.

ANN PETRY

This famous preacher, abolitionist, and lecturer was born Isabella Bomefree, a slave. She was freed in 1827, and in 1843 she became an itinerant preacher, taking the name Sojourner Truth. A fiery orator, she spoke out on subjects ranging from abolition to temperance, prison reform, and woman suffrage. (SCHOMBURG CENTER)

Truth, Sojourner (c. 1799–1883)

Sojourner Truth, abolitionist and woman's rights activist, is one of the two most widely known nineteenth-century black women; the other, **Harriet Tubman**, was also a former slave who was not formally educated. While Tubman is known as the "Moses of her People" for having led hundreds of slaves to freedom, Truth is remembered more for her speeches than for her post–Civil War work in freedpeople's relief. She is most closely identified with the question "and a'n't I a woman?" which demands that women who are poor and black be included within the category of woman. Disrupting assumptions about race, class, and gender in American society, Truth's twentieth-century persona works most effectively within the politically minded worlds of black civil rights and feminism. During her lifetime, however, she was deeply immersed in the Second Great Awakening's propagation of Methodist-inflected and unconstrained religiosity. Hence the making of her modern reputation entails the creative reworking of much of her life, an elaboration that began during her lifetime and that she encouraged. The emblematic character of Sojourner Truth—the slave woman who asks "and a'n't I a woman?"—is constructed upon a peculiarly nineteenth-century life experience that is nearly as obscure as the symbolic figure is well known.

The symbol of Sojourner Truth that is most popular today turns on two speeches of the 1850s: one in Akron, Ohio, in 1851, the other in Silver Lake, a small town in northern Indiana, in 1858. Like everything that happened to Truth after 1849, both events are known only through reports from other people. Truth was illiterate, and even her *Narrative of Sojourner Truth* (1878) was dictated to someone else in the late 1840s. Feminist abolitionist Frances Dana Gage recorded the popular version of Sojourner Truth's speech before a woman's rights convention held in Akron, Ohio, in May 1851. According to Gage, Truth said:

> Wall, chilern, whar dar is so much racket dar must be somethin' out o' kilter. I tink dat 'twixt de niggers of de Souf and de womin at de Norf, all talkin' 'bout rights, de white men will be in a fix pretty soon. But what's all dis here talkin' 'bout? Dat

man ober dar say dat womin needs to be helped into carriages, and lifted ober ditches, and to hab de best place everywhar. Nobody eber helps me into carriages, or ober mud-puddles, or gibs me any best place! And a'n't I a woman? Look at me! Look at my arm! (and she bared her right arm to the shoulder, showing her tremendous muscular power). I have ploughed, and planted, and gathered into barns, and no man could head me! And a'n't I a woman? I could work as much and eat as much as a man—when I could get it—and bear de lash as well! And a'n't I a woman? I have borne thirteen chilern, and seen 'em mo's all sold off to slavery, and when I cried out with my mother's grief, none but Jesus heard me! And a'n't I a woman?

Truth's 1851 speech demands that definitions of female gender allow for women's strength as well as their suffering attendant upon poverty and enslavement. Her 1858 gesture, recorded by abolitionist William Hayward, again reclaims her female gender and defies critics who seek to silence an eloquent critic of slavery and sexism. Faced with a hostile audience that questioned a black woman's right to speak in public and that intended to shame her out of presenting her case, Truth confronted men who claimed she was too forceful a speaker to be a woman. After they demanded that she prove her sexual identity through a performance intended to humiliate, Truth bared her breast in public, turned the imputed shame back on her tormenters, and, transcending their small-minded test, turned their spite back on them also.

Based on these words and gestures, the symbol of Sojourner Truth is an eloquent, inspired ex-slave who made her experience of work and victimized motherhood into an alternate model of womanhood. In a world that saw women as white and men as black, she is a woman who is also black and a black who is also a woman. Although several black women worked for the abolition of slavery and the achievement of women's rights in the middle of the nineteenth century (e.g., **Sarah Mapps Douglass, Frances Ellen Watkins Harper, Sarah Remond**), the ex-slave Sojourner Truth has become the emblematic nineteenth-century black woman and the symbol of the conjunction of sex and race.

Sojourner Truth was born about 1799 in Ulster County, New York, on the west side of the Hudson River, some eighty miles north of New York City, in a region dominated culturally and economically by people of Dutch descent. She was the second youngest of ten or twelve children, and her parents, James and Elizabeth Bomefree, named her Isabella. Their first language was Dutch. As a child Isabella belonged to several owners, the most significant of whom was John Dumont, for whom she worked from 1810 until a year before she was emancipated by state law in 1827. She kept in touch with the Dumont family until they moved west in 1849.

When she was about fourteen years old, Isabella was married to another of Dumont's slaves, an older man named Thomas. Thomas and Isabella had five children: Diana, Sophia, Elizabeth, Peter, and, perhaps, Hannah. In 1826–27, the year before she became free, Isabella had several critical experiences. She left her long-time master Dumont of her own accord and went to work for the family of Isaac Van Wagenen. When her son's owner illegally sold him into perpetual slavery in Alabama, Isabella went to court in Kingston, New York, and sued successfully for his return. She also had a dramatic conversion experience and joined the recently established Methodist church in Kingston, where she met a Miss Grear, with whom she journeyed to New York City after her emancipation. Leaving her daughters in Ulster County at work or in the care of their father, Isabella took Peter, a troubled young teenager, with her.

In New York City in the early 1830s Isabella supported herself through household work. She attended the white John Street Methodist Church and the black African Methodist Episcopal Zion Church, where she briefly encountered three of her older siblings. She also began to preach at the camp meetings held around the city and attracted the attention of white religious mavericks, some of whom became her employers. Through the dissident Methodist Latourette family, Isabella encountered the Magdalene Society, a mission for prostitutes founded by Arthur Tappan, who became a leading abolitionist in the mid–1830s. In the Magdalene Society she met Elijah Pierson, and through Pierson, the self-proclaimed prophet Matthias (Robert Matthews).

Between 1832 and 1835, Isabella was a follower of Matthias and lived in his "kingdom," a commune in Sing Sing underwritten by Pierson and a wealthy merchant family. The only black follower among Matthia's adherents, Isabella was also one of only two of the commune's working-class members. Like that of many other independent popular prophets of the early nineteenth century, Matthia's message was eclectic and idiosyncratic. Having begun his public life as an ardent advocate of temperance and a fiery anti-Mason, Matthias advocated several of the enthusiasms that were current in the

1830s. He claimed to possess the spirit of God and taught his followers that there were good and evil spirits and that the millennium was imminent. The virtually corporeal existence of spirits was also a central tenet of the kingdom. Matthias and his followers did not believe in doctors, reasoning that illness was caused by evil spirits that must be cast out. Members of the kingdom fasted often and followed a diet that emphasized fresh fruit and vegetables and prohibited alcohol. Although other communities with which Sojourner Truth would be connected held many of these same convictions, Matthia's kingdom was the only one organized around so autocratic and charismatic a prophet.

Matthia's kingdom collapsed in 1835, after an accusation of murder and a free love scandal brought the community tremendous notoriety. Matthias left for the West, and Isabella resumed household work in New York City for another eight years. Her *Narrative* contains no record of her activities between the breakup of the Matthias commune and her assumption of a new identity in the midst of economic hard times in 1843.

The *Narrative* does indicate that in 1843 Isabella was profoundly influenced by the millenarian movement inspired by a religiously independent farmer named William Miller. Making his own calculations based on biblical prophesies, Miller had figured that the world would come to an end in 1843. Scores of itinerant preachers, who addressed hundreds of camp meetings, coordinated by several well-run newspapers (including the New York *Midnight Cry*), spread Miller's message. Believing herself to be part of what she called a great drama of robbery and wrong, Isabella felt that she must make a definitive break with her old way of life. On the first of June 1843, she changed her name to Sojourner Truth, which means itinerant preacher. Without informing her family or friends, she set out eastward, exhorting people to embrace Jesus, as the Spirit had commanded her. Following a network of Millerite camp meetings, she made her way from Brooklyn, across Long Island, into Connecticut, and up the Connecticut River Valley. By December 1843, the Millerites were facing the reality of the Great Disappointment, and Sojourner Truth had joined the utopian Northampton Association, located in what is now Florence, Massachusetts.

A utopian community dedicated to the cooperative manufacture of silk, the Northampton Association attracted relatively well-educated people whose reforming sentiments were broad and deep-running. Unusual at the time, the Northampton Association did not draw the color line, and there Truth encountered the retired black abolitionist David Ruggles, who was a permanent resident, and Frederick Douglass, who visited occasionally. William Lloyd Garrison also spent months at a time at the Northampton Association, staying with his brother-in-law George Benson, who was one of the association's founders. Between residents and visitors at the association, Truth lived for the first time in an environment permeated with liberal reforms like feminism and abolitionism. Even before the association collapsed in 1846 and its lands were subdivided and sold, Truth began to address antislavery audiences, taking her preacher's forensic skills into a new field. After 1846 she stayed on in Florence, where she bought a house on Park Street. In 1849, she joined George Thompson, an antislavery British Member of Parliament, on the antislavery and women's rights lecture circuit,

selling her *Narrative* to pay off the mortgage on her house. Florence remained her base until she moved to Battle Creek, Michigan, in 1856.

As an antislavery feminist speaker, Sojourner Truth quickly gained a reputation for pungent wit and insight. Whether she said that women deserved equal rights with men, that slavery should be abolished, or that freedpeople should be allocated government lands in the West, she always prefaced her remarks and authenticated her authority by recalling her experience in slavery. In time she overstated both the duration of her enslavement and the particulars of her suffering. In the "a'n't I a woman?" speech she says she lost thirteen children to the slave trade, which more nearly approximates her mother's tragic experience than her own. After the Civil War, Truth routinely spoke of having spent her mother's forty, rather than her own thirty, years as a slave. Stressing her identification with slavery, Truth gauged her audiences well, for she, rather than her free, educated, and ladylike black colleagues, found a fond place in American memory.

Truth continued to lecture to antislavery and women's rights audiences until she went to Washington, D.C., in 1863 to help the black refugees who were fleeing the warfare of northern Virginia. As she nursed and taught domestic skills among destitute former slaves, she realized that the old clothes and handouts of charitable aid could not address the fundamental causes of poverty among the freedpeople: lack of paying jobs and material resources. In 1867, she initiated a job-placement effort that matched refugee workers with employers in Rochester, New York, and Battle Creek, Michigan. When that operation became too cumbersome for volunteers to manage, she drew up a petition to Congress that demanded that western land be set aside for a freedpeople's settlement. In 1870 and 1871 she traveled throughout New England and the Midwest, including Kansas, collecting signatures on her petition, on which no action was taken. In 1879, however, scores of black Southerners—who were called Exodusters—migrated to Kansas spontaneously. The Exodusters were acting independently on the same kind of millenarian fear of imminent transformation that Truth had experienced in 1843. Fearing (rightly) that ascendant Democrats would seek to reenslave them, Exodusters from Mississippi, Louisiana, Texas, and Tennessee flocked to the state that they knew as Free Kansas. By the late 1870s Sojourner Truth was in very poor health, but she applauded the Exoduster's venture. She died in Battle Creek in 1883, and was mourned as a stalwart of antebellum reform.

Well before her death Truth had begun to enter historical memory. Writing down her autobiography, which Truth published in 1850 as *The Narrative of Sojourner Truth*, Olive Gilbert preserved the first portrait of Sojourner Truth. Harriet Beecher Stowe wrote a widely circulated profile entitled "Sojourner Truth, The Libyan Sibyl," which was published in the *Atlantic Monthly* in April 1863 and reprinted in the 1875–78 edition of *The Narrative of Sojourner Truth*. Stowe's article motivated Frances Dana Gage to write her own recollections of Truth, which were republished in the 1875–78 edition of *The Narrative of Sojourner Truth* and volume one of Elizabeth Cady Stanton et al., *History of Woman Suffrage* (1881). Subsequent Sojourner Truth biographies, long and short, have mostly repeated material from these three mid–nineteenth-century sources.

Because she was so singular and eloquent a person who knew how to appeal to educated American audiences without revealing her inner self, Sojourner Truth's persona changed to reflect the needs and tastes of her audiences since she entered the public realm in the early 1830s. In camp meetings around New York City she gained renown as a preacher and singer, a reputation that she retained well after she became Sojourner Truth, the itinerant preacher, in 1843. As an antislavery lecturer, her first famous phrase, uttered in the late 1840s, as Frederick Douglass was doubting the possibility of ending slavery peaceably, was, "Frederick, is God dead?" This rhetorical question established her as a Christian of exquisite faith, in accordance with nineteenth-century evangelical sensibilities. But this phase's popularity had begun to fade by the century's end. Modern audiences are more likely to know Truth as a feminist who redefined womanhood along contemporary lines. To reinforce the power of this black feminist persona, it is now common practice to collapse her 1851 words and 1858 actions into one event. This combination produces an angry, defiant character that may suit modern tastes but that does not match the evangelical qualities of the historic Sojourner Truth.

NELL IRVIN PAINTER

Tubman, Harriet Ross (c. 1821–1913)

Running away was one way to resist slavery. Until recently, running away has been described in general terms as a predominantly masculine form of resistance. Because of their roles as mothers, wives, and daughters, women slaves, it was argued, resorted instead to strategies consonant with their biology and with social expectations. They poisoned food, injured livestock, committed arson, aborted pregnancies, feigned illness, and some physically fought mistresses, masters, and overseers. The fact that Harriet Tubman ran away repudiates the comfortable dichotomy of race and sex in resistance strategies.

Harriet Ross Tubman has achieved mythic fame as the best known conductor on the Underground Railroad. Her heroic exploits included at least fifteen trips into the South to rescue over 200 slaves and deliver them to freedom. Since Underground Railroad operators did not keep records of their activities, the exact number of trips Tubman made is unknown. Tubman herself remembered the number as eleven.

Born around 1821 in Dorchester County on Maryland's eastern shore to Benjamin and Harriet Greene Ross, Harriet was one of eleven children. Called Araminta when young, she later chose her mother's name, Harriet. Like most slave children, Harriet performed a variety of domestic chores, including attending the owner's children and cleaning house, before becoming a field hand. Harriet preferred fieldwork since it afforded a measure of autonomy and moments of respite from the close scrutiny and relentless demands of the slave owner. An added benefit of fieldwork was that it enabled her to develop considerable muscular strength and physical endurance.

One incident in her youth left Tubman with a lifelong affliction. An owner or overseer (accounts vary) intent on reprimanding a fleeing slave instead struck Harriet on the head. As a result of this nearly fatal head injury, Harriet suffered recurring narcolep-

tic seizures. In 1844, Harriet married John Tubman, a free black man. Harriet yearned to be free, but John failed to share her mounting anxiety about being sold into the Deep South or of the possible dispersal of her family should her owner die. In 1849, upon learning that her worst fears were soon to become reality, Harriet escaped. John refused to accompany her, and when she returned for him months later, he had taken another wife. John died soon after the Civil War and in 1869, Harriet married Civil War veteran Nelson Davis.

Harriet Tubman is often thought of as a figure in the distant American past, yet she lived into the twentieth century. She is shown here in a photograph taken shortly before her death in 1913. (SCHOMBURG CENTER)

After her escape, Tubman made her way to Philadelphia where she worked as a domestic, saving her meager earnings until she had the resources and contacts to rescue her sister, Mary Ann Bowley, and her two children. This was the first of many rescue missions Tubman would undertake as an agent of the Underground Railroad, a network of way stations situated along several routes from the South to the North to Canada, providing runaways with assistance in the form of shelter, food, clothing, disguises, money, or transportation. Most conductors on the Railroad who ventured South to seek prospective escapees and to guide them to freedom were black station masters. In her numerous trips South, Tubman followed various routes and used different disguises. She might appear as a hooded, apparently mentally impaired, wretchedly dressed man loitering about or talking in tongues or as an old woman chasing hens down the street. She usually chose a Saturday night for the rescue since a day would intervene before a runaway advertisement could appear. She carried doses of paregoric to silence crying babies and a pistol to discourage any fugitive slave from thoughts of disembarking the freedom train. Within two years of her own escape she had returned to Maryland's eastern shore to lead more than a dozen slaves to freedom in Northern states. Maryland planters regarded her as such a threat that they offered $40,000 for her capture.

Tubman eventually developed close, mutually supportive relationships with black abolitionist William Still of Philadelphia and white abolitionist Thomas Garrett of Wilmington, Delaware. Still was the leading black figure in the Underground Railroad. He described Tubman as "a woman of no pretensions; indeed a more ordinary specimen of humanity could hardly be found among the most unfortunate-looking farm hands of the South. Yet in point of courage, shrewdness, and disinterested exertions to rescue her fellowman, she was without equal." As early as 1830, Garrett, a Quaker, had become actively involved in the Underground Railroad. By August 1854, Garrett had assisted 1,853 runaways. On numerous occasions, Tubman relied on these men and on others for assistance as she escorted fugitives North.

The Fugitive Slave Law of 1850 placed fugitive cases under federal supervision and empowered special U.S. commissioners to receive $10 for each arrest that returned a slave to his or her owner. With the passage of this legislation, the entire federal government machinery and power could be called upon to assist in the capture and return of escaped slaves in any section of the country. This law cast an ominous shadow over the lives of all free African Americans in Northern communities. Tubman, having been forced to relocate many fugitives to Canada, herself moved to Saint Catharines, Ontario, just beyond Niagara Falls.

In December 1851, Harriet went South and returned with eleven slaves, including her brother and his wife. The following year she made another trip into Maryland and retrieved nine more slaves. On December 29, 1854, Thomas Garrett wrote, "We made arrangements last night, and sent away Harriet Tubman, with six men and one woman to Allen Agnew's (in Pennsylvania) to be forwarded across the country to the city. Harriet and one of the men had worn their shoes off their feet, and I gave them two dollars to help fit them out but do not yet know the expense." On June 4, 1857, Tubman achieved a long-desired goal when she rescued her parents and took them to Garrett's house in Wilmington. She made her last rescue in late 1860 when she returned to Dorchester County to free Steven Ennets, his wife, Maria, and their three children. Tubman took great pride in having never lost a passenger. These long journeys of courage and faith inspired her friends and the runaways to call her "Moses."

As is true with any social movement, a culture developed around the antislavery or abolitionist movement. Its luminaries included Frederick Douglass, William Lloyd Garrison, David Ruggles, and Gerrit Smith. Among the many newspapers supporting the cause were the *Liberator*, *North Star*, *National Anti-Slavery Standard*, and the *Genius of Universal Emancipation*. Meetings, conventions, lectures, petitions, fund-raising and political activities, and dramatic rescue attempts generated newspaper headlines and kept antislavery sentiments alive. Tubman, in addition to her rescues, participated fully in this culture. Although illiterate, Tubman gave speeches and personal testimony. She conspired with John Brown in his doomed effort to provoke a massive armed slave rebellion by raiding the federal arsenal at Harpers Ferry, although illness prevented her direct participation in the raid.

When the Civil War began, free African Americans eagerly anticipated participation in this long-awaited opportunity to help strike down slavery. Harriet Tubman, **Sojourner Truth**, Frederick Douglass, and other black leaders, therefore, were shocked and angered by President Abraham Lincoln's denial that the purpose of the war was to free the slaves and his initial reluctance to accept black volunteers into the Union Army. Eventually, Lincoln gave in to pressure and issued the preliminary Emancipation Proclamation declaring that slaves in states still in rebellion on January 1, 1863, would be set free, and early in 1863, the enlistment of African Americans into the Union Army began in earnest.

Tubman, like more than 186,000 fellow African Americans, willingly put her life on the line in the quest for emancipation. She earned distinction as the only woman in American military history to plan and execute an armed expedition against enemy forces. Serving in numerous capacities, Tubman was a spy, scout, and nurse for the Union Army stationed in the Carolinas and Florida. Her most famous adventure during the war was as assistant to Colonel James Montgomery on a raid from Port Royal, South Carolina, inland up to the Combahee River in June 1863, during which many plantations that had been providing food for Confederate troops were destroyed. Tubman was also present at the Fort Wagner battle and was purported to have served the last meal to Colonel Robert Gould Shaw of the black Massachusetts Fifty-Fourth Regiment, celebrated in the 1990 film *Glory*. She recorded a powerful description of the battle that ended in the death of approximately 1,500 black troops: "Then we saw de lightening, and that was de guns; and then we heard de thunder, and that was de big guns; and then we heard de rain falling, and that was de drops of blood falling; and when we came to get in de crops, it was dead men that we reaped."

Following the Civil War, Tubman recounted her life story to her friend, Sarah Elizabeth Bradford, and received a small stipend from the sale of the resulting biography, *Scenes in the Life of Harriet Tubman* (1869). For thirty years, Tubman fought to receive a pension from the U.S. government for her military services and eventually won a $20 per month stipend. She purchased a home in Auburn, New York. On land she had purchased from New York governor W. H. Seward before the Civil War as a home for her parents, she established a permanent home for aged ex-slaves who could no longer perform strenuous jobs. Her postwar social reform efforts to provide relief for the recently freed slaves and the families of black soldiers paralleled the work of many black women, such as **Harriet Jacobs** and **Elizabeth Keckley.** These women organized relief associations, raised funds, and rendered invaluable aid. Harriet Tubman died in March 1913.

Frederick Douglass wrote to Harriet Tubman on August 28, 1868, and eloquently summed up her life.

> The difference between us is very marked. Most that I have done and suffered in the service of our cause has been in public, and I have received much encouragement at every step of the way. You, on the other hand, have labored in a private way. I have wrought in the day—you the night. I have had the applause of the crowd and the satisfaction that comes of being approved by the multitude, while the most that you have done has been witnessed by a few trembling, scared, and foot-sore bondmen and women, whom you have led out of the house of bondage, and whose heartfelt "God bless you" has been your only reward. The midnight sky and the silent stars have been the witness of your devotion to freedom.

On May 30, 1974, the Department of Interior declared the Harriet Tubman Home for Aged and Indigent Colored People a national historic landmark. The U.S. Postal Service issued in 1978 its first stamp in the black Heritage USA Series, appropriately enough commemorating Harriet Tubman. She was a great leader determined to gain freedom for herself and others or to die in the effort.

DARLENE CLARK HINE

V

Vashon, Susan Paul (1838–1912)

Susan Paul Vashon was a distinguished teacher, school principal, and organizer of numerous groups for women and young people, but she is perhaps best remembered for her efforts during the Civil War when she raised money and cared for wounded soldiers and black refugees.

Susan Paul Vashon was born on September 19, 1838, in Boston, Massachusetts. Her father was Elijah W. Smith, a skilled musician and composer. Her mother, Anne Paul Smith, was a daughter of Reverend Thomas Paul, who was renowned for his abolitionist work and his efforts on behalf of black people generally and one of the most influential black leaders in Boston in his time. Paul was founder and pastor of the Joy Street Church, the only refuge for the American Anti-Slavery Society in Boston. The African school conducted in the basement of Paul's church educated black children who were denied admittance to the city's segregated public schools.

Her mother died when Vashon was very young, and she then moved into the house of her maternal grandmother, Katherine Paul. Also living there was Vashon's aunt, Susan Paul, a hard-working abolitionist and advocate of woman's rights for whom Susan had been named. At sixteen, Vashon graduated from Miss O'Mear's Seminary in Somerville, Massachusetts, a private, non-segregated school. Vashon, the only black student in her class, graduated as valedictorian. After graduation, she went to Pittsburgh, Pennsylvania, where her father lived, and began to work as a teacher in the city's only school for black children.

The principal of her school was George Boyer Vashon, who like Vashon, came from a family dedicated to working both for black education and the abolitionist movement. They were married in 1857 and had seven children. It is probable that as newlyweds the Vashons were helpers in the Underground Railroad. Both George Vashon and his father, John Bethune Vashon, are known to have been conductors for the railroad. During the years 1864–65, Vashon helped organize a series of highly successful sanitary relief bazaars, raising thousands of dollars that were used to nurse sick and wounded soldiers as well as house black refugees in Pittsburgh.

After the family moved to Washington, D.C., in 1872, Vashon returned to public school teaching. She later became principal of the Thaddeus Stevens School, a position she held until 1880. Vashon was widowed in 1878, and in 1882 she and her four surviving children moved to St. Louis, Missouri, where she worked with church groups and women's organizations. In 1902, she served as president of the Missouri State Federation of Colored Women's Clubs of the **National Association of Colored Women's Clubs**. She also played a pivotal role in the formation of the St. Louis Association of Colored Women's Clubs. She was active too in the Mother's Club for young women and the Book Lover's Club. Her children went on to hold respected positions in St. Louis, and Vashon High School was named in recognition of the family's outstanding community achievements.

Having led a busy and successful life as mother, teacher, and community organizer, Susan Paul Vashon died in 1912.

FENELLA MACFARLANE

W

Washington, Josephine (1861–1949)

As a writer and educator, Josephine Washington was committed to freeing America from what she described as the "monster of prejudice whose voracious appetite is appeased only when individuals are reduced to abject servitude and are content to remain hewers of wood and drawers of water." Washington was concerned with social issues from an early age, and in her teaching and many writings she was a powerful advocate of women's rights and racial justice.

Born on July 31, 1861, in Goochland County, Virginia, Washington was the daughter of Augustus and Maria Turpin. Her education began at home and continued through normal and high schools to the Richmond Institute, which later became the Richmond Theological Seminary. She entered **Howard University**'s college department and graduated in 1886. While at the university, Washington spent her summer vacations working as a copyist for Frederick Douglass, during his tenure as recorder of deeds for the District of Columbia. Following her marriage to Dr. Samuel H. H. Washington, she moved to Birmingham, Alabama, in 1888. She later taught at Richmond Theological Seminary, Howard University, and Selma University, Alabama. Her commitment to education led Washington to play an important role in the development of Selma University, an educational institution for teachers and ministers alike.

Washington's literary efforts began as a teenager. Her first story, "A Talk about Church Fairs," in which she criticized the sale of wine at church fund-raisers, was published in the *Virginia Star*—to a favorable reaction—when she was only sixteen years old. While her writing, and perhaps

Writer and educator Josephine Turpin Washington was committed to freeing America from what she described as the "monster of prejudice whose voracious appetite is appeased only when individuals are reduced to abject servitude and are content to remain hewers of wood and drawers of water." (MOORLAND-SPINGARN)

especially her poetry, has largely been neglected, Washington addressed herself to many of the important issues of her day. Essays such as "Higher Education for Women," published in the *People's Advocate,* and her introduction to Lawson A. Scrugg's *Women of Distinction* (1893) display her concern with an array of issues affecting black people, including job opportunities, education, motherhood, and relations between women and men. In the latter essay she powerfully defends the "progressive woman" who seeks to successfully participate in both professional and domestic spheres. While chairperson of the Executive Board of the Alabama State Federation of Colored Women's Clubs, Washington also wrote their Federation Hymn, "Mother Alabama." Her work appeared in numerous publications, including the *New York Freeman,* the *New York Globe,* the *AME Review,* the *Christian Recorder,* the *Virginia Star,* the *Colored American Magazine,* and the *People's Advocate.*

Writing in 1904 for the *Colored American Magazine* on the sixth annual meeting of the State Federation of Colored Women's Clubs, held in Mobile, Alabama, Washington reported not only on the delegate's focus on black womanhood, standards of morality, and the setting up of a youth reformatory but also on the pervasive effects of segregation and racial prejudice within the city itself. With an eye to discrimination on all levels of society, Washington noted, for instance, the playgrounds that were set aside for the exclusive use of white children, while black children "look on longingly, but dare not touch the sacred structure."

While as yet little is known about the later years of her life, and the details of her death in 1949, Washington's numerous writings remain as testimony to her religious faith, her belief in the equality of women, and her strong commitment to ending racial discrimination.

FENELLA MACFARLANE

Washington, Margaret   (c. 1865–1925)

Few people manage to rise above the culture of their time. When someone does—**Ida B. Wells-Barnett** or **Sojourner Truth**—she lights the way for those who follow. Margaret Murray Washington was among the great majority. Her achievements were remarkable, but she remained anchored to the attitudes, prejudices, and customs of the world in which she lived.

Margaret James Murray was born in Macon, Georgia, on March 9, 1865, according to her gravestone. Evidence suggests, however, that she was actually born four years earlier. She was the daughter of Lucy Murray, who was a washerwoman, and a white father whose identity is unknown. He was apparently an Irish immigrant, and he died when Margaret was seven years old. At his death, the girl went to live with a Quaker family, a brother and sister. When she was fourteen, they suggested that she become a teacher, and she did.

Six years later, Murray decided to enter Fisk University's preparatory school. At that time, many young women were teaching with scarcely more formal education than some of their students. It is at this point, perhaps, that Murray subtracted those four years from her age, thinking twenty an advanced age to begin her high school education. At any rate, that is the speculation of Louis R. Harlan, editor of the *Booker T. Washington Papers.*

Murray, working to pay her way, finished both the preparatory and college courses. She was associate editor of the student newspaper and president of one of the campus literary societies. She met her future husband, Tuskegee's Booker T. Washington, at a senior class dinner just before commencement and went to Tuskegee Institute to teach the next fall. One year later she became lady principal. A year after that, in 1891, Washington proposed. Murray was not sure, however, that she wanted to marry. For one thing, Washington had a daughter and two sons, and she did not much care for children. Paula Giddings quotes a letter from Murray to Washington in which she writes, "You do not have much sympathy with me because I feel as I do in regard to little folks. I get annoyed at myself but the feeling is there just the same." She particularly disliked Washington's daughter, Portia, and Portia felt the same about her.

Margaret Murray did marry Booker T. Washington, and she and Portia learned to live with one another. She kept her position at Tuskegee after her marriage and combined her authority on the faculty with her new authority as the president's wife to accomplish what she thought was best for the school and the surrounding community. She was instrumental in the establishment of an industrial department for women, housed in Dorothy Hall, and served on the committee that administered the institute when her husband was away.

Some of her most important work took place away from the campus. On March 2, 1895, she gathered together thirteen women who were connected with the institute—on the faculty or married to faculty members—to form the Tuskegee Woman's Club. One of the major activities of the club was a

Margaret Murray Washington's achievements were remarkable, but she remained anchored to the attitudes, prejudices, and customs of the world in which she lived. She worked fiercely and effectively for social improvement, never stinting herself in the service of her people, but she could not or would not take the final step into political action. (LIBRARY OF CONGRESS)

series of mother's meetings that took place every Saturday in rented rooms above a black grocery store. While students entertained the children in one room, their mothers heard a talk and enjoyed a discussion in another. The talks were on subjects such as "When Shall a Girl Be Permitted to Receive Her First Company" and "Mother's Relation to the Teacher." Eventually, these meetings attracted almost 300 women every week.

The club, under Washington's leadership, also started a school for the children of poor workers on a nearby plantation settlement. Washington persuaded the county to allocate $15 a month toward the teacher's salary, and parents contributed what they could. The Woman's Club paid the rest. Children were taught advanced farming methods and household industries in addition to basic literacy skills. Members of the Woman's Club also worked on weekends for twelve years with the families on the plantation, teaching Sunday school, organizing boy's clubs, girl's sewing classes, and newspaper-reading clubs for men. Washington also started a small public library staffed by members of the Woman's Club.

In 1910, Washington and twelve other women who had been excluded from the annual Tuskegee Negro conference met separately. During their meeting, they conceived the Town Night School. The school taught reading, cooking, sewing, carpentry, bricklaying, painting, and tailoring to the people of the town of Tuskegee. To keep the children occupied while their mothers were in class, they were taught cooking. For a time, the school was listed in the Tuskegee catalog as an extension program, but two years after it opened, Tuskegee withdrew its support. The Woman's Club took over. They were able to keep the school open eight months of the year, supporting 103 night classes and thirty-seven day classes, including cooking for the children.

Eventually, the night school began to offer some academic courses. The most successful of these was Negro history, and Washington promoted the teaching of the subject in other schools around the country. She also worked in the club movement on a national level. She was president of the National Federation of Afro-American Women, which she helped found in 1896. The organization united thirty-six women's clubs in twelve states. One year after its founding it merged with the National League of Colored Women. Together they formed the **National Association of Colored Women** (NACW). Washington served as president of that group from 1912 to 1918.

Some attempts were made at about this time to bring black and white clubwomen together. Washington's home was the site of one such attempt. Nine Southern white women, at the invitation of Lugenia Hope, met in Atlanta with a group of black women. After considerable initial mistrust, the black women began to share their daily fears, and the white women agreed to organize a conference to explore how they could help in such areas as child welfare, education, protection of black girls, and the eradication of lynching.

The conference took place in October 1920. Many of the foremost black women of the time spoke. Then, as Dorothy C. Salem (1990) put it, "the conference became a model for interracial meetings of the next decade. Sympathetic white women worked with articulate black women to improve the conditions for the 'educated and developed Negro,' while leaving the general system of segregation unchallenged."

A seven-point statement was issued by the black women calling for, among other things, free exercise of the ballot and an end to lynching and unfair trials. However, the statement did not reach the white women as drafted. It was changed by Carrie Parks Johnson, leader of the Woman's Missionary Council. She had organized the conference and she took it upon herself to eliminate any reference to suffrage. To the point about lynching and injustice she added a qualifier deploring the actions of black men that supposedly incited mob violence. A preamble that had articulated a feeling of pride and militance on the part of the black women was omitted. The statement was politically gutted. Margaret Murray Washington advised black clubwomen to respond with moderation. **Lugenia Hope** and others blasted the white leadership of the conference.

The process of this event is highly revealing. Washington was involved in the earliest parts of the process, as she so often was. She offered her own resources to make things happen, as she so often did. She participated actively, but then came down firmly on the side of compromise and concession. It was the keynote of Washington's life that she could work fiercely and effectively for social improvement, never stinting herself in the service of her people, but that she could not or would not take the final step into political action.

Margaret Murray Washington continued to work for Tuskegee and in the black women's club movement until her death on June 4, 1925.

KATHLEEN THOMPSON

Wheatley, Phillis (c. 1753–1784)

Phillis Wheatley was America's first black published author. The volume was her collection *Poems on Various Subjects, Religious and Moral* (1773). She was America's second woman to publish a book of poems; Anne Bradstreet was the first.

Because she herself identifies Gambia in "Philli's Reply" as the land of her birth and because her slender facial features (long forehead, thin lips, well-defined cheekbones, and small nose) remarkably resemble those of present-day Fulani, a people who occupied the region of the Gambia River during the eighteenth century, most scholars conclude that Phillis Wheatley was born of the Gambian Fulani. At the time of her purchase in Boston on or about July 11, 1761, she was

losing her front baby teeth, suggesting that she was seven or eight at that time, and that she was born c. 1753. The name of the slaveship that transported her was the *Phillis,* and we can only speculate about the discomfort that this intelligent and sensitive child experienced because she was named after this ill-fated vessel. Her name must have served as a lifetime, moment-to-moment reminder of the horrid middle passage from Africa to America.

The only memory of her mother that Wheatley cared to recall to her white captors was that she was "out water before the sun at his rising," but this self-same sun subsequently became the central image of her poetry. On the numerous occasions when the poet employs solar imagery, she seldom articulates the commonly occurring eighteenth-century Western pun on sun-Son (Christ); rather, her sun is more often simply the life-giving sun of nature, echoing her mother's devotion. Her mother's practice of this daily ritual suggests a syncretization of hierophantic solar worship (usually practiced by the African aristocracy) and Islam, which by the mid–eighteenth century had established a presence within the Gambian region of West Africa. Wheatley's later blending in her poems of solar imagery, Judeo-Christian thought and figures, and images from ancient classicism bespeaks complex multicultural commitments, not the least of which is to her African heritage.

Wheatley's principal biographer, Margarita Matilda Oddell, recorded that Wheatley "was frequently seen," very shortly after her purchase by John and Susanna Wheatley, "endeavoring to make letters upon the wall with a piece of chalk or charcoal." Perhaps these letters were Arabic characters, but in any case her efforts seem to have prompted

Mary Wheatley, one of the Wheatley twins (Nathaniel was the other), to teach Phillis how to read the English Bible. Her master John wrote in a letter dated November 14, 1772 (a portion of which appears in the prefatory material of her 1773 *Poems*) that "by only what she was taught in the Family, she, in sixteen Months Time from her Arrival, attained the English Language." He noted, "She has a great Inclination to learn the Latin Tongue, and has made some Progress in it." Indeed, she had by the next year mastered Latin so well that for *Poems* she rendered into heroic couplets the Niobe episode from Ovid's *Metamorphoses* with such dexterity that she created one of the best English translations of it. Significantly, Wheatley did not stop with mere translation; she added so many elements to Ovid's original (such as invocation to the muse, long speeches by Niobe and a goddess, and machinery of the gods) that she has effectively recast the Latin to create an epyllion, or short epic.

Her first memorable composition appears to have been a letter to Samson Occom, the Mohegan minister, recorded in the letter by her master as written in 1765. Her first published poem was printed on December 21, 1767, in the *Newport Mercury*, a colonial newspaper of Newport, Rhode Island, where her black friend Obour Tanner resided. Some have speculated provocatively that Wheatley and Tanner came over together on the *Phillis*. In any event, Wheatley corresponded with Tanner with greater tenacity than with any other known correspondent. Recent evidence has suggested that these two visited one another frequently as well, with Wheatley traveling round-trip from Boston to Newport.

Wheatley, as a young woman, may have socialized with the other young women of Boston who joined the regular meetings of the singing schools conducted by William Billings, America's first full-time composer-choirmaster. Evidence that Wheatley and Billings knew each other has surfaced from the publication of Wheatley's elegy on Samuel Cooper's death, for appended to a six-page version of the Cooper elegy is a two-page anthem "set to Musick by Mr. Billings" to be sung at Cooper's funeral. In Billings' 1770 *The New England Psalm-Singer,* the first collection of original anthems published by an American, he included one piece entitled "Africa," which may well have been a paean to Wheatley. As early as October 2, 1769, Billings ran an ad in the *Boston Gazette* that read: "John Barrey and William Billings Begs Leave to inform the Publick, that they propose to open a Singing School This Night, near the Old South Meeting-House, where any Person inclining to learn to sing may be attended upon at said School with fidelity and Dispatch." To be sure, the Old South Boston Meeting House was Wheatley's church and the designation "any Person," not limiting sex or race, could have appealed to her.

One possible motivation for Wheatley's patriot political position might have been her close association with Old South Church itself. This church was the site of the town meeting that followed the Boston Massacre and that resulted in the expulsion of the royal governor. Wheatley's non-extant poem "On the Affray in King Street, on the Evening of the 5th of March" was most likely about the Boston Massacre and would surely have celebrated the martyrdom of Crispus Attucks, the black man who organized the "affray." "To Samuel Quincy, Esq; a Panegyrick," also non-extant, doubtless extolled Quincy, attorney for the Wheatley family and prosecutor of the British troops who fired on the American colonists in the massacre. This same Old South Church became the site of the massacre's anniversary orations, one of which was delivered by John Hancock, who signed Wheatley's letter of attestation as well as the Declaration of Independence. Here also was held the organizational meeting of the Boston Tea Party.

Still, Wheatley would not have required a building as a setting in which to learn the meaning of freedom. As a slave until mid-October 1773, this poet hardly chose the American quest for independence by accident. Indeed, American patriot rhetoric must have held an inexorable attraction for one who struggled so determinedly in her poetry for freedom. The fact that Wheatley was a communicant of the largely patriot Old South Church, though John and Susanna Wheatley attended the more loyalist New South Church, has gone relatively unnoticed. For example, as recently as 1982, J. Saunders Redding published in the *Dictionary of American Negro Biography* a sketch of Wheatley in which he claimed she was, along with the entire Wheatley family, a faithful loyalist.

Little could be further from the truth. Not only was Mary Wheatley married, by January 1771, to the fiery patriot John Lathrop, minister of Old North Church (largely a patriot congregation), but Wheatley herself wrote no poetry on behalf of the Torie's predicament. It is true that John and Susanna were indeed loyalists, and it is likely that their son Nathaniel, the other twin, who remained in England when Wheatley returned to Boston in September 1773, was a

staunch loyalist as well, for Benjamin Franklin, who was in England at the same time as Wheatley, remarks in a letter dated July 7, 1773, that "I went to see the black Poetess and offer'd her any Services I could do her. Before I left the House, I understood her Master was there and had sent her to me but did not come into the Room himself, and I thought was not pleased with the Visit." The poet's political stance must have been uncomfortable to maintain in view of the divisive attitudes within the family.

Wheatley addressed patriot themes throughout her career, writing poems dedicated to George Washington, General David Wooster, and to the declaration of peace in the 1783 Treaty of Paris, for this last occasion the poem "Liberty and Peace." Such a political position, doubtless known by the citizens of Boston, may have discouraged publication of a volume of Wheatley's poems in Boston in 1772. Whether or not the poet's politics played a role in this, racism definitely did play a decisive role, for the Boston public would not support "anything of the kind" to be printed. Wheatley was, however, soon to find a more sympathetic backer in England. Largely because of the publication in 1770 of her most famous elegy, "On the Death of Mr. George Whitefield," a poem widely printed in broadside on both sides of the Atlantic, the poet came to the attention of Selina Hastings, Countess of Huntingdon, a wealthy philanthropist whose personal chaplain had been Whitefield. When the Countess heard that Boston would not endorse Wheatley's volume, she agreed to financially back its appearance in London.

Wheatley's first proposal for a volume was made on February 29, 1772, and almost a year and a half elapsed before the volume finally went to press in July 1773. The collection as originally proposed was quite different from what was published; in effect it was two separate volumes. Such titles as "On America," "On the Death of Master Seider [Snider], who was killed by Ebenezer Richardson, 1770" (Snider was arguably, according to Wheatley, "the first martyr for the common good" [Wheatley 1988]), "On the Arrival of the Ships of War, and the Landing of the Troops," "On the Affray in King-Street, on the Evening of the 5th of March," and "To Samuel Quincy, Esq; a Panegyrick" had all been eliminated by July 1773 and replaced by such new titles as "To Maecenas," "Thoughts on the Works of Providence," "Hymn to the Morning," "Hymn to the Evening," "Isaiah," "On Recollection," "On Imagination," "Hymn to Humanity," "To S.M.," and "Niobe in Distress."

Though the earlier volume would have had much more appeal to an American patriot audience, Wheatley may have hoped that the 1773 *Poems* would appeal aesthetically to an audience that would find pro-American poems inflammatory. The 1772 volume's subject was American patriot politics; if published, Wheatley arguably could have been the author of the first book of Revolutionary War poems, challenging Philip Freneau's claim to this distinction. The 1773 *Poems*, however, has for its subject poetry, or rather how and why one Phillis Wheatley should write poetry.

Nonethelesss, the poems that Wheatley added to the 1773 volume are among her best; the year and a half between March 1772 and July 1773 was unusually productive, a period in which the poet matured as an artist. Finding her freedom still unattainable, Wheatley turned inward to construct a poetics of liberation. In her most powerful and best poem, "On Imagination," as a poet with absolute power over her words she can "with new worlds amaze th'unbounded soul." In the very next line of this piece, she constructs a new world not bound by winter's iron bands, but instead populated by fragrant flowers and forests heavy with verdant leaves. This world into which she escapes is more redolent of her African Gambia than of a Christian paradise. As the consummate romantic poet John Keats was to learn some forty years later, Wheatley realizes that no poet can indefinitely sustain a poetic world; hence she reluctantly leaves "the pleasing views" and returns to a winter whose starkest reality is the condition of slavery.

The poet's letter of October 18, 1773, to David Wooster, enumerating her activities in London during the past summer, announces the following: "Since my return to America my Master has at the desire of my friends in England given me my freedom." She was freed, then, because of events that occurred in England. This same letter reveals that while Wheatley was in London she met such dignitaries as Thomas Gibbons, Granville Sharp, Brook Watson, and the earl of Dartmouth. Dartmouth gave Wheatley five guineas with which he encouraged her to purchase Alexander Pope's *Complete Works* "as the best he could recommend to my perusal." While it is certain that Wheatley was well-acquainted with many of Pope's works before this time (for instance, her familiarity with Pope is demonstrated in "To Maecenas"), Dartmouth's recommendation that she examine Pope's complete opus suggests either that the earl was unaware of Wheatley's knowledge of Pope or that she was not as thoroughly steeped in Pope's works as has heretofore been assumed.

Regarding Wheatley's attitude toward slavery, in a letter to Samson Occom dated February 11, 1774, she presents her most eloquent and emphatic condemnation of slavery when she declares: "In every human Breast, God has implanted a Principle, which we call Love of Freedom; it is impatient of Oppression, and pants for Deliverance." This magnificent indictment of slavery the poet issued after her own manumission had been accomplished, hence putting the lie to the notion that she was unconcerned for her still-enslaved black brothers and sisters. The letter saw almost a dozen reprintings in New England newspapers before 1780.

In October 1775, Wheatley wrote a poem in honor of George Washington. She mailed the piece to the commander in chief of the Continental Army, and received an enthusiastic reply from the general and an invitation to visit him at his headquarters. Washington passed on Wheatley's encomium to a friend; subsequently the poem was printed several times as an instrument for the patriot cause. Wheatley accepted Washington's invitation, and met with him privately for thirty to forty-five minutes in his Cambridge headquarters. This poem and Wheatley's visit may have contributed to Washington's anguish about the slavery question in his later years.

In Wheatley's final years, nevertheless, she met with disappointment after disappointment. In 1778, the year of her marriage to John Peters, John Wheatley died, leaving her with greatly limited resources. The very next year, one senses almost a desperation in the impulse behind her decision to try to publish a new volume of poems. This attempt may have failed not because of racism but because a country in revolution has little

time or money for poetry. Even so, this volume projects some three hundred pages of poetry, only a small portion of which has been reclaimed. Until that manuscript is recovered (many think Peters took the manuscript south to Philadelphia after his wife's death), poems by Wheatley will probably continue to surface. During the last year of her life, Wheatley published what is perhaps her most moving funeral elegy on the death of her mentor, Samuel Cooper, as well as a poem celebrating the victory and peace of the American Revolution and another elegy. The elegy on Cooper describes its subject as "A Friend sincere, whose mild indulgent rays/Encouraged oft, and oft approv'd her lays." The paean to the Revolution boldly asserts, "And new-born Rome shall give *Brittania* Law."

While neither of these poems suggests a weakening of her poetic powers, "An Elegy on Leaving M——" does imply that the poet's career may indeed be coming to an end, for she bids farewell to "friendly bow'rs" and streams, protesting that she leaves "with sorrow each sequester'd seat." She seems uncannily to know she will soon cease to visit in imagination the plains and shepherds of the pastoral land of pure poetry. Yet even in her estranged condition, "sweet Hope" may "Bring calm content to gild my gloomy seat."

America's first internationally respected author, Wheatley was only about thirty-one when she died. On December 5, 1784, she died in Boston, unattended, of complications arising from the birth of her third child. This child apparently died mercifully with her, the other two children had also died.

Phillis Wheatley Peters (as she signed her name after her marriage) deserves to be remembered not only as a first-rate author but also for the other firsts she accomplished. Wheatley is the first American woman author who tried to earn a living by means of her writing. Henry Louis Gates, Jr., identifies Wheatley as "the progenitor of the black literary tradition" and "the black woman's literary tradition." In the history of American letters, Wheatley's sponsors and supporters comprised the first community of women devoted to insuring the success of one of their sex. Moreover, she and her work were promoted by Susanna Wheatley, her mistress, who encouraged her literary pursuits until her death; Mary Wheatley, daughter of Susanna, who apparently taught her to read the Bible; Obour Tanner, Wheatley's black soulmate (after William Robinson) with whom she commiserated throughout her life; and Selina Hastings, countess of Huntingdon, who financed Wheatley's publication of her 1773 *Poems*. All of these women nourished this young artist and without their assistance her talents and achievements may never have seen the light of day.

JOHN C. SHIELDS

World's Columbian Exposition, 1893

The World's Columbian Exposition, also known as the Chicago World's Fair, in 1893 in Chicago, Illinois, celebrated the four-hundred-year anniversary of the "discovery" of America. The 27 million people who attended saw the latest innovations in technology and heard the latest developments in intellectual thought. Moreover, spectators, for the first time, witnessed the significantly active role of women at the fair.

During the planning stages of the fair, black Americans recognized that this grand celebration also symbolized and reflected the growing tide of racism and segregation nationwide. The fair, dubbed by most Americans the "White City" because the fair commission planned for all the buildings to have white exteriors, was for black Americans a "white city" because they were not adequately represented in the celebration. In the process of protesting the exclusion and organizing appropriate representation, black women contributed to the growing efforts to develop an effective national agenda and voice for black women.

A 117-member Board of Lady Managers was appointed in 1890 by the commission to approve applications for space in the female exhibits. Included on the board were several prominent Chicago women—Bertha Honore Palmer, wife of tycoon Potter Palmer, Phoebe Couzins, women's rights advocate, and Matilda Carse, fund-raiser for the Women's Christian Temperance Union. No black women were appointed to the board nor were there plans to include exhibits from black women.

In November 1890, a group of black women in Chicago sent a resolution admonishing the commission because "no provisions have, as yet, been made . . . for securing exhibits from the colored women of this country, or the giving of representation to them . . . and . . . under the present arrangement and classification of exhibits, it would be impossible for visitors to the Exposition to know and distinguish the exhibits and handwork of the colored women from those of the Anglo-Saxons." Thus, the group resolved that "for the purpose of demonstrating the progress of the colored women since emancipation and of showing to those who are yet doubters . . . that the colored women have and are making rapid strides in art, science, and manufacturing, and of furnishing to all information as to the educational and industrial advancement made by the race, and what the race has done, is doing, and might do . . . we, the colored women of Chicago request the World's Columbian Commission to establish an office for a colored woman whose duty it shall be to collect exhibits from the colored women of America." The commission promptly sent the letter to the Board of Lady Managers.

Still, a black woman was not appointed to the board, though the concerns of black women did become a central issue. The board appointed a Southern white woman, Mary Cecil Cantrill, to represent black women's interests. Cantrill, a friend of Palmer, was suspected by black leaders of being just as paternalistic as other board members, and her appointment was a major disappointment to the black community.

Because of the constant and consistent agitation by black women, a board majority voted to provide the "same latitude and opportunity" for black women. As a conciliatory gesture, **Fannie Barrier Williams** was appointed to "help supervise the installation of all exhibits in the Woman's Building." She later became secretary of the art department of the woman's branch of the Congress Auxiliaries for the fair.

Williams was also asked to address the departmental congress of the National Association of Loyal Women of American Liberty at the World's Congress of Representative Women in May 1893. A few months later, Williams was invited to speak before the World's Parliament of Religions. Although Williams was not the only black woman who spoke at the meetings, she undoubtedly played an important role in opening the doors for several other black women to speak before the predominantly white groups. **Anna**

Julia Cooper, Sarah J. Early, Hallie Quinn Brown, and **Frances Harper** were other black women participants.

Meanwhile, **Ida B. Wells** was busy soliciting funds for the publication of a protest pamphlet, *The Reason Why the Colored American Is Not in the Columbian Exposition*, to expose the problems inherent in white racism. With the aid of several black Chicago women and with the $500 raised to finance the venture, 20,000 copies of the pamphlet were printed. Contributions from Frederick Douglass, Ferdinand Barnett, and I. Garland Penn, a journalist and editor, enhanced the pamphlet's popularity. Douglass, former minister to Haiti, provided Wells with a desk in the Haitian building at the fairgrounds where she "spent the days putting this pamphlet in the hands of foreigners." By the end of the fair, thousands of copies had been sold.

The black women who participated in the five-month world celebration had integrated the fair. In the process, these women put the concerns of black Americans on the national agenda and reshaped the image of black womanhood.

WANDA HENDRICKS

Wright, Elizabeth Evelyn (1872–1906)

Elizabeth Wright was born in a three-room cabin in Talbotton, Georgia, the seventh of twenty-one children of John Wesley Wright and Virginia Rolfe. Her father was a former slave and an illiterate carpenter. Her mother, also unschooled, was a full-blooded Cherokee. Elizabeth Wright grew up in an impoverished black section of Talbotton known as Smith Hill. She received a haphazard primary education because the school she attended at St. Philip's Church operated only periodically. Perhaps it was her own difficulty in securing an education that made Wright so determined to provide better opportunities for others. She persisted doggedly, despite violent opposition, financial constraints, and her own deteriorating health. Her persistence made possible Voorhees College in Denmark, South Carolina.

Without parental support and possessing a meager education, Wright enrolled at Tuskegee Institute in 1888. She worked days in the kitchen and attended night classes in language, reading, spelling, and mathematics as well as dressmaking, millinery, and cooking. She was physically weak and chronically sick. She could not maintain the rigorous schedule. With the help of Olivia Davidson Washington, she secured financial aid from Massachusetts judge George W. Kelley. In poor health, she interrupted her education at Tuskegee in 1892 and taught for a year at a school in McNeill's, South Carolina, operated by a Northerner, Almira S. Steele. White locals opposed the efforts of this Northern white woman to educate black people and they set fire to the school, completely destroying it.

Elizabeth Wright returned to Tuskegee, finished her fifth year, and graduated in 1894. Thoroughly impressed by Booker T. Washington and fully imbued with the self-help ideology of Tuskegee, she set out to establish a similar institution in South Carolina. Repeated failure and persistent opposition did not daunt this determined woman. When Wright attempted to organize a school in McNeill's, locating it on the nine-acre site that Judge Kelley purchased from Steele, white locals burned the building materials before construction began. A second school organized in McNeill's did not survive. Her third school, opened at Hampton Court House in 1896, incited white opposition and Wright was driven out. A fourth school established at nearby Govan lasted only briefly.

Wright finally met with success in Denmark, South Carolina, when she opened Denmark Industrial School on April 14, 1897, on the second floor of a local store. With the support of a local white attorney and state senator, Stanwix G. Mayfield, she purchased twenty acres of land, moved the school, and opened it to 236 students on October 4, 1897. With the aid and persistent encouragement of Jessie Dorsey, a nurse and teacher from Coshocton, Ohio, the school grew steadily if uncertainly. Some black people led by a local clergyman opposed the school and questioned the religious commitment of the two women, especially Dorsey, who was a Seventh-Day Adventist.

Wright served as principal of the Denmark school, supervising instruction, construction, farming, and fund-raising. Devoted to industrial and agricultural education and intensely moralistic, she was convinced tl.at hard work, self-discipline, and the acquisition of skills combined with honesty, cleanliness, and reliability would elevate people of color. In her second annual report, she explained her mission: "We feel it is our duty to work for the ennobling of our race, and as they rise to a higher standard of citizenship and become stronger morally, physically, and intellectually, they will be a blessing to American civilization instead of a curse, and other races will be helped indirectly by them."

She was an intrepid fund-raiser. In 1901, Ralph Voorhees, a New Jersey philanthropist, donated $4,500 to purchase 200 acres of land. The school moved to the new site and was renamed Voorhees Industrial

School. Kennerly Hall and Voorhees Hall were constructed and several new programs were added, including carpentry, blacksmithing, and printing. The farm expanded with the arrival of contributions in the form of horses, mules, hogs, and poultry.

On June 2, 1906, Wright married Martin Menafee, a Tuskegee graduate and the business manager-treasurer of Voorhees. Four months later, after Wright suffered another of her repeated illnesses, Dr. James Harvey Kellogg operated on her for gastritis in Battle Creek, Michigan. She seemed to be recovering when she suffered a relapse and died on December 14.

As her legacy, Voorhees survived and prospered. It maintained its industrial mission for most of the first half of the twentieth century. In 1924, the Episcopal Church began to support Voorhees. In 1929, a junior college was added to its elementary and high school programs. In 1964, it became a four-year college.

WILLIAM C. HINE

Y

Yates, Josephine Silone   (1859–1912)

Josephine Silone Yates, second president of the **National Association of Colored Women** (NACW), from 1901 to 1906, made her most significant mark on the world as a teacher. She was also a writer—mainly for newspapers and sometimes under the pen name R. K. Potter—and lecturer.

Born in 1859 in Mattituck, New York, to a well-respected and solidly established family, Josephine Silone was taught reading, writing, and arithmetic at home before entering school. She received the favorable attention of her teachers early on for her unusual intelligence and eagerness to learn. At the age of eleven, she was sent to live with an uncle so that she could have the opportunity to study under **Fanny Jackson Coppin** at the **Institute for Colored Youth**. This, her first opportunity to interact with other black students, seems to have been a rewarding and meaningful experience. She returned home a year later when her uncle accepted a post at **Howard University** but, at the age of fourteen, she accepted the invitation of an aunt to live with her in Newport, Rhode Island. This arrangement was probably made in order to provide young Josephine with the opportunity to attend the larger, and presumably better, Newport schools.

The only black student in her high school, Yates completed the four-year course of study in three years and was the valedictorian of the class of 1877. She then attended the Rhode Island State Normal School, taking teaching courses, and graduated with honors. Again, she was the only black student in her class. After receiving the highest score that had ever been recorded on the state teacher's examination, she became the first black person to be certified to teach in Rhode Island.

Yates had shown an interest in and ability for science, particularly chemistry, from an early age. In 1879, she moved to Jefferson City, Missouri, to teach chemistry at the Lincoln Institute where, not long after becoming the first woman professor, she became the head of the department of natural science. Her reputation grew and she was asked by Booker T. Washington to become the "lady principal" of Tuskegee Institute, an offer she declined.

In 1889, Josephine Silone resigned her teaching position to marry W. W. Yates, the principal of the Wendell Phillips School in Kansas City. She did not, however, give up her intellectual pursuits. Although no longer teaching, she continued writing, mainly for newspaper publications, on a variety of subjects, including such wide-ranging topics as economics and Russian literature.

Yates also worked in the club movement, organizing the Kansas City Women's League in 1893 and joining, in 1896, the NACW.

After her husband's death in 1910, Yates returned to teaching for two years. She died on September 3, 1912.

JAN GLEITER

Chronology

1619

Twenty Africans, three of them women, are put ashore off a Dutch ship at Jamestown, Virginia.

1624

In Jamestown, Virginia, a woman known to us only as Isabel, wife of Antoney, gives birth to William, the first black child born in English North America.

1641

Massachusetts is the first colony in North America to recognize slavery legally; Connecticut follows in 1650.

1661

Virginia legally recognizes slavery; Maryland in 1663; New York and New Jersey, 1664; South Carolina, 1682; Rhode Island and Pennsylvania, 1700; North Carolina, 1715; Georgia, 1750.

1662

Virginia law establishes that children born in the colony will be free if the mother is free and slave if the mother is slave.

1692

Tituba, a West Indian slave accused of witchcraft in Salem, Massachusetts, is the catalyst for the infamous Salem witchhunt and trials.

1708

At least one black woman is involved in a Newton, Long Island, New York, slave revolt in which seven whites are killed.

1712

Slave men and women in New York City initiate a revolt that results in the deaths of nine white men and the stiffening of restrictions on slaves.

1746

Lucy Terry Prince writes "Bars Fight," the first known poem by an African-American in the United States; the poem is not published until 1895.

1765

Jenny Slew sues for her freedom in a Massachusetts court and wins.

1773

Phillis Wheatley publishes *Poems on Various Subjects Religious and Moral,* the first book published by a black person and the second by a women in North America.

1776

Margaret Corbin fights for the colonies during the Revolutionary War. Known as "Captain Molly," she is wounded during an attack on Fort Washington, New York.

1777

Vermont abolishes slavery.

1780

Pennsylvania passes a law that gradually frees slaves in the state. Similar laws are enacted in Connecticut and Rhode Island in 1784; New York, 1799; New Jersey, 1804.

1781

Los Angeles, California, is founded by forty-four settlers, of whom at least twenty-six are black women, men, and children.

Elizabeth Freeman, also known as Mum Bett, sues for her freedom on the grounds that the 1780 Massachusetts state constitution declares that all men are born free and equal. Her petition is designed to establish slavery as inconsistent with state law and thus secure freedom for all Massachusetts slaves. Freeman is granted her freedom and 30 shillings in damages as restitution for a beating by her mistress.

1782

Deborah Sampson (Gannett), disguised as a man, begins a seventeen-month stint in the Continental Army. Sources disagree as to whether Sampson was African American.

1784

The first black Catholic community in the United States is established in St. Augustine, Florida, by escaped slaves who build the fortified town of Gracia Real de Santa Teresa de Mose.

1787

The U.S. Constitution, with three clauses protecting slavery, is approved at the Phila-delphia Convention.

The Northwest Ordinance prohibits slavery in the territory that will eventually become Michigan, Ohio, Illinois, Indiana, and Wisconsin.

The Free African Society is established in Philadelphia. It is the first African-American secret and beneficial society in the United States.

The first African Free School is established in New York.

Mary Butler, the daughter of Mary and William Butler, who had sued for their freedom in 1771 and lost, takes her own case to court and wins.

1790

The black population of the United States totals 757,181. Of this number, 59,557 are free and 697,624 are held in slavery.

1793

The first fugitive slave law is enacted by Congress, making it a crime to harbor or prevent the arrest of a fugitive slave.

The Female Benevolent Society of St. Thomas is founded by black women in Philadelphia.

A former slave, **Catherine Ferguson**, having purchased her freedom, opens Katy Ferguson's School for the Poor in New York. She enrolls both black and white children from a local poorhouse.

1796

The first woman to argue before the U.S. Supreme Court is Lucy Terry Prince. She represents her own family against a white man and wins.

1800

The black population of the United States totals 1,002,037. Of this number, 108,435 are free and 893,602 are held in slavery.

Nanny Prosser joins her husband, Gabriel, and other slaves in planning a revolt near Richmond, Virginia. The revolt fails.

1804

The Ohio legislature enacts the first of a series of black Laws restricting the rights and movements of free blacks. Similar laws are passed throughout the North.

1809

The African Female Benevolent Society of Newport, Rhode Island, is founded.

1810

The black population of the United States totals 1,377,808. Of this number, 186,446 are free and 1,191,362 are held in slavery.

1816

The African Methodist Episcopal (AME) Church is founded.

1817

Jarena Lee is authorized by African Methodist Episcopal Bishop Richard Allen to lead prayer meetings in her house. She is, in this limited sense, the first woman minister in the AME.

1818

The Colored Female Religious and Moral Society of Salem, Massachusetts, is founded.

1820

The black female population of the United States totals 870,860. The total black population is 1,771,656. Of this number, 233,634 are free and 1,538,022 (750,010 women) are held in slavery.

Eighty-six African Americans, sailing out of New York City, emigrate to Sierra Leone, West Africa.

The African Company, the first black dramatic company, is founded. It performs in the African Grove Theatre in Greenwich Village in New York City. Black women are seen on stage for the first time we know of.

1821

The African Methodist Episcopal Zion (AMEZ) Church is founded.

Two hundred working-class women in Philadelphia form the Daughters of Africa mutual benefit society.

1826

Nashoba, a colony for free blacks near Memphis, Tennessee, is established by Frances "Fanny" Wright.

1827

The first black newspaper, *Freedom's Journal*, is published in New York. Among its main financial supporters is the Female Literary Society of New York City.

The African Methodist Episcopal Daughters of Conference organizations are officially allowed to provide material assistance to ministers.

The African Dorcas Association is founded by black women in New York City to supply clothing to children in the African Free Schools.

1828

The Coloured Female Roman Catholic Beneficial Society of Washington, D.C., is founded.

1829

Following a race riot, more than 1,000 black women, men, and children leave Cincinnati, Ohio, and immigrate to Canada.

The **Oblate Sisters of Providence**, the first Roman Catholic religious community of black women in the United States, is established in Baltimore, Maryland. **Elizabeth Lange,** originally from Saint-Domingue, is the Mother Superior.

St. Francis Academy of Colored Girls, a boarding school founded by the Oblate Sisters of Providence, opens in Baltimore, Maryland.

1830

Women are 1,162,366 of a total U.S. black population of 2,328,642. Of the total, 319,599 are free and 2,009,043 (996,220 women) are held in slavery. As a result of gradual emancipation laws, only 2,780 African Americans remain enslaved in the Northern states.

1831

The first National Negro Convention meets in Philadelphia.

The Female Literary Association of Philadelphia and the Afric-American Female Intelligence Society of Boston are founded.

The History of Mary Prince, a West Indian Slave is the first slave narrative published by a black woman in the Americas.

1832

The Female Anti-Slavery Society of Salem, Massachusetts, is founded by free women of color, including Mary A. Battys, Charlotte Bell, Eleanor C. Harvey, and Dorothy C. Battys.

Maria Stewart becomes the first native-born U.S. woman to begin a public-speaking career when she lectures before a male and female audience in Boston's Franklin Hall, under the sponsorship of the African-American Society.

Former slave **Marie Bernard Couvent** provides in her will for the "establishment of a free school for orphans of color." It opens in New Orleans in 1848 and becomes the oldest black Catholic school in the United States.

1833

The Philadelphia Library of Colored Persons is established to house books and sponsor concerts, lectures, and debates.

The interracial **Philadelphia Female Anti-Slavery Society** is founded, with nine black women among the charter members.

Prudence Crandall, a white Quaker schoolteacher, opens a "High school for young colored Ladies and Misses" in Canterbury, Connecticut, enrolling fifteen students. The townspeople burn the school.

1835

Oberlin College becomes the first U.S. college to admit students without regard to race or sex.

1836

A group of black women rush a Boston courtroom and carry away to freedom two fugitive slave women before they can be returned to those claiming to be their masters. A similar rescue is executed by black women in New York.

Jarena Lee publishes *The Life and Religious Experiences of Jarena Lee, a Coloured Lady...* the first autobiography of an American black woman.

1837

When the first Antislavery Convention of American Women meets in New York, at least one-tenth of the members are African American. Grace Bustill Douglass is elected a vice president and **Sarah Forten**'s poem "We are thy sisters" is printed by the convention.

1838

The Memoirs of Elleanor Eldridge, one of the few narratives of the life of an early nineteenth-century free black woman, is published.

1840

Women total 1,440,660 in a U.S. black population of 2,873,648. Of the total population, 386,293 are free and 2,487,355 (1,240,948 women) are held in slavery.

1841

Ann Plato writes *Essays, including Biographies and Miscellaneous Pieces in Prose and Poetry.*

1842

Henriette Delille founds the second black Roman Catholic religious congregation in the United States, the Sisters of the Holy Family, in Louisiana.

1843

Sojourner Truth leaves New York and begins abolitionist work.

1844

The African Methodist Episcopal Church General Conference defeats the first petition to license women to preach.

1846

The Colored Female Benevolent Society of Louisiana is founded in New Orleans.

Zilpha Elaw publishes *Memoirs of the Life, Religious Experience, Ministerial Travels and Labors of Mrs. Zilpha Elaw.*

1848

Boston officials bar Sarah Roberts from a neighborhood white school and require her to pass five other white schools to attend a school designated for black children. Her father, Benjamin Roberts, files the first school integration suit on her behalf. In its 1849 ruling in *Sarah C. Roberts* v. *City of Boston,* the Massachusetts state supreme court upholds the legality of segregation, justifying it with the first recorded use of the "separate but equal" doctrine.

Ellen Craft, with her husband, William, escapes from slavery. Ellen dresses as a slaveholder, and William acts as her valet.

1849

The Women's Association of Philadelphia is organized to raise money to support Frederick Douglass' newspaper, the *North Star.*

Harriet Tubman escapes from slavery. She will return South more than a dozen times to bring hundreds of others out of slavery.

At a suffrage meeting in Ohio, a group of black women threaten to leave if they are not allowed to speak during discussions. The meeting decides that they can participate.

1850

Women total 1,827,550 in a U.S. black population of 3,638,808. Of the total population, 434,495 are free and 3,204,313 (1,601,779 women) are held in slavery.

Following the passage of the Fugitive Slave Law, which gives virtually unlimited authority to any white man claiming a black person as his runaway slave, thousands of African Americans flee to Canada.

Lucy Sessions earns a literary degree from **Oberlin College**, becoming the first black woman in the United States to receive a college degree.

1851

In Christiana, Pennsylvania, armed black men and women resist an effort to recapture four escaped slaves. Federal troops are sent to defeat the resisters, thirty-six of whom are charged with treason. All are eventually acquitted in court.

During her speech at an Akron, Ohio, women's rights convention, Sojourner Truth (Isabella Baumfree) speaks her now-famous words, "And a'n't I a woman?"

Elizabeth Taylor Greenfield ("The Black Swan"), the first black American concert singer, makes her debut in Buffalo, New York.

1852

The **Institute for Colored Youth** is founded in Philadelphia by the Society of Friends. It is the first coeducational classical high school for African Americans.

The Norman School for Colored Girls is founded in Washington, D.C., by Myrtilla Miner, a white educator.

Mary Ann Shadd (Cary) publishes *A Plea for Emigration or Notes on Canada West, in Its Moral, Social, and Political Aspect: With Suggestions Respecting Mexico, W. Indies and Vancouvers Island for the Information of Colored Emigrants* to educate black people on the advantages of emigrating to Canada.

1853

Mary Ann Shadd (Cary) becomes editor and financier of the *Provincial Freeman*, published in Windsor, Canada, becoming the first black woman editor of a newspaper in North America.

Rachel Parker wins her freedom in a Maryland state court.

1854

Twenty-nine black women delegates make up one-third of the participants at the National Emigration Convention. Mary E. Bibb is elected second vice president of the convention.

Elizabeth Jennings sues the Third Avenue Railroad Company, winning $225 in damages and a court ruling that "colored persons, if sober, well-behaved and free from disease" can ride the New York City horsecars without segregation.

Frances Ellen Watkins (Harper) publishes *Poems on Miscellaneous Subjects*.

Elizabeth Taylor Greenfield gives a command performance at Buckingham Palace for Queen Victoria.

1855

Mary Ann Shadd (Cary) addresses the National Negro Convention in Philadelphia, where she is the first female corresponding member.

1856
Mary E. Bibb and Mary Ann Shadd (Cary) are elected to the Board of Publications at the National Emigration Convention.

Sarah Parker Remond becomes lecturer for the American Antislavery Society.

When **Biddy Mason's** master returns to the South, she stays behind in California. A local court agrees that she is free, and she becomes an affluent landowner and activist.

1857
Elizabeth Thorn Scott-Flood opens what is probably the first black school in Alameda County, California.

1858
Mary Ellen Pleasant, the "mother of the Civil Rights Struggle in California," finances the defense of Archy Lee in California's famous fugitive slave case.

1859
In Philadelphia, **Rebecca Cox Jackson** founds the first black Shaker community.

Sarah Parker Remond begins a two-year lecture tour on the abolition of slavery to Scotland, Ireland, England, and France.

Harriet E. Wilson's *Our Nig: or Sketches from the Life of a Free Black,* the first novel published in the United States by an African American. Wilson is the fifth African American to publish fiction in English, and one of the first two black women to publish a novel in any language.

A graduate of Oberlin College, **Sarah Jane Woodson Early** becomes the first black woman on the faculty of an American uni-

versity when she joins that of Wilberforce University in Ohio.

1860
Women total 2,225,086 in a U.S. black population of 4,441,830. Of the total population, 488,070 are free and 3,953,760 (1,971,135 women) are held in slavery.

1861
The Civil War begins. Thousands of slave women and men flee to Union lines and join their efforts to those of the Union soldiers.

Mary Peake opens a one-room day school in Hampton, Virginia, with the help of the American Missionary Association (AMA).

The Port Royal Commission is begun in the Sea Islands near South Carolina, with **Charlotte Forten (Grimké)** as the only black teacher in the experiment. She is joined by **Susan King Taylor** in 1864.

Harriet Jacobs' *Incidents in the Life of a Slave Girl* is published under the pseudonym Linda Brent.

Early civil rights activist Mary Ellen Pleasant leads a successful petition drive fighting for the passage of a law guaranteeing African Americans the right to testify in court.

1862
Congress abolishes slavery in Washington, D.C.

Elizabeth Keckley helps form the Contraband Relief Association to raise money to aid freedpeople.

Susan King Taylor, at fourteen, becomes the first African-American army nurse in the United States.

Mary Jane Patterson earns a B.A. degree from Oberlin College, making her the first black woman to earn a Bachelor's degree from an accredited United States college.

Mary Ellen Pleasant sues the San Francisco Car Company to correct rude treatment given her and other black women.

1863

Harriet Tubman leads Union troops in a raid along the Combahee River in South Carolina.

1864

Maryland abolishes slavery.

Mary Ann Shadd Cary receives a commission as a recruiting officer from Governor O.P. Morton of Indiana, becoming the only woman given official recognition as a recruiter during the Civil War.

Rebecca Lee (Crumpler) becomes the first African-American woman to graduate from a U.S. college with a formal medical degree.

1865

The Thirteenth Amendment to the U.S. Constitution, abolishing slavery, is adopted.

The Bureau of Refugees, Freedmen, and Abandoned Lands (Freedmen's Bureau) is established by Congress to coordinate aid and relief efforts, including educational opportunities, for newly emancipated slaves.

Thousands of African-American women, individually and through their organizations, become depositors in the Freedman's Savings and Trust Company, chartered by the U.S. Congress, with business limited to African Americans. Most of them lose their money when the bank suspends operations in 1874.

Atlanta University (Georgia) and Shaw Institute (Raleigh, North Carolina) are founded.

Fanny Jackson (Coppin) is the second Af-rican-American woman to receive an A.B. degree when she graduates from Oberlin College.

1866

Fisk University (Nashville, Tennessee), Rust College (Holly Springs, Mississippi), and Lincoln University (Jefferson City, Missouri) are founded.

Three days of racial violence break out in Memphis, Tennessee.

Washerwomen in Jackson, Mississippi, organize a strike and submit a formal petition to the mayor, notifying him of their intentions to demand reasonable wages.

Sarah Woodson Early is appointed preceptress of English and Latin and lady principal and matron at Wilberforce University, becoming the first African-American woman on a college faculty.

1867

Howard University (Washington, D.C.), Talladega College (Alabama), Morgan State College (Baltimore, Maryland), Johnson C. Smith College (Charlotte, North Carolina) and St. Augustine's College (Raleigh, North Carolina) are founded.

Rebecca Cole, the second black woman to receive a medical degree in the United States, graduates from the Women's Medical College of Pennsylvania in Philadelphia.

1868

The Fourteenth Amendment is ratified, extending citizenship rights to African Americans.

Hampton Normal and Agricultural Institute (Virginia) is founded.

The African Methodist Episcopal Church General Conference creates the position of stewardess, the first official position for women in the denomination.

Elizabeth Keckley publishes her autobiography, *Behind the Scenes: or Thirty Years a Slave and Four Years in the White House.*

1869

The American Equal Rights Association, the umbrella universal suffrage organization, splits over the questions of black male suffrage and woman suffrage. The National Woman Suffrage Association and the American Woman Suffrage Association are created in its absence.

Clark College (Atlanta, Georgia), Claflin College (Orangeburg, South Carolina), Straight College (now Dillard, New Orleans, Louisiana), and Tougaloo College (Mississippi) are founded.

Howard University Medical School opens its doors to women, both black and white. By 1900, 103 women have enrolled. Of the forty-eight who graduate, twenty-three are black and twenty-five are white.

Mary Ann Shadd Cary chairs the Committee on Female Suffrage at the Colored National Labor Union (CNLU) convention and becomes the only woman elected to the CNLU's executive committee.

Fanny Jackson (Coppin) is named principal of the Institute for Colored Youth in Philadelphia, becoming the first black woman to head an institution for higher learning in the United States.

Woman suffragist **Louisa Rollin** addresses the South Carolina House of Representatives on behalf of universal suffrage.

1870

Women total 2,486,746 in a U.S. black population of 4,880,009.

The Fifteenth Amendment to the U.S. Constitution is ratified and interpreted as providing black male citizens with the right to vote. Its enfranchisement of men sparks a debate within African-American communities over women suffrage.

The Colored Methodist Episcopal (CME) Church is founded.

Allen University (Columbia, South Carolina), Benedict College (Columbia, South Carolina), and Le Moyne–Owen College (Memphis, Tennessee) are founded.

Upon graduation from the New York Medical College for Women, Susan McKinney Steward becomes the third black woman doctor in the United States.

1871

The first tour of the **Fisk Jubilee Singers,** in the United States, England, Scotland, Ireland, Holland, and Switzerland, raises $50,000 for their university.

Mary Ann Shadd Cary addresses the U.S. House of Representatives Judiciary Committee, speaking on woman suffrage.

1872

Alcorn A&M College (Lorman, Mississippi) is founded.

Following her graduation from Howard University Law School, **Charlotte E. Ray,** using the initials C. E. to avoid discrimination against women, is admitted to the District of Columbia bar. She is the first black woman lawyer in the United States.

1873

Bennett College (Greensboro, North Carolina), Wiley College (Marshall, Texas), and Alabama State College (Montgomery) are founded.

1874

The federally sponsored Freedman's Savings and Trust Company closes, with 61,000 black depositors losing nearly $3 million.

1875

The Civil Rights Bill of 1871 provides for equal access to public accommodations without regard to race.

Alabama A&M College (Normal), Knoxville College (Tennessee), and Lane College (Jackson, Tennessee) are founded.

Black women armed with clubs patrol polling places on election day in South Carolina.

1876

Prairie View A&M College (Texas) is founded.

Harriet Purvis is the first African-American woman to be elected vice president of the National Woman Suffrage Association.

The first permanent black musical-comedy troupe, the **Hyers Sisters** Comic Opera Company, is organized.

Lucy Parsons joins the Workingmen's party and later becomes the first black woman to have a major role in the Socialist Party.

1877

On the heels of the Great Strike of 1877, which crippled the nation's railroad industry, domestic workers in Galveston, Texas, organize a strike.

The all-black town of Nicodemus, Kansas, is founded.

Jackson State College (Mississippi) is founded.

1878

Two hundred and six black emigrants set sail from Charleston, South Carolina, for Liberia, West Africa, on board the *Azor*.

1879

As many as 6,000 African Americans migrate to Kansas in the space of a few months. This is part of a larger westward movement of approximately 25,000 Southern black people in the late 1870s and early 1880s.

Livingston College (Salisbury, North Carolina) is founded.

Mary Eliza Mahoney is the first African American in the United States to receive a diploma in nursing.

Julia A. J. Foote publishes *A Brand Plucked from the Fire! An Autobiographical Sketch*.

1880

Women total 3,327,678 in a total U.S. black population of 6,580,793.

Southern University (New Orleans, later Baton Rouge, Louisiana) is founded.

Mary Ann Shadd Cary, Mrs. Nichols, Anna Montgomery, Miss Jennings, Mrs. Robinson, Mrs. Jerris, and Mrs. Monroe organize the Colored Women's Progressive Franchise Association in Washington, D.C. to gain the vote for women and to establish black women in business.

1881

Tennessee passes a state railroad segregation law. Similar laws are passed in Florida (1887); Mississippi (1888); Texas (1889); Louisiana (1890); Alabama, Arkansas, Georgia, Kentucky (1891); South Carolina (1898); North Carolina (1899); Virginia (1900); Maryland (1904); and Oklahoma (1907).

In the largest mass migration from South Carolina, 5,000 black women, men and children leave Edgefield and relocate in Alabama. They equal approximately one-fifth of the Edgefield population.

Tuskegee Institute (Alabama) is founded.

The Atlanta Baptist Female Seminary is founded in Atlanta, Georgia; the name is changed to Spelman Seminary in 1884.

Washerwomen in Atlanta form the Washing Society and organize the largest known strike by black women to date. At its peak, 3,000 strikers and supporters are mobilized.

1882

Virginia State College (Petersburg) is founded.

1882-1927

At least twenty-six black women are lynched in the United States.

1883

The U.S. Supreme Court declares the Civil Rights Act of 1875 unconstitutional.

Hartshorn Memorial College for Women is founded in Richmond, Virginia. It becomes (in 1888) the first educational institution in the United States chartered as a *college* for black women.

Mary Ann Shadd Cary becomes the second black woman to earn a law degree when she graduates from Howard University.

Rebecca Lee Crumpler, M.D., publishes *A Book of Medical Discourses in Two Parts.* It offers advice to women on how to provide medical care to themselves and their children.

1884

Anna Julia Cooper, Mary Church (Terrell), and Ida A. Gibbs (Hunt) graduate from Oberlin College.

1885

Gertrude Mossell launches the woman's column in the *New York Age* with her article "Woman's Suffrage."

Sara E. Goode is the first black woman to receive a U.S. patent, for her folding cabinet bed.

1886

The Colored Farmers' Alliance is founded. By 1901 it has organized in twenty states, with a membership of 1,125,000.

Kentucky State College (Frankfort) is founded.

Lucy Craft Laney opens a grammar school in Augusta, Georgia, which becomes the **Haines Normal and Industrial Institute.**

The first school for black nursing students is established at Spelman Seminary in Atlanta, Georgia.

Louise "Lulu" Fleming is the first black woman to be commissioned for career missionary service by the Women's Baptist Foreign Missionary Society of the West.

1887

Florida A&M College (Tallahassee) and Central State College (Wilberforce, Ohio) are founded.

Mary Ellen Morrison earns a pharmaceutical doctoral degree from Howard University's School of Medicine.

Amanda America Dickson becomes one of the wealthiest women in Georgia after the Georgia Supreme Court upholds her right to inherit her white father's estate.

1888

Our Women and Children begins publication. Founded by Dr. William J. Simmons, it employs a number of black women journalists, including **Lucy Wilmot Smith** as head of the woman's department, Mary V. Cook as editor of the educational department, **Ida B. Wells (Barnett)** as editor of the home department, and Ione E. Wood as editor of the temperance department.

Cornelia Bowen founds Mt. Meigs Institute in Mt. Meigs, Alabama.

Sarah Woodson Early becomes superintendent of the Colored Division of the Women's Christian Temperance Union and serves until 1892.

Sarah E. Gorham becomes the first woman missionary of the African Methodist Episcopal Church to be appointed to a foreign field.

Nancy Jones is the first unmarried black woman commissioned by the Congregational American Board as a missionary to Africa.

Miriam E. Benjamin is awarded a patent for a "Gong and Signal Chair." It is later adopted for use in the U.S. House of Representatives to signal pages.

1889

The federal government opens Oklahoma Territory to homestead settlement. More than 7,000 African Americans migrate to the territory during the first year of settlement.

Ida B. Wells (Barnett) is elected secretary of the National Afro-American Press Association. Wells also becomes part owner and editor of the *Memphis Free Speech and Headlight*.

Maria Louise Baldwin becomes the first African-American female principal in Massachusetts and the Northeast. She supervises white faculty and a predominantly white student body at Agassiz Grammar School in Cambridge.

Josephine A. Silone Yates becomes professor and head of the Natural Sciences Department at Lincoln University (Jefferson City, Missouri).

1889-93

At least eight black women are lynched.

1890

Women total 3,753,073 in a U.S. black population of 7,488,676.

The National Afro-American League is founded.

The all-black town of Langston City, Oklahoma, is founded.

Savannah State College (Georgia) is founded.

Janie Porter Barrett establishes the Locust Street Settlement House in Hampton, Virginia. It is one of the first African-American settlement houses.

Clarence and Corinne or God's Way, by Amelia E. Johnson, is the first book by a woman to be published by the American Baptist Publication Society and the first Sunday school book published by an African American.

Ida Gray is the first African-American woman to receive the Doctor of Dental Surgery degree.

Octavia R. Albert's book *House of Bondage*, is published. It includes seven slave narratives.

1891

Delaware State College (Dover), North Carolina A&T College (Greensboro), and West Virginia State College (Institute) are founded.

Daniel Hale Williams founds Provident Hospital in Chicago, site of the second nursing school for African-American students.

Lucy Parsons begins publishing her newspaper, *Freedom: A Revolutionary Anarchist-Communist* Monthly.

Julia Ringwood Coston edits and publishes *Ringwood's Afro-American Journal of Fashion.*

Minnie Cox is appointed postmistress of Indianola, Mississippi.

1892

Ida B. Wells (Barnett) launches the first phase of the antilynching movement, with her articles and editorials in the Memphis *Free Speech* and the *New York Age* and the publication of *Southern Horrors.*

The **Woman's Loyal Union** is founded in New York City, with **Victoria Earle Matthews** as its first president.

The Colored Woman's League of Washington, D.C., is founded.

Mary Moore Booze, Harriet Amanda Miller, and Dixie Erms Williams graduate with B.S. degrees from Hartshorn Memorial College, the first college degrees granted by a black women's institution.

Anna Julia Cooper publishes *A Voice from the South by a Black Woman of the South.*

Frances Ellen Watkins Harper publishes her novel *Iola Leroy: or, Shadows Uplifted.*

The international opera star **Sissieretta Jones** sings before President Benjamin Harrison at the White House.

1893

The Women's Home and Missionary Society of the African Methodist Episcopal Church is founded.

Anna Julia Cooper, Fanny Jackson Coppin, and Fannie Barrier Williams address the Women's Congress at the World's Columbian Exposition in Chicago, on the theme "The Intellectual Progress of Colored Women of the United States Since Emancipation."

Meharry Medical College, founded in 1876 in Nashville, Tennessee, awards its first medical degrees to women, Georgianna Patton and Anna D. Gregg.

The Women's Era Club is founded in Boston.

Myrtle Hart, pianist and harpist, plays at the British exhibit at the Chicago World's Fair.

1894

The *Women's Era,* later to become the official organ of the National Association of Colored Women, begins publication.

Julia A. J. Foote is the first female ordained deacon in the A.M.E. Zion Church.

Gertrude (Mrs. N. F.) Mossell publishes *The Work of the Afro-American Women.*

1894-98

At least fifteen black women are lynched.

1895

The Church of God in Christ is founded.

Black Baptist churches throughout the country organize the National Baptist Convention.

The National Medical Association is founded.

Fort Valley State College (Georgia) is founded.

Josephine St. Pierre Ruffin organizes the first National Conference of Colored Women, meeting in Boston.

The National Federation of Afro-American Women is founded, with **Margaret Murray Washington** as president and Josephine St. Pierre Ruffin as vice president.

Victoria Earle Matthews begins a tour of the South to report on the status of southern African-American women for the National Federation of Afro-American Women.

Ida B. Wells (Barnett) publishes *Red Records: Tabulated Statistics and Alleged Causes of Lynchings in the United States, 1892–1894* after completing lecture tours in England.

Mary Church Terrell is appointed to the Washington, D.C., Board of Education, becoming the first African-American woman to serve on a board of education.

1896

In the precedent-setting *Plessy* v. *Ferguson,* the U.S. Supreme Court rules "separate but equal" facilities are constitutional.

South Carolina State College (Orangeburg) is founded.

The *Laurada* sets sail from Savannah, Georgia, with 321 African Americans emigrating to Liberia, West Africa.

The National League of Colored Women and the National Federation of Afro-American Women merge to form the **National Association of Colored Women**, with Mary Church Terrell as the first NACW president.

Sissieretta Jones organizes the Black Patti Troubadours.

1897

The First Hampton Negro Conference is held. At the first conference, Fanny Jackson Coppin speaks on industrial education. Later conferences include sessions organized by state and national women leaders on topics such as women's education, community services, and health issues.

The American Negro Academy is founded to promote scholarly work and fellowship among leading intellectuals. Anna Julia Cooper is the only woman elected to membership.

Langston University (Oklahoma) is founded.

Elizabeth Evelyn Wright, with the help of Jessie Dorsey, founds the Denmark Industrial School in Denmark, South Carolina (later Voorhees Industrial School, now Voorhees College).

Spelman Seminary begins a College Department, with collegiate courses offered on Atlanta Baptist (Morehouse) campus.

Victoria Earle Matthews founds the **White Rose Mission** in New York City to serve as a community center, with special emphasis on assistance to black women emigrating from the South.

1898

A Slave Girl's Story, Kate Drumgold's autobiographical narrative, is published.

1899-1903

At least four black women are lynched.

Bibliography

GENERAL BOOKS USEFUL TO THE STUDY OF BLACK WOMEN IN AMERICA

Reference Books

African-Americans: Voices of Triumph. Three volume set: *Perseverance, Leadership,* and *Creative Fire.* By the editors of Time-Life Books, Alexandria, Virginia, 1993.

Estell, Kenneth, ed., *The African-American Almanac.* Detroit, Mich., 1994.

Harley, Sharon. *The Timetables of African-American History: A Chronology of the Most Important People and Events in African-American History.* New York, 1995.

Hine, Darlene Clark, ed., Elsa Barkley Brown and Rosalyn Terborg-Penn, associate editors. *Black Women in America: An Historical Encyclopedia.* Brooklyn, New York, 1993.

Hine, Darlene Clark. *Hine Sight: Black Women and The Re-Construction of American History.* Brooklyn, New York, 1994.

Hornsby, Alton, Jr. *Chronology of African-American History: Significant Events and People from 1619 to the Present.* Detroit, Michigan, 1991.

Kranz, Rachel. *Biographical Dictionary of Black Americans.* New York, 1992.

Logan, Rayford W., and Michael R. Winston, eds. *Dictionary of American Negro Biography,* New York, 1982.

Low, W. Augustus, and Virgil A. Clift, eds. *Encyclopedia of Black America.* New York, 1981.

Salem, Dorothy C., ed. *African American Women: A Biographical Dictionary.* New York, 1993.

Salzman, Jack, David Lionel Smith, and Cornel West. *Encyclopedia of African-American Culture and History.* Five Volumes. New York, 1996.

Smith, Jessie Carney, ed., *Notable Black American Women.* Two Volumes. Detroit, Mich., Book I, 1993; Book II, 1996.

General Books about Black Women

Giddings, Paula. *When and Where I Enter: The Impact of Black Women on Race and Sex in America,* New York, 1984.

Guy-Sheftall, Beverly. *Words of Fire: An Anthology of African-American Feminist Thought.* New York, 1995.

Hine, Darlene Clark, Wilma King, and Linda Reed, eds. *"We Specialize in the Wholly Impossible": A Reader in Black Women's History.* Brooklyn, N.Y., 1995.

Jones, Jacqueline. *Labor of Love, Labor of Sorrow: Black Women, Work, and the Family from Slavery to the Present.* New York, 1985.

Lerner, Gerda, ed. *Black Women in White America: A Documentary History.* New York, 1972.

BOOKS ON PRE-TWENTIETH-CENTURY AFRICAN AMERICANS

Bibliography

Yellin, Jean Fagan, and Cynthia Bond, compilers. *The Pen Is Ours: A Listing of Writings by and about African-American Women before 1910 With a Secondary Bibliography to the Present*. New York, 1991.

Books

Berlin, Ira. *Slaves without Masters: The Free Negro in the Antebellum South*. New York, 1974.

Blassingame, John W. *The Slave Community: Plantation Life in the Antebellum South*. Rev. ed. New York, 1979.

Cell, John W. *The Highest Stage of White Supremacy: The Origins of Segregation in South America and the American South*. Cambridge, Mass. 1982.

Curray, Leonard P. *The Free Black in Urban America, 1800-1865: The Shadow of the Dream*. Chicago, 1987.

Fox-Genovese, Elizabeth. *Within the Plantation Household: Black and White Women of the Old South*. Chapel Hill, N.C. 1988.

Foner, Eric. *A Short History of Reconstruction*. New York, 1990.

Frey, Sylvia R. *Water from the Rock: Black Resistance in a Revolutionary Age*. Princeton, N.J., 1991.

Genovese, Eugene. *Roll, Jordan, Roll: The World the Slaves Made*. New York, 1974.

Gutman, Herbert G. *The Black Family in Slavery & Freedom, 1750-1925*. New York, 1976.

Huggins, Nathan I. *Black Odyssey: The Afro-American Ordeal in Slavery*. New York, 1977.

Litwack, Leon F. *Been in the Storm So Long: The Aftermath of Slavery*. New York, 1979.

Loewenberg, Bert James, and Ruth Bogin, eds. *Black Women in Nineteenth-Century American Life*. University Park, Pennsylvania, 1976.

Miller, Randall M., and John David Smith, eds. *The Dictionary of Afro-American Slavery*. New York and Westport, Conn. 1988.

Nash, Gary B., and Jean Soderlund. *Freedom by Degrees: Emancipation in Pennsylvania and Its Aftermath*. New York, 1991.

Sterling, Dorothy, ed. *We Are Your Sisters: Black Women in the Nineteenth Century*. New York, 1984.

Stevenson, Brenda E. *Life in Black and White: Family and Community in the Slave South*. New York, 1996.

White, Deborah G. *Ar'n't I a Woman? Female Slaves in the Plantation South*. New York, 1985.

Williamson, Joel. *The Crucible of Race: Black-White Relations in the American South Since Emancipation*. New York, 1984.

Woodward, C. Vann. *The Strange Career of Jim Crow*. 3rd revised ed. New York, 1974.

Contents of the Set

(ORGANIZED BY VOLUME)

Brown, Linda Beatrice
Burroughs, Margaret
Butler, Octavia E.
Campbell, Bebe Moore
Cary, Lorene
Chase-Riboud, Barbara
Cleage, Pearl
Cliff, Michelle
Clifton, Lucille
Cooper, J. California
Cortez, Jayne
Danner, Margaret Essie
Davis, Thadious
Davis, Thulani
Delaney Sisters
DeVeaux, Alexis
Dove, Rita
Drumgold, Kate
Dunbar-Nelson, Alice
Dunlap, Ethel Trew
Fauset, Jessie Redmon
Giddings, Paula
Giovanni, Nikki
Golden, Marita
Greenfield, Eloise
Guy, Rosa
Hamilton, Virginia Esther
Harper, Frances Ellen Watkins
hooks, bell
Hopkins, Pauline Elizabeth
Hunter, Kristin
Hurston, Zora Neale
Johnson, Georgia Douglas
Jones, Gayl
Jordan, June
Kincaid, Jamaica
Larsen, Nella
Lorde, Audre
Madgett, Naomi Long
Marshall, Paule
McElroy, Colleen J.
McMillan, Terry
Meriwether, Louise
Morrison, Toni
Naylor, Gloria
Petry, Ann Lane
Polite, Carlene
Sanchez, Sonia
Sanders, Dori

Shockley, Ann Allen
Southerland, Ellease
Spencer, Anne
Taylor, Mildred
Thomas, Joyce Carol
Vroman, Mary Elizabeth
Walker, Alice
Walker, Margaret Abigail
Wallace, Michele
West, Dorothy
Williams, Sherley Anne
Wilson, Harriet E.

Dance, Sports, and Visual Arts

Dance
Asante, Kariamu Welsh
Baker, Josephine
Blunden, Jeraldyne
Brown, Joan Myers
Collins, Janet
DeLavallade, Carmen
Dunham, Katherine
Forsyne, Ida
Hinkson, Mary
Jamison, Judith
Johnson, Virginia
Primus, Pearl
Turney, Matt
Waters, Sylvia
Yarborough, Sara
Zollar, Jawole Willa Jo

Sports
Ashford, Evelyn
Bolden, Jeanette
Brisco-Hooks, Valerie
Brown, Alice
Brown, Earlene
Cheeseborough, Chandra
Coachman, Alice
Daniels, Isabel
Dawes, Dominique
DeFrantz, Anita
Devers, Gail
Edwards, Teresa
Faggs, Mae

Ferrell, Barbara
Franke, Nikki
Gallagher, Kim
Garrison, Zina
Gibson, Althea
Glenn, Lula Mae Hymes
Harris-Stewart, Lusia
Hudson, Martha
Hyman, Flora
Jacket, Barbara J.
Jackson, Nell Cecilia
Jones, Barbara
Jones, Leora "Sam"
Joyner, Florence Griffith
Joyner-Kersee, Jackie
Love, Lynette
Matthews, Margaret
McDaniel, Mildred
McGuire, Edith
Miller, Cheryl
Mims, Madeleine Manning
Murray, Lenda
Patterson-Tyler, Audrey, (Mickey)
Pickett, Tydie
Powell, Renee
Rudolph, Wilma
Stokes, Louise
Stone, Lyle (Toni)
Stringer, C. Vivian
Thomas, Debi
Thomas, Vanessa
Tyus, Wyomia
Washington, Ora
White, Willye B.
Williams, Lucinda
Woodard, Lynette

Visual Arts
Beasley, Phoebe
Blount, Mildred E.
Brandon, Barbara
Burke, Selma
Catlett, Elizabeth
Fuller, Meta
Gafford, Alice
Humphrey, Margo
Hunter, Clementine
Jackson, May Howard

Jackson-Jarvis, Martha
Jones, Lois Mailou
Lewis, Mary Edmonia
Maynard, Valerie
McCullough, Geraldine
Moutoussamy-Ashe, Jeanne
Owens-Hart, Winnie
Pindell, Howardena
Piper, Adrian
Pogue, Stephanie
Powers, Harriet
Prophet, Nancy Elizabeth
Ringgold, Faith
Roberts, Malkia
Saar, Alison
Saar, Betye
Savage, Augusta
Sklarek, Norma Merrick
Thomas, Alma
Waring, Laura Wheeler
Woodard, Beulah Ecton

Business and Professions

Andrews, Rosalyn
Avant, Angela
Baker, Augusta
Beasley, Delilah
Bowen, Ruth
Bowser, Yvette Lee
Bradford, Martina
Bragg, Janet Harmon
Bricktop (Ada Smith)
Britton, Mary E.
Brooks, Hallie
Brown, Willa Beatrice
Brunson, Dorothy
Cadoria, Sheridan Grace
Cardozo Sisters
Clayton, Xernona
Coleman, Bessie
Coston, Julia Ringwood
Day, Carolyn Bond
Delaney, Sara "Sadie"
de Passe, Suzanne
Diggs, Ellen Irene

Dunnigan, Alice
Early, Charity Adams
Fisher, Ruth Anna
Florence, Virginia
Fudge, Ann
Gillespie, Marcia Ann
Gleason, Eliza Atkins
Hare, Maud Cuney
Harris, Marcelite
Harsh, Vivian Gordon
Haynes, Elizabeth Ross
Houston, Drusilla Dunjee
Hunter-Gault, Charlayne
Hutson, Jean Blackwell
Jefferson, Lucy
Jemison, Mae C.
Jenkins, Carol
Johnson, Eunice Walker
Jones, Clara Stanton
Jones, Virginia Lacy
Julian, Anna Johnson
King, Reatha Clark
Latimer, Catherine Allen
Lewis, Ida Elizabeth
Major, Gerri
Malone, Annie Turnbo
Malveaux, Julianne
Matthews, Miriam
McClain, Leanita
Morgan, Rose
Murray, Joan
Nelson, Jill
Oglesby, Mary
Payne, Ethel L.
Phinazee, Alethia
Pleasant, Mary Ellen
Procope, Ernesta G.
Proctor, Barbara Gardner
Quarles, Norma R.
Randolph, Lucille
Rhone, Sylvia
Rollins, Charlemae Hill
Saunders, Doris
Simmons, Judy
Simpson, Carole
Sims, Naomi
Smith, Ida Van
Smith, Jessie Carney
Stewart, Pearl

Taylor, Susan
Thompson, Era Bell
Villarosa, Linda
Walker, Madam C. J.
Washington, Sarah Spencer
Wattleton, Faye
Wesley, Dorothy Porter
White, Eartha Mary
Willis, Gertrude

Music

Addison, Adele
Akers, Doris
Allen, Geri
Anderson, Ernestine
Anderson, Marian
Armstrong, Lillian "Lil"
Arroyo, Martina
Ashby, Dorothy Jeanne
Austin, Lovie
Bailey, Pearl
Baiocchi, Regina Harris
Baker, Anita
Baker, LaVern
Barnett, Etta Moten
Barrett, "Sweet Emma"
Barton, Willene
Battle, Kathleen
Blige, Mary J.
Bonds, Margaret
Braxton, Toni
Brice, Carol
Brown, Anne Wiggins
Brown, Cleo Patra
Brown, Ruth
Bryant, Clora
Bryant, Hazel Joan
Bumbry, Grace
Caesar, Shirley
Calloway, Blanche
Campbell, Lucie E.
Capers, Valerie
Cara, Irene
Carlisle, Una Mae
Carter, Betty
Chapman, Tracy
Chiffons, The
Coates, Dorothy

Religion and Community

Social Activism

Science, Health, and Medicine

Contents of the Set

(LISTED ALPHABETICALLY BY ENTRY)

Index

Page numbers in **boldface** indicate main entries. *Italic* page numbers indicate illustrations.